MASTERING EXPERT TESTIMONY
A Courtroom Handbook
for Mental Health Professionals

Ken –
Many thanks for your help.
I hope ours is a lot better
than this one.
Bill

MASTERING EXPERT TESTIMONY
A Courtroom Handbook
for Mental Health Professionals

William T. Tsushima
Straub Clinic and Hospital, Honolulu
Robert M. Anderson, Jr.
American School of Professional Psychology, Honolulu

LEA LAWRENCE ERLBAUM ASSOCIATES, PUBLISHERS
1996   Mahwah, New Jersey

Lawrence Erlbaum Associates, Inc., Publishers
10 Industrial Avenue
Mahwah, New Jersey 07430

Cover design by Semadar Megged

Library of Congress Cataloging-in-Publication Data

Tsushima, William T.
 Mastering expert testimony : a courtroom handbook for
mental health professionals / William T. Tsushima, Robert M.
Anderson, Jr.
   p.   cm.
 Includes bibliographical references and index.
  ISBN 0-8058-1888-X (cloth : alk. paper). — ISBN 0-8058-
1889-8 (pbk. : alk. paper)
  1. Forensic psychiatry—United States. 2. Evidence, Expert—United States. I. Anderson, Robert M., 1943–. II.
Title.
KF8965.T78 1996
347.73'67—dc20
[347.30767]
                                                  96-22752
                                                      CIP

Books published by Lawrence Erlbaum Associates are printed on
acid-free paper, and their bindings are chosen for strength and
durability.

Printed in the United States of America
10 9 8 7 6 5 4 3 2 1

CONTENTS

FOREWORD

Patrick H. DeLeon, PhD, JD
U.S. Senate Staff

The courtroom represents an exciting and highly challenging arena for most mental health professionals. It truly is uncharted territory, for which the majority of our colleagues possess very little formal training.

Thus, for the practicing clinician, an intimate appreciation for the inner workings of the court—its unique language, procedures, and expectations—is critical. Well-prepared and reasoned mental health experts can contribute significantly to the court's decision-making process. Conversely, those who do not appreciate the nuances of the judicial system, or who are unprepared, will soon feel its wrath—for, "fools are not suffered gladly." The judicial process—unlike the underlying tenants of the mental health field—is above all else, an adversarial one.

This practice-oriented handbook impressively accomplishes its objective of effectively assisting experienced practitioners from all of the mental health disciplines in understanding and contributing meaningfully to the court's deliberations. Its unique approach of providing specific examples of typical courtroom dialogues between attorneys and mental health professionals, including suggesting "effective" responses, represents a refreshing approach to continuing education. The extensive courtroom experience of the authors facilitates an appreciation for differentiating between meaningful versus insignificant issues. Foundations are laid, in both legal and psychological terms, explaining the different approaches taken by the law and the mental health field to such critical issues as confidentiality, the role of experts, and client–professional relationships.

Addressing the ever-feared classic courtroom confrontation—the rhetorical, "are you a real doctor?"—helpful tips are provided. Underlying issues addressed include cross-examination of testing results, determination of patient malingering, and maintaining one's professional credibility. Throughout, one clear message constantly comes through: the ultimate importance of being effectively prepared and thoroughly professional in one's work. For example, the political usefulness of "taking that extra step"—such as by reviewing outside records or confirming background information with unbiased third parties (school teachers, police officers, etc.)—that one might not usually take when doing evaluations is discussed because such information must be expected to be carefully scrutinized by opposing counsel. The references provided are timely, up to date, and include many of the classics that opposing counsel might use.

The American judicial system is unquestionably an adversarial process—an approach that many mental health professionals initially find uncomfortable and fundamentally foreign to their instincts and training. Psychologists, psychiatrists, and other mental health professionals have much to contribute to our system of jurisprudence, which has served this nation admirably for generations.

PREFACE

From their daily clinical work in therapy and counseling, mental health professionals are known to be skilled communicators and verbally facile in responding to the full array of personal interactions. Thus, the possibility of being unable to explain their ideas and struggling to articulate their thoughts is anathema to clinicians. No wonder the prospect of testifying in a courtroom has a chilling effect on these practitioners.

It is common knowledge that clinicians in the courtroom experience high levels of apprehension because they are not prepared to cope with aggressive questioning in an unfamiliar arena. We believe that with some familiarity with forensic testifying, the practitioner can learn to respond in a highly effective manner, thus enabling him or her to contribute substantially to the court's fuller understanding of the relevant mental health issues in the case.

This volume is designed to serve as a practical handbook that assists practitioners from all mental health disciplines. It is unique with its emphasis on the typical courtroom dialogue between attorneys and mental health professionals who are either testifying about their psychotherapy clients or who are hired by attorneys specifically to provide expert opinions. With our extensive experience in the courtroom, we offer well thought-out effective responses as contrasted with impulsive and weak answers to attorney's queries. Sample cases are employed to illustrate typical challenges in various legal areas, including criminal law, child custody hearings, and personal injury cases. Certain forensic issues, such as the scientific bases of expert opinions, the accuracy of psychological versus medical tests, and malingering, are emphasized throughout the chapters.

The book is based on the belief that exposure to courtroom dialogue enhances the awareness of appropriate professional responses to an attorney's cross-examination and greatly alleviates the fears toward a situation that is known to provoke intense levels of anxiety. We realize that graduate schools and medical programs offer minimal training in forensic testimony, and we believe this book fills an invaluable educational need for mental health professionals.

Although this volume is written alluding to the forensic psychologist or psychiatrist, the strategies for the witness are readily applicable in most instances to all mental health professionals. Issues such as therapist bias, unconfirmed observations, and cultural and ethnic factors, are clearly relevant to all who provide mental health services. Furthermore, chapter 13 is devoted specifically to challenges that nondoctoral witnesses may face in testifying. Thus, this volume is recommended reading for psychologists, psychiatrists, social workers, psychiatric nurses, marriage and family therapists, speech therapists, occupational therapists, school counselors, and vocational rehabilitation counselors as well as graduate students, interns, residents, and trainees in these mental health disciplines. Attorneys will also find value in reviewing the samples of mental health expert witness testimony throughout this book.

This book is intended for educational purposes only and is not a rendering of legal or other professional services. If legal advice or other expert assistance is desired, the reader should seek the assistance of a competent professional with knowledge of the law. Names and situations depicted in various scenarios throughout the book do not represent actual persons or legal cases.

ACKNOWLEDGMENTS

Mental health professionals with interests in forensic work have been helped by several books that have preceded this one. The voluminous work by lawyer-psychologist Jay Ziskin is well-known, especially to attorneys who, thanks to Ziskin, are now even more formidable in the courtroom when challenging mental health witnesses. Books by Theodore Blau, Stanley Brodsky, Michael Maloney, Gary Melton and his associates, Richard Rogers and David Shapiro are valuable resources, and we are grateful to these authors for many of the ideas included in this book. We want to thank especially our friends and colleagues, Howard Luke, Jack Annon, and Kenneth Nakano, for their encouragement and critique of our material. Finally, our efforts to complete this book could not have occurred without the support of our wives, Jean Tsushima and Demetria Leong-Anderson, and we want to acknowledge our appreciation to them.

William T. Tsushima
Robert M. Anderson, Jr.

CHAPTER 1

THE ART OF EXPERT WITNESSING

"Who is an expert witness and what does an expert do?"

In this initial chapter, we present a description of the expert witness and basic guidelines for the mental health professional who is called in to provide expert testimony in the courtroom. Several books have been published by those experienced in forensic work, and their many suggestions are summarized here.

CHARACTERISTICS OF EXPERT WITNESSES

The definition of an expert witness is, by law, a well-defined concept, yet it is poorly understood by many. During the "trial of the century," *People v. O.J. Simpson*, the defense called as a witness, Robert Huizenga, MD, a specialist in internal medicine. Regarding Mr. Simpson's rheumatoid arthritis condition, Dr. Huizenga was asked if he would defer to the opinion of a pre-eminent *expert* who was a Stanford University professor and author in a standard textbook on rheumatoid arthritis. Dr. Huizenga would not yield, and quipped that there are many definitions of an expert and that he had heard as a Harvard University medical student that an expert was "a bastard from Boston with slides." In a court of law, an expert is defined more precisely.

According to Rule 702 of the Federal Rules of Evidence, an *expert* is a person who, due to specialized training and experience, may provide testimony to assist the trier of fact in understanding evidence that is beyond the layperson's knowledge, or to determine a fact in issue (Moore, 1985). Thus, the expert must be knowledgeable with the scientific literature in the area of expertise and have the ability to explain technical information in a clear and comprehendible

1

manner. (And in the Simpson example, Dr. Huizenga, who had conducted a physical examination of the defendant, was correct in not deferring to the "pre-eminent expert" who had never examined Simpson.)

A mental health professional can become involved as an expert in legal matters in three different ways. First, practitioners may become expert witnesses inadvertently, when their client is embroiled in litigation, such as in divorce proceedings and personal injury cases. In these situations, therapists may be ordered to appear in court to provide testimony regarding the client's mental health condition. Second, mental health professionals could be hired by one of the parties in litigation to provide an opinion about someone not previously seen or treated. Finally, mental health professionals can be appointed by the court to provide expert testimony, such as in sanity proceedings. The latter two situations often involves professionals who regularly participate in forensic examinations.

The expert witness should be thoroughly informed about the specific facts and issues in a legal case, so that the testimony can be proffered in a competent and professional manner. The expert is able to form opinions based on known facts and objective evidence, not only on theory. Testimony should be presented in a confident but not arrogant or condescending way. A glib and witty style may impress some courtroom intellectuals but would not be well received by the average juror.

Although often hired by one side in a legal matter, the expert witness does not serve as an advocate, as do the attorneys involved, but remains completely objective and impartial. Having strong convictions based on a professional analysis is a good thing; arguing to win a case for the client or attorney is not. The expert's role is to help the jury understand the case and not to decide its outcome.

The expert witness is able to communicate opinions in a clear, succinct, and persuasive manner, while avoiding technical terminology and jargon. The expert can answer questions directly and completely without volunteering unsolicited information. When faced with a challenging cross-examination, the expert remains calm and responds constructively to vigorous inquiry. Even when the questioning turns hostile, the expert witness' demeanor should remain polite and nonargumentative.

Mental health professionals approach the task of testifying with a range of concerns and emotions. Many have an appropriate fear of dealing with a strange and unknown professional experience. Others look on testifying with painful levels of anxiety and apprehension, with the perceived threat of being publicly embarrassed or feeling helpless, whereas still others consider the experience of testifying with the same fondness they have for proctoscopic examinations. Not all professionals have such negative perceptions about going to court. There are those who relish the intellectual and personal challenges presented in testifying and regard the activity as invigorating and rewarding. Sharing one's professional knowledge and assisting in the search for truth can be an uplifting experience for many.

GUIDELINES FOR THE MENTAL HEALTH EXPERT

Most mental health professionals have had little or no experience in legal activity, and few are prepared to cope effectively with the various phases of the court process. Those who take on forensic responsibilities should consider the following facets of expert witnessing: (a) preparations for forensic practice and testifying, (b) consulting with the referring attorney, (c) forensic evaluations, (d) direct examination by the referring attorney, and (e) cross-examination by the opposing attorney.

Preparations for Forensic Practice and Testifying

1. Obtain education and training pertinent to forensic practice (Grisso, 1988b).

Psychologists, psychiatrists, and other mental health professionals typically do not have, as an integral part of their graduate education, formal courses in forensics. In the absence of doctoral, internship, or postdoctoral training and experience, professionals should undertake their own self-study program. This could involve planned readings and consultation with an experienced forensic psychologist, psychiatrist, or other mental health professional—a mentor. Didactic sessions with the mentor and observation of the mentor in depositions and courtroom testifying would lead to doing cases under the supervision of the mentor. Periodic workshops and symposia on forensic activity would also increase skills in this area.

2. Become and stay current in your area of expertise (Applebaum & Gutheil, 1991; Brodsky, 1991).

As an expert, your opinion and the information you are providing the court should issue from a thorough and current knowledge base in your area of expertise. With the increasing presence of mental health experts in legal matters, attorneys themselves are becoming more sophisticated in their grasp of psychological issues, and you want to be able to respond with state-of-the-science information. Your ongoing education will help you in the courtroom as well as in your clinical practice.

3. Be clearly aware of the limits of your knowledge and do not venture beyond them (Pope, Butcher, & Seelen, 1993).

It is important to clearly understand the limits of your expertise and to make these limits clear to attorneys, other individuals, or institutions who wish to make use of your services as an expert. You should refrain from accepting cases outside your area of expertise. For example, being a clinical psychologist does not automatically confer expertise in neuropsychology or behavioral medicine. Having these limits clearly in mind can also be helpful when a cross-examining attorney asks questions outside your area of expertise. You can respond that the question is outside your area of expertise and that you do not know the answer. Finally, within your scope of specialized knowledge, testify with opinions based on reasonable probability as contrasted with speculations, gut feelings and hunches.

4. Become familiar with the legal terms and law relevant to your area of expertise (Ewing, 1985; Hambacher, 1994).

Know what terms like *subpoena, deposition, competency, joint custody*, and *disability* mean. This can be accomplished by reading, attending seminars, and obtaining supervision. Certain cases, such as in criminal law and divorce court, will have specific relevant legal terminology. To assist you, the referring attorney may be able to define the legal terms and issues relevant to a given case. Although it is important to understand basic aspects of the law, never assume to be an expert in anything other than your own field, and confer with the attorney on important points of law. Let the lawyers be the legal professionals and you remain the mental health professional.

5. Maintain a copy of organizationally endorsed guidelines for forensic work in your specialty.

For psychologists, the American Psychology–Law Society and Division 41 of the American Psychological Association have adopted *Specialty Guidelines for Forensic Psychologists* (Committee on Ethical Guidelines for Forensic Psychologists, 1991).

6. Familiarize yourself with the courtroom (Brodsky, 1991; Maloney, 1985).

Know where the courthouse is, what parking is available, and how the courtroom is structured. This can involve visiting the courtroom and observing a seasoned expert witness, possibly your mentor, testifying in court. Pope et al. (1993) recommended reading books such as *The Trial Lawyers* (Couric, 1988), *The Litigators* (Jenkins, 1989), *The Best Defense* (Dershowitz, 1982), and *The Trial Masters* (Warshaw, 1984) to obtain an understanding and feel for the legal process. *Trials of an Expert Witness* (Klawans, 1991) describes the process from the point of view of an expert witness. A relatively recent development, *Court TV*, a network television channel, provides frequent opportunity to watch psychiatrists and psychologists in well-publicized trials, such as the trials of

O.J. Simpson and the Menendez brothers in Los Angeles, usually with reviews by experienced trial lawyers and judges.

Consulting With the Referring Attorney

1. Maintain objectivity (Applebaum & Gutheil, 1991; Brodsky, 1991). Avoid becoming an advocate (Group for the Advancement of Psychiatry, 1991; Shapiro, 1991).

When working closely with a client or the attorney, it is easy to become emotionally involved and to want to please the parties you are working with. Avoid partiality and advocacy. The role of the expert is to provide an objective, scientific opinion. Ideally, your opinion would be the same regardless of which side of a dispute is retaining you. Your job is to present truthful testimony, not to win the case for the attorney.

2. Request all available information that is relevant to the legal case (Sadoff, 1988).

Forensic evaluations must be thorough and based on all of the available relevant information. Thus, criminal experts will review arrest records, and personal injury specialists will peruse various medical and psychological documents in preparation for their testimony. Educational and work records can be extremely pertinent. When possible, verify information by interviewing family members, coworkers, and the like.

3. Reserve your opinion until after you have received sufficient information and have conducted your evaluation (Ewing, 1985).

Attorneys may invite the expert to commit to a position prior to examining the client and all information. This may involve an attempt to determine whether the expert will provide an opinion favorable to the attorney's client or perhaps to ensure that the expert will not be able to play any role in the case (Pope, Butcher, & Seelen, 1993). Try to obtain as much relevant information as possible before forming any conclusions. The expert who changes diagnoses, even when legitimate because of additional relevant data, may be perceived as unreliable or lacking in certainty.

4. If possible, obtain a retainer or a written agreement of your fee from the attorney. Never work on a contingency fee basis (Applebaum & Gutheil, 1991; Ewing, 1985; Pope et al., 1993; Shapiro, 1991).

Although most attorneys and clients are honorable in terms of their payment for professional services rendered, sometimes it is difficult to collect your fees after the fact, especially when the outcome is not favorable. A written agreement avoids any disputes or misunderstandings. It is unethical to link your fees to the outcome of the trial. By not working on a contingency fee basis, you are able to maintain objectivity and avoid the charge of advocacy.

5. Have some information that can be used by the attorney to establish your expertise (Brodsky, 1991).

Attorneys may not be aware of your relevant training and experience, or any teaching or research you conduct. Your resume or curriculum vitae (CV) can be very handy for the hiring attorney to inform the court about your specialized professional knowledge, as well as the limits of your expertise.

Forensic Evaluations

1. Be sure that the examinee understands the nature and circumstances of the evaluation and the limits on confidentiality (Pope et al., 1993).

It may not be obvious to the client that you will be sharing your findings with the referring attorney and eventually the court. The usual restrictions pertaining to client confidentiality may not apply when legal proceedings are involved. If there is any doubt, you may want to consult your attorney to be certain of your responsibilities and the client's rights.

2. Be thorough in your evaluation (Ewing, 1985).

In any legal case—in criminal court, civil court, and family court—the consequences are substantial, and the expert must perform a competent and thorough examination. Obtain all relevant documents, including health, education, work, and criminal records, and when possible interview individuals familiar with the client to verify information.

3. Know precisely the chain of reasoning that leads from your data to your conclusions (Brodsky, 1991).

Be prepared to explain to laypersons how you used your findings to arrive at your conclusions. The average juror does not share the same assumptions and beliefs as yourself, and will need careful and clear explanations of your conclusions.

4. Consider the role that faking and malingering may play in the evaluation (Brodsky, 1991; Pope et al., 1993).

Assessing the honesty of an examinee may be one of the most difficult tasks for the mental health professional, but it is a vital aspect of your testimony. Be familiar with the research related to the detection of faking and whatever methods you can rely on to assess the client's honesty and attempts at impression management.

Direct Examination by the Referring Attorney

1. Before the trial, prepare the attorney (Applebaum & Gutheil, 1991; Shapiro, 1991).

It is perfectly acceptable to meet with the attorney before going to court so that you can be apprised of the critical issues in the case and so that the attorney is thoroughly familiar with your testimony. Assist the attorney with the kinds of questions that should be asked in order to elicit your opinion most effectively. Anticipate the challenges that may be made to your opinion and help the attorney in determining how these may be dealt with during direct examination.

2. Wear dark, conservative, semiformal clothes with muted accessories (Blau, 1984; Mangiaracina, 1991).

Although Brodsky (1991) suggested that a primary concern in choice of clothes for the courtroom is the witness' comfort level in the clothes, experts generally recommend semiformal conservative dress (Maloney, 1985). It is easier for the jury to accept the opinions of a professional from one who has the appearance of a professional person.

3. Allow yourself to relax before your court appearance (Brodsky, 1991).

Bringing a book or paper work can ease the tensions of waiting outside the courtroom. It is inappropriate to converse with the opposing attorney or other witnesses.

4. Listen carefully to each question, and look at the jury during your responses (Brodsky, 1991).

If the question is vague or confusing, you may request that the question be rephrased.

5. Explain your conclusions and your reasoning to your conclusions in everyday language. Define any technical terms in easy-to-understand language (Ewing, 1985; Maloney, 1985).

Technical obscurities and jargon hurt one's testimony because whatever point you are emphasizing may be lost by the average juror.

6. Refrain from answering the ultimate legal questions, such as legal sanity. Answer the psychological questions (Brodsky, 1991) that allow the jury or judge to reach these legal decisions.

However, there may be a "slippery slope" between psychological and legal questions. Answers to the psychological questions may approach so close to answers to legal questions as to be indistinguishable. In many jurisdictions the expert is allowed to testify to "the ultimate issue." For example, a psychiatrist or psychologist may be asked whether the facts of a criminal case met the definition of insanity at the time of the alleged offense. Unless the psychological issues are closely relevant to the legal issues, your response may be considered useless by the court (Applebaum & Gutheil, 1991).

7. Be sure that you understand the meaning of "reasonable medical certainty," or "reasonable psychological probability" in your jurisdiction (Applebaum & Gutheil, 1991; Rogers, 1987).

The expert is commonly asked whether he or she has an opinion within reasonable medical or psychological probability. This commonly means "more probable than not" but may have other meanings in some jurisdictions. Do not offer speculations or conjecture; limit yourself to opinion for which there is reasonable probability.

Cross-Examination by Opposing Attorney

The direct examination typically proceeds smoothly because your input is welcomed by the referring attorney who is asking questions to enhance your findings. In contrast, the purpose of the cross-examination is to refute your contributions by questioning any aspect of your testimony, from your qualifications as an expert to your evaluation methods and conclusions.

1. As in direct examination, listen carefully to each question and look at the jury during your responses to cross-examination (Brodsky, 1991).

In cross-examination, an overly apprehensive witness may be on guard to look for hidden meanings behind questions and not answer directly to simple and clear questions. Respond to each question in a straightforward manner. If a question is not clear, you are permitted to request that the question be restated.

2. In cross-examination, attorneys often ask leading questions that require a simple "yes" or "no" response, such as "You're the therapist for the defendant, aren't you?" If the attorney tries to limit you to a "yes" or

"no" response, you can ask the court for permission to fully explain (Brodsky, 1991).

3. Don't succumb to the temptation to argue with the cross-examining attorney (Ewing, 1985; Group for the Advancement of Psychiatry, 1991).

You are not likely to win a battle of the wits in the lawyer's territory, and even if you do, you may appear petty, arrogant and adversarial rather than professional and objective.

4. Cross-examining attorneys may offer science-based attacks on mental health testimony. You can acknowledge the critical research and yet assert confidence in your findings in the particular case (Group for the Advancement of Psychiatry, 1991).

Ziskin (1995; Faust & Ziskin, 1988; Faust, Ziskin, & Hiers, 1991; Ziskin & Faust, 1988) authored a number of well-known books and articles designed to discredit mental health expertise and to provide attorneys with information, methods, and questions that can be used to impeach the testimony of mental health experts. Brodsky (1991) suggested that the expert acknowledge the contribution that the research cited by Ziskin, Faust, and Hiers has made to the improvement of accountability in mental health assessment. In addition, the expert can point out that many of the studies cited by Ziskin and Faust in support of their contention that psychiatric diagnosis is unreliable were performed long ago, before advances in diagnostic sophistication (Applebaum & Gutheil, 1991). It is wise for mental health professionals engaging in forensic work to be familiar with the voluminous works of Ziskin and his associates.

Appendix A provides an annotated list of books written for mental health professionals, with more background information regarding expert witnessing and abundant suggestions as to courtroom testifying. The appendix also lists relevant forensic journals and professional organizations.

CLOSING ARGUMENTS

This chapter presented the definition and general characteristics of expert witnesses. It also provided helpful tips for the mental health expert in the various phases of forensic activity, including: (a) preparations for forensic practice and testifying, (b) consulting with the referring attorney, (c) forensic evaluations, (d) direct examination by the referring attorney, and (e) cross-examination by the opposing attorney.

Clearly the role of expert witness is not for everyone, certainly not for those whose anxiety will inhibit clear reasoning and articulate responses, nor for those who are readily angered by the forcefulness and sarcastic tone of the skilled cross-examiner. Mental health experts must be willing to accept the critical statements made about their profession, the controversies in their field, and any flaws in their own data gathering and reasoning processes.

Such attacks should never be taken personally. The expert witness realizes that opposing attorneys, as part of an adversarial system, are merely emphasizing points that strengthen their arguments and have nothing personally against the witness. The expert who rebounds from the assaults of the cross-examining attorney and provides well-reasoned opinions based on objective evidence will have made valuable contributions to the trial process and the search for truth.

CHAPTER 2

WITNESS QUALIFICATION

"Doctor, how can you claim to be an expert?"

The first series of questions a psychologist/psychiatrist encounters is aimed at establishing one's qualifications as an expert witness. The attorney who sees value in your professional opinions has requested or subpoenaed your presence in the courtroom, and will ask in direct examination a standard series of questions about your background that will enhance your credibility as an expert. Inquiry about one's education, clinical experience, and academic activities will highlight the expert's professional strengths.

The qualification process is designed to persuade the judge and jury of the expert's credibility and the authority of the opinions rendered. After identifying and introducing into evidence the expert's resume, the attorney will attempt to stress favorable points, including the following educational or technical training:

- formal professional education (schools, degrees, dates)
- clinical internship and clerkships
- specialization training
- continuing professional education
- honors, recognitions
- license, certifications
- professional memberships and activities

The attorney also wants to elicit information about the expert's practical experiences, such as:

- current employment and duties
- prior relevant jobs and activities
- description of experience regarding specific subjects matters
- teaching positions and activities
- research and publications
- prior experience as expert witness

This will be the easy part.

DIRECT EXAMINATION

Qualifying a Psychologist

The direct examination is conducted by the attorney who has called the witness to court and consists of standard questions to validate the witness' qualifications to testify.

> **Q. Doctor, could you tell us about your educational background, beginning with your undergraduate studies?**
> A. I received my bachelor's degree in ____ in 19__ from the University of_____. I obtained my master's degree in_____ in 19___ from the University of _____and my PhD in clinical psychology in 19___ from the University of _____.
> **Q. Since you received your PhD, where have you practiced or been employed?**
> A. From 19___ to 19___ I was employed by _____, and since 19___ to the present I have been _____.
> **Q. Are you licensed to practice in the State of _____?**
> A. Yes, I received my license in 19___.
> **Q. Are you a member of any professional organizations?**
> A. Yes, I am a member of the American Psychological Association and of the_____State Psychological Association. I also belong to_____.

Qualifying a Psychiatrist

A psychiatrist is asked similar initial questions that include schooling, residency training, licensing, and board certification.

> **Q. Where did you receive your undergraduate education?**
> A. I attended _____ University, and received my bachelor's degree in chemistry in 19___.
> **Q. What medical school did you attend?**
> A. I went to _____ University Medical School.

Q. Where did you do your residency?
A. My residency in psychiatry was at _____ Medical Center.
Q. How long did your residency take?
A. I did 3 years of residency training in adult psychiatry.
Q. Are you board certified in the field of psychiatry?
A. Yes. I am certified by the American Board of Psychiatry and Neurology.
Q. What are the requirements for board certification in psychiatry?
A. Completion of medical school, and residency in psychiatry, ____ years
   of experience in psychiatry, as well as passing a written and oral exami-
   nation in psychiatry and neurology.
Q. What work have you done since you completed your residency?
A. Since my residency training 4 years ago, I have been employed at the
   Mental Health Clinic at the _____ Hospital.
Q. Where are you licensed to practice psychiatry?
A. I am licensed to practice medicine in this state. There is no state license
   for any specialized field of medicine, such as psychiatry or pediatrics.
Q. What is the nature of your current position?
A. I am a staff psychiatrist in an outpatient mental health clinic.

MORE SPECIFIC QUESTIONS

After this initial query of a general nature, the psychologist/psychiatrist may be
asked more specific questions pertinent to the trial at hand. The following
example pertains to a criminal trial of an alleged rape.

**Q. In the course of your training and practice, have you seen persons
   who have, as a part of their history, been victims of sexual assault?**
A. Yes, I have.
Q. How many such patients have you seen?
A. That's hard to say. About 100.
**Q. How many persons have you evaluated or treated specifically for
   injuries from sexual violence?**
A. About 15 to 20.
**Q. Have you assisted in court proceedings before by providing expert
   psychological/psychiatric testimony for the court?**
A. Yes.
**Q. On approximately how many occasions have you provided expert
   testimony in court?**
A. About 5 or 6 times.

The attorney may want to emphasize some of the unique strengths you bring
to the courtroom as a clinical expert. Questions to bring out your special assets
might include:

Q. Are you board certified?

Q. How many years have you specialized in studying or treating_____?

Q. Have you done any research in your area of specialty?

Q. Do you have any publications in your field?

Q. Have you presented any lectures or workshops in your area of expertise?

Q. Do you do any teaching or supervising?

Q. Have you held an office in any of your professional organizations?

Information pertaining to these questions may be summarized in your resume or CV. Nonetheless, it is helpful for you to highlight for the attorney prior to court time certain aspects of your resume to be included during this initial phase of your testimony. If the CV is impressive, the attorney may consider marking it as an exhibit and offering it into evidence so that the jury can later review the qualifications and accomplishments of the expert witness. Admission into evidence of the CV is discretionary with the court.

VOIR DIRE AND CROSS EXAMINATION

After the professional's credentials have been extolled on direct questioning, the opposing counsel has the opportunity to question the witness. This procedure, known as *voir dire,* is very similar to cross-examination in that it is conducted by the opposing attorney, who may use leading questions. The voir dire normally occurs when the opposing attorney requests permission "to take the witness on voir dire." The judge will invariably permit the opposing attorney to do so.

The *voir dire* procedure can be quite dramatic, because it allows the opposing attorney the opportunity to interrupt the proponent's direct examination. Keep in mind, however, that the voir dire has a limited purpose, which is to test and challenge the qualifications of the expert and his or her competency to testify in the area for which the expert was called. Although one attorney is eager to underscore your professional expertise, the opposing attorney in the courtroom perceives that your testimony may negatively affect the case and will try to flush out in a cross-examination the limitations of your knowledge by noting gaps in your professional training and work experience. There may even be an attempt to disqualify you as a witness by arguing your lack of adequate credentials or background, or by claiming that your contribution is irrelevant or unduly biased. Note that, unlike the direct examination where the examining attorney is strictly prohibited from asking leading questions, in cross-examination the attorney will use leading questions almost exclusively to discredit the expert.

Challenging a Psychologist's Qualifications

A psychologist's expertise may be challenged in cross-examination by an opposing counsel who typically accentuates the absence of medical training, because concepts such as *mental illness*, *brain damage*, or *pain* are at the center of the courtroom discussion.

Q. You're not a medical doctor, are you?
A. No.
Q. What kind of degree do you have?
A. A PhD in clinical psychology.
Q. Is that a doctor of philosophy?
A. Yes.
Q. Not a doctor of medicine, right?
A. Yes.
Q. Have you taken any medical courses?
A. No, but I have taken courses in psychobiology and have attended several seminars in medically related subjects.
Q. Can you tell me all the courses you've taken in graduate school that related to medicine?
A. Well, I've taken_____.
Q. So, you've taken four courses that sort of relate to medicine, is that right?
A. Yes.
Q. Since you've obtained your PhD, what kind of training or courses have you taken that relate to medicine?
A. Let's see. I've taken _____
_____.
Q. So, what you're telling us is that you've had practically no medical training, have you?
A. Yes, I have had limited medical training.
Q. Are you board certified?
A. No.
Q. Have you published any articles in a medical journal?
A. No, I haven't.

Although the lack of training, certification, and publications may reflect on a professional's degree of expertise, these factors do not exclude a psychologist from being a qualified expert.

Challenging a Psychiatrist's Qualifications

A similar approach can be taken to cast aspersions on the qualifications of a psychiatrist, focusing on the relative lack of training in psychology, in psychometric assessment, or in cognitive and behavioral treatments.

Q. What kind of degree do you have?
A. An MD or doctor of medicine degree.

Q. You're not a psychologist, are you?
A. No, I'm a psychiatrist.
Q. In medical school, did you take any specific courses in psychology?
A. No, but in medical school I had introductory training in psychiatry, and after medical school I had 3 years of residency training in psychiatry, much of which relates to psychology.
Q. During your medical training, how many formal courses in psychology have you taken?
A. None.
Q. During your residency training, how many formal courses in psychology have you taken?
A. None.
Q. Have you had any training in psychological testing or in behavior therapy?
A. No.
Q. So, Doctor, you would agree with me that, as compared to a person with a PhD in psychology, you have had almost no formal courses in psychology, right?
A. That's right.
Q. Have you published any papers in psychology or psychiatry?
A. No.

As before, the absence of certain training or research experiences reflects one's degree of expertise, but it does not preclude a psychiatrist from being qualified as an expert witness.

MORE AGGRESSIVE CHALLENGES

With a more aggressive attack, some attorneys try to intimidate the expert witness, hoping to arouse enough anxiety, defensiveness, or anger to render the witness less effective. For example, the lawyer might emphasize studies that have found that highly trained and experienced clinicians are no more accurate in their evaluations than secretaries and high school students (Faust & Ziskin, 1988). It is not easy to respond to questions asked in a hostile or sarcastic manner, but it is important to maintain a professional demeanor from the start of the cross-examination to its end. Engaging in clever repartee in a one-up-manship contest is not advisable.

Intimidated witnesses often blurt out defensive retorts to counteract the aggressive questioning. Rather than enhancing one's position, these impulsive comments could quickly undermine the credibility and effectiveness of the expert witness. The following are a variety of aggressive challenges for a psychologist followed by responses that are not well thought out.

For the Psychologist

1. **Q. You're not saying that psychology is an exact science like physics and chemistry, are you?**
   a.[1] Physics and chemistry aren't that exact either, so we're not that different.

2. **Q. Since there are so many different theories in psychology, how do we know that the theory you follow is correct?**
   a. I'm not sure. How do we know if any theory is right?

3. **Q. Do I address you as Mister or Doctor?**
   a. Call me Doctor, of course.

4. **Q. You're not a real doctor, are you?**
   a. The doctor of philosophy degree historically preceded the medical degree, so *we* are the real doctors.

5. **Q. You can't testify about mental illness when you've had no training in neurology, anatomy, and physiology, can you?**
   a. Mental illness has to do with the mind, and you don't need to have medical knowledge.

6. **Q. You mean you haven't written any scientific articles, not even one?**
   a. I'm sorry. I haven't written any published articles.

7. **Q. How much experience have you had with multiple sclerosis [MS] patients who have had a closed head injury?**
   a. She's the first MS patient I've seen who's had a head injury.

8. **Q. You're not qualified to render an opinion about the medical condition of a patient's brain, are you?**
   a. No, I'm not.

9. **Q. Okay, you're telling us that you have had several years of experience, but aren't there several reputable studies that show that experience doesn't insure more accurate diagnoses?**
   a. I don't accept the studies that say that experience doesn't matter. It doesn't make sense to me.

10. **Q. Is there any study showing that a person who is board certified, like yourself, is more accurate in evaluating patients than a psychologist who is not board certified?**
    a. I don't know of any such study.

11. **Q. Since you have always testified in the past for your patients who are plaintiffs, couldn't you be biased against defendants?**
    a. I can't help it if I'm only called by patients or their lawyers to testify.

12. **Q. You've worked for this law firm several times. Aren't you just a hired gun?**
    a. Just because I get paid for my services doesn't make me a hired gun. I resent the implication.

---

[1]Throughout this book, weak and ineffectual responses are preceded by a small "a," whereas better answers are indicated by a capital "A.")

For the Psychiatrist

Psychiatrists also encounter varied aggressive challenges and may succumb to the following weak and damaging answers:

1. **Q. You psychiatrists are not as scientific or objective as cardiologists and surgeons, right?**
   a. I don't need to defend my profession today. I'm here to testify about the patient.

2. **Q. You're a medical doctor—are you telling us that you are able to arrive at a medical opinion even without doing any physical examination of your patients?**
   a. Psychiatrists shouldn't examine their patients. It's a complex matter pertaining to the therapist–patient relationship that you wouldn't understand.

3. **Q. Isn't it true that behavioral scientists assert that the concept of mental illness is inappropriate for understanding psychological problems?**
   a. The mental illness concept has been criticized, but it has nothing to do with this case.

4. **Q. Your medical school background may sound impressive, but your training in medicine has nothing to do with this custody hearing, isn't that true?**
   a. We're not talking about medicine here. I can't argue that.

5. **Q. You testified that you read primarily psychiatric journals. Don't psychological journals report important findings in the diagnosis and treatment of mental disorders?**
   a. Yes, but I learn enough about mental disorders from my own professional journals.

6. **Q. You mean you've never administered a single psychological test? Not one?**
   a. I'm an experienced psychiatrist and I don't need a psychological test to tell me about my patients.

7. **Q. Isn't it true that psychiatric diagnoses, as in *DSM–IV*, were derived by popular consensus and not by scientific research?**
   a. I think you're right. The diagnoses were derived at by committee decisions.

8. **Q. You rely primarily on what the patient tells you, and not on objective medical tests, right?**
   a. We all have to rely on what patients tell us.

9. **Q. Isn't psychology the appropriate specialty for the understanding of psychological problems, such as those of this patient?**
   a. Psychiatrists study psychology, too, and understand psychological problems.

10. Q. This case involves alleged pyromania. Isn't it true that you have had little or no experience with pyromaniacs?
    a. It's true I haven't dealt with many pyromaniacs, but I've read a lot about them, so I know how to treat them.

11. Q. Are you an expert just in psychiatry or specifically in the insanity plea?
    a. I don't know. I'm not sure what the requirements of an expert are.

12. Q. Since you have always testified in the past for your patients who are criminal defendants, couldn't you be biased against the prosecution?
    a. After seeing several wrongly accused defendants, I may have a problem with these kinds of cases. Wouldn't you?

MORE THOUGHTFUL RESPONSES

By the Psychologist

Instead of the previous impulsive, self-destructive statements, a calmer, more thoughtful response for psychologists is clearly preferred, such as:

1. Q. You're not saying that psychology is an exact science like physics and chemistry, are you?
   A. I'm not sure what you mean by "exact," but psychology has been long accepted as a discipline based on scientific theory and methodology. It is taught in all of our universities as the science of human behavior.

2. Q. Since there are so many different theories in psychology, how do we know that the theory you follow is correct?
   A. The best way to evaluate a theory is by empirical research, that is, by proof through experiments. The theory I follow has been supported by numerous experiments and studies, with findings published in reputable journals.

3. Q. Do I address you as Mister or Doctor?
   A. I have a PhD in Clinical Psychology, and my patients refer to me as Doctor.

4. Q. You're not a real doctor, are you?
   A. I am not a medical doctor. I have a PhD degree in clinical psychology, and my colleagues and I have traditionally been referred to as doctors.

5. Q. You can't testify about mental illness when you've had no training in neurology, anatomy, and physiology, can you?
   A. I have not had specific courses in neurology, anatomy, and physiology, but graduate training in psychology provides sufficient bases in the biological aspects of mental illness. Courses in the psychological aspects of medical illness have also been an important part of our training.

6. **Q. You mean you haven't written any scientific articles, not even one?**

A. I am not a researcher and, therefore, haven't published any papers. My specialty and expertise is in doing clinical work, such as in this case.

7. **Q. How much experience have you had with multiple sclerosis patients who have had a closed head injury?**

A. I have not had many MS patients with head injuries, but I have a wealth of experience with varied neurological patients with different kinds of brain complications.

8. **Q. You're not qualified to render an opinion about the medical condition of a patient's brain, are you?**

A. I'm not a physician and, therefore, I provide no medical opinions. I'm a neuropsychologist and I am qualified to assess a person's brain through tests of cognitive and mental functioning. I am trained to diagnose and treat brain injured persons, such as this patient.

9. **Q. Okay, you're telling us that you have had several years of experience, but aren't there several reputable studies that show that experience doesn't insure more accurate diagnoses?**

A. I am aware that there are studies which state that experience does not guarantee greater diagnostic accuracy. However, these are but a few investigations pertaining to specific disorders, such as brain injury. I believe, in my case, my experience over the years has added to the knowledge I gained in my formal education and training.

10. **Q. Is there any study showing that a person who is board certified, like yourself, is more accurate in evaluating patients than a psychologist who is not board certified?**

A. Although no such study exists, psychologists should demonstrate their clinical skills by passing specialty board examinations and not simply rely on their degree and state license.

11. **Q. Since you have always testified in the past for your patients who are plaintiffs, couldn't you be biased against defendants?**

A. My responsibility, regardless of who calls me to court, is to provide professional, objective, scientifically based opinions. My responsibility is to tell the truth.

12. **Q. You've worked for this law firm several times. Aren't you just a hired gun?**

A. I have been an expert witness for this law firm, but I have also testified in court for patients on many occasions. My duty is to testify truthfully, not to be an advocate as an attorney must be.

By the Psychiatrist

For psychiatrists, similarly calm and more reasoned comments are desirable. For example:

1. **Q. You psychiatrists are not as scientific or objective as cardiologists and surgeons, right?**

   A. I'm not sure what you mean by objective, but psychiatry relies on observable and quantifiable data and has long been accepted as one of the major disciplines in the medical profession. What patients tell us is valuable objective data not only for psychiatrists but for all medical doctors.

2. **Q. You're a medical doctor—are you telling us that you are able to arrive at a medical opinion even without doing any physical examination of your patients?**

   A. Psychiatrists do not ordinarily perform physical examinations. When a medical evaluation is needed, I refer the patient to a specialist, such as an internist.

3. **Q. Isn't it true that behavioral scientists assert that the concept of mental illness is inappropriate for understanding psychological problems?**

   A. The mental illness concept has been criticized but that does not mean that psychiatrists are unable to diagnose and treat psychological problems, such as in this case.

4. **Q. Your medical school background may sound impressive, but your training in medicine has nothing to do with this custody hearing, isn't that true?**

   A. My medical training has included 3 years of psychiatric residency, which has prepared me to understand the family dynamics and emotional needs of the children involved in this custody hearing.

5. **Q. You testified that you read primarily psychiatric journals. Don't psychological journals report important findings in the diagnosis and treatment of mental disorders?**

   A. Important psychological research is reported in psychiatric journals as well, so I am kept abreast of current scientific findings in psychology.

6. **Q. You mean you've never administered a single psychological test? Not one?**

   A. Although psychological tests are often helpful, in cases such as this, I believe I can provide a thorough assessment without having had administered any test.

7. **Q. Isn't it true that psychiatric diagnoses, as in *DSM–IV*, were derived by popular consensus and not by scientific research?**

   A. The diagnoses in *DSM–IV* have proven to be clinically reliable and have been subjected to numerous studies since its inception. The *DSM–IV* diagnoses are relied on to define clinical disorders in many research investigations.

8. **Q. You rely primarily on what the patient tells you, and not on objective medical tests, right?**

A. I depend not only on what the patient tells me, but I include a review of the patient's history and medical records, and I observe closely the patient's behavior during the session. When appropriate, I gather input from family members and others who are familiar with the patient's background.

9. **Q. Isn't psychology the appropriate specialty for the understanding of psychological problems, such as those of this patient?**

A. The patient's psychological problems constitute a diagnosable psychiatric disorder which I am trained to treat.

10. **Q. This case involves alleged pyromania. Isn't it true that you have had little or no experience with pyromaniacs?**

A. Yes, I've treated very few pyromaniacs. However, over the years, I've examined and treated many patients suffering from different compulsive disorders, such as kleptomania or sexual compulsions. There is a similarity among these compulsive disorders which I believe applies to this case of pyromania.

11. **Q. Are you an expert just in psychiatry or specifically in the insanity plea?**

A. I am an expert in psychiatry, and with my training and experience I am also an expert in forensic psychiatry, including the insanity plea.

12. **Q. Because you have always testified in the past for your patients who are criminal defendants, couldn't you be biased against the prosecution?**

A. It's true that I've testified only for a criminal defendant in the past. However, if I were to be called by a prosecutor to evaluate someone I would be willing to help.

And Nothing But the Truth

"I'm one of the best in the business in this town."

If there is a First Commandment for expert witnesses, it must be "Thou shalt not lie" or even have the appearance of lying. Unfortunately, some witnesses overreact to the intimidating atmosphere of the courtroom by embellishing their professional credentials with half-truths and exaggerations. Note the following examples:

1. **Q. When you provided your educational background, you stated you attended Stanford University. What was the extent of your attendance at Stanford?**

a. I had a 6-week intensive training in brain function analysis at a Stanford University laboratory.

2. **Q. You testified that you've had 10 years of experience as a psychologist. Didn't you receive your PhD in 1990?**

    a. Yes. But I included in the 10 years my predoctoral clinical experience as well as the time I was a professor's assistant in my undergraduate and graduate school years.

3. **Q. You included hypnosis as one of your skilled areas. What formal training have you had in hypnosis?**

    a. Three years ago I completed a 2-day course in hypnosis, but I don't practice hypnosis very much.

4. **Q. Do you call yourself a neuropsychologist because you have been trained in neuropsychology?**

    a. Not exactly. I call myself a neuropsychologist because I administer neuropsychological tests, like the Bender–Gestalt and the Wechsler Memory Scale.

5. **Q. As an adjunct professor of psychiatry, do you actually teach courses?**

    a. No. Periodically the medical school calls me to give a lecture to medical students.

6. **Q. You cited as a publication, an article you wrote in *General Hospital Proceedings*. Is that a refereed journal publication?**

    a. No. It's a hospital newsletter.

7. **Q. What does your title, "President, Society for the Advancement of Self-Esteem" mean?**

    a. It's not a formal organization. I head the monthly meetings of persons who gather at my office to discuss self-esteem issues.

These efforts at self-aggrandizement and overstatement are clearly transparent and raise significant ethical concerns. Whether it is a function of insecurity or of manipulativeness, being less than perfectly honest is perhaps the most self-damaging mistake to make in the courtroom.

CLOSING ARGUMENTS

There may be attempts to disqualify the expert witness altogether. It could be contended that the issue on which testimony is offered is not one requiring professional expertise. For example, a psychologist is not needed to testify that a job promotion would lead to a better self-image. An expert could also be excluded if the proffered area of expertise is irrelevant. For instance, a mental health evaluation of a robbery victim is usually not relevant in a criminal courtroom. Finally, the attorney could argue that the professional witness has inadequate training or experience in the relevant issue, such as when a psychiatrist who normally treats adults evaluates a distressed child.

    This chapter described the qualification and *voir dire* process, which is usually a series of routine questions about the witness' educational and clinical experiences. On occasion, the opposing attorney may want to prevent the mental health professional from offering any testimony or at least diminish the weight of the testimony by a probing critique of the witness' professional background. The chapter provided samples of impulsive and inadequate replies to such challenges, as well as better thought out responses. Finally, the futility of self-enhancement and exaggerating of one's credentials is shown.

More often than not the professional witness' qualifications are not aggressively challenged and are accepted with little dispute (Blau, 1984). This is particularly true when the expert is experienced or is known to have impressive professional credentials. In this initial phase of courtroom questioning, the two opposing attorneys are primarily attempting to verify the strengths and limitations of the expert witness. But because the witnesses' expertise outside the courtroom is usually honored by their clients, colleagues, and students without much question, doctors invariably feel offended by these initial attacks on their intelligence and professional integrity.

Experts need to be mindful that the courtroom is the attorney's home turf, and the mental health professional should never succumb to the temptation to be more verbally adroit than the cross-examiner. Even more important, you should never engage in sarcastic repartee with the opposing attorney. An expert will never impress a jury with courtroom one-upmanship. In fact, an experienced attorney will quickly unveil the professional mask of the expert and expose you as a petty or pompous show-off. Once this has been accomplished, the value of your testimony has been diminished. For this initial phase of witness qualification, it is important to remain calm and not exert too much effort in defending your background. This is just the start of what could be a prolonged inquisition, and you are advised to conserve energy for more critical questions that are likely to be asked in cross-examination.

CHAPTER 3

THE CLINICAL EXAMINATION

"So, after one session with the patient, you're prepared to testify in this case?"

After the doctor has been qualified by the court to testify as an expert witness, the next series of questions is directed at the actual examination of the client. In nearly every instance, the lawyers have a copy of the mental health evaluation, that includes a description of the evaluation procedures. You will be asked to explain how the examination was conducted, what findings were obtained, and what conclusions were reached.

DIRECT EXAMINATION

The attorney who called the witness to testify proceeds with the direct examination. Standard questions are asked of a psychologist (or psychiatrist) in order to reveal the process that led to the witness' professional conclusions. For ease of reading, the following example consists of the minimum basic questions rather than a more detailed and prolonged direct examination.

Q. Doctor, in your practice, have you had occasion to see Ms. Annette Anderson?
A. Yes.
Q. When did you first see her?
A. On August 9, 19__.
Q. Was she referred to you by anyone?
A. Yes, she was referred by her gynecologist, Dr. Jean Bernstein.

Q. What was the reason for the referral?

A. Dr. Bernstein telephoned me and asked if I would evaluate and possibly treat her patient, Ms. Anderson, who reportedly had been sexually assaulted and was emotionally upset.

Q. On how many occasions have you seen Ms. Anderson?

A. Four times.

Q. Where were these visits held?

A. In my office where I have my private practice.

Q. What are your normal procedures for conducting an examination such as this?

A. I interview the patient, that is, ask a number of questions to obtain her recollection of the assault and its aftermath. I also take a total history, which means asking about her childhood, education, work experience, health, and social background. I try to assess her current emotional symptoms and any need for psychiatric treatment.

Q. How long is each evaluation or treatment session?

A. About 50 minutes.

Q. What are your findings as a result of your examination of Ms. Anderson?

A. Ms. Anderson has suffered significant emotional distress, including depression and anxiety reactions. She has frequent nightmares and flash-backs of the incident. She continues to exhibit symptoms of what I diagnose as prolonged post-traumatic stress disorder, or PTSD.

Q. Have your reached an opinion, to a reasonable degree of medical (or psychological) probability as to the cause of Ms. Anderson's PTSD?

A. Yes.

Q. And what is that opinion?

A. In my opinion, the PTSD is a direct result of the sexual assault she suffered last year.

The most significant questions in the courtroom usually occur toward the end of the witness' testimony and begin with the words, "Do you have an opinion based on a reasonable degree of medical (or psychological) certainty …" There is no precise definition of "reasonable certainty" or "reasonable medical probability." However, in a criminal case in which a defendant's freedom or even life is at stake, the least amount of error is tolerated, and the degree of proof is "beyond a reasonable doubt." In civil litigation, the demand for proof is less stringent, and the degree of proof is "preponderance of evidence" or "more likely than not," although the weight of medical/psychological testimony may vary from jurisdiction to jurisdiction.

Using Measurement Instruments

If an examiner, in addition to clinical interviews, also uses questionnaires or behavior assessment techniques, the following questions might be asked:

Q. Doctor, how do you normally conduct your examination of a possible sexual assault victim?

A. I interview the patient regarding the severity and type of sexual assault, the level of violence involved in the assault, and other factors such as the number of assailants and whether the victim's life was threatened. I also administer several questionnaires for further information about the patient.

Q. What type of questionnaires do you administer?

A. I administer the Cornell Medical Index to assess current illness symptoms, the Modified Fear Survey to evaluate anxiety and fears, and the Sexual Experience Survey to assess the person's sexual victimization history.

Q. How long is the examination?

A. About 4 or 5 hours altogether, sometimes longer, depending on the psychological condition and reading ability of the individual.

Q. Did Mrs. Fernandez undergo the 4-to 5-hour examination that you just described?

A. Yes, she did.

Q. As a result of your examination of Mrs. Fernandez, do you have an opinion, to a reasonable degree of psychological probability, as to any injuries the patient suffered from the sexual assault?

A. Yes.

Q. What is that opinion?

A. In my opinion, the patient shows no evidence of psychological distress. In other words, although the patient had an apparently serious sexual and physical encounter, there is no evidence of any emotional disorder related to the assault.

CROSS-EXAMINATION: CHALLENGING A CLINICAL EXAMINATION

The clinical interview method has innate flaws, and the cross-examining attorney will attempt to underscore any and all of them in order to discredit the testimony so that the court will devalue or even disregard it. As mentioned in the previous chapter, unlike the direct examining attorney, the cross-examining attorney has the freedom to ask leading questions so as to attack and discredit the expert's opinions. Many opposing attorneys are generally polite as they proceed with a firm and persuasive manner to probe the witness. Others choose to be less cordial and do not hesitate to argue tenaciously that the witness' testimony be ignored or even impeached. This is the time for you to remain calmly professional and respond with authority.

The cross-examining attorney may explore the following issues:

- interview reliability
- standardization and norms
- validity of assessment tools
- duration of examination
- limits of data
- situational effects
- use of *DSM–IV*
- precision of diagnosis
- malingering and faking
- avoiding conflicting findings

Interview Reliability

"How reliable can an unstructured interview be?"

The very nature of the free-flowing unstructured interview will be challenged because of its potential for yielding different information by different examiners. The result of an unstructured interview may be substantially varying information and clinical impressions because of the differences between interviewers and the reliability of data obtained by this approach (Lanyon & Goodstein, 1982; Matarazzo, 1990). Because most clinicians employ the clinical interview to evaluate their patients, you are likely to face the following cross-examination:

Q. Doctor, would you describe your examination of the patient as a clinical interview?

A. Yes.

Q. You don't have a predetermined set of questions, such as in a structured interview, isn't that true?

A. That's correct, although I do have in mind the goal of obtaining certain kinds of relevant information about the person.

Q. And aren't clinical interviews subject to error, because examiners can misunderstand what is said, misrecord what is heard, or misinterpret what is meant?

A. Yes, that's true.

Q. Well then, Doctor, wouldn't you agree that the clinical interview is an unreliable method of examining a patient?

a. I can't disagree with you, but most clinicians depend on interviews to examine patients, and it is an accepted standard of practice.

To testify that an unreliable method is an acceptable practice does not bolster the expert witness' testimony. It is better to point out the positive contributions of the clinical interview approach.

A. The clinical interview is not a foolproof method of examining a patient, but the clinical interview method has also been found to be useful and effective, and in some cases superior to structured tests because the interview allows more flexibility to address the individual concerns of the patient and needs of the examination.

Standardization and Norms

"So, what is the gold standard for PTSD?"

A similar cross-examination will query as to the scientific and objective aspects of the clinical evaluation.

Q. When you examine for PTSD, do you ask the same questions of each person who is evaluated for the existence of PTSD?
A. No, the questions in every interview differ, depending on the situation.
Q. When you interview a person with PTSD, do you have a precise measure of the disorder, such as its severity?
A. No, I don't.
Q. Is your interview a scientific litmus test for PTSD?
A. No, it isn't.
Q. Then, Doctor, isn't it true that a clinical interview, like the one you conducted, is not a rigid, precise and scientific procedure?
a. An interview is not rigid or precise, but we try to be as objective as we can.

This response may not impress the jury because experts are presumed to be doing their best. A stronger reply reminds the court that one's findings are based on proven professional methods, such as the following:

A. Although an interview is not a rigid procedure, a clinical examination, like the one I conducted, is based on scientific findings and produces reliable and valid diagnoses.

There may be inquiry as to whether the examination was a standardized method, that is, whether it was a procedure with measurable scores and relevant normative data.

Q. Is there a standardized interview procedure with comparative norms used in the evaluation of PTSD?
a. There are a few tests with normative data, but I don't know of a standardized procedure to diagnose PTSD.

Admitting to the lack of a standardized technique suggests that the evaluation may be unprofessional or invalid. There are, of course, different ways to objectively examine any clinical disorder, and the diversity of methods does not, per se, preclude a competent clinical assessment. A more convincing response would be:

A. It is true that there is no single way to evaluate PTSD. It is extremely important that all examinations must be conducted rigorously by a clinician who has the knowledge and understanding of mental disorders and applies the recognized standard criteria for PTSD. Those criteria are provided in the *Diagnostic and Statistical Manual for Mental Disorders*, which is also known as the *DSM–IV*.

Validity of Assessment Tools

"How do we know that your test is valid for this client?"

The use of questionnaires and inventories engenders different kinds of challenging questions. Typically, data from assessment tools are criticized in terms of their reliability and validity (Ziskin & Faust, 1988).

Q. **Does the Sexual Experience Survey have norms so that you can compare the patient with a relevant population of normal and impaired persons?**

A. No, there are no norms, as such. The Sexual Experience Survey has been used in several studies and found to be reliable and useful in terms of measuring severity levels of victimization.

Q. **Were individuals from this community included in these studies?**

A. I don't believe so.

Q. **Aren't there many factors in different communities, such as social class, culture, and environment, that influence psychological measurements?**

A. Yes.

Q. **Then, Doctor, aren't questionnaires based on individuals from other parts of the country inappropriate to use for this patient?**

A. Certainly local studies would be ideal; however the use of questionnaires developed elsewhere has been found to be satisfactory in the practice of clinical psychology. In other words, it was appropriate to utilize this instrument with this patient, based on available studies.

Many challenges to mental health examinations make comparisons to other medical examinations and technology, which are presumed to be more scientific and accurate, such as the following:

Q. As a test for patients, psychological questionnaires are far from being as accurate as other high-tech medical procedures, like a CT scan or MRI, isn't that correct?

a. Yes, that's true, but that doesn't mean that psychological questionnaires aren't accurate or reliable.

This reply confirms that other medical techniques may be more accurate diagnostic procedures, but it suggests that psychometric instruments lack precision. A better reply would inform the jury that different information are obtained from different tests and that psychological questionnaires provide unique information about the brain.

A. Although the CT scan and MRI are accurate for certain conditions, like locating brain tumors, psychological questionnaires are much more informative about a person's emotional functioning, such as anxiety and anger, and that is what I am testifying about in this case.

Duration of Examination

"Wouldn't you know the patient better if you saw her more?"

A frequent attack on a psychiatrist's or psychologist's evaluation focuses on the limited duration spent with the examinee or the limited data obtained about the individual. In those cases the following questions could follow:

Q. You said you saw Ms. Anderson four times. How long was each meeting?

A. About 50 minutes.

Q. So, you spoke with her for less than 3 1/2 hours, is that right?

A. Yes.

Q. Doctor, isn't it true that you usually see patients for more than four occasions?

A. Yes.

Q. Do you think that talking with Ms. Anderson for less than 3 1/2 hours is enough time to testify about her?

A. Well, I do ...

Q. Doctor, but don't you learn more about that person as you spend more and more time with that person?

A. Yes.

Q. And haven't you changed your diagnosis on occasion because you uncover different things about the patient after several visits?

A. Yes.

Q. **Don't you think you would also learn more about Ms. Anderson if you spent more time with her?**

A. Yes.

Q. **And yet, Doctor, are you telling us that in this case, talking with Ms. Anderson for less than 3 1/2 hours was enough time for you to reach an opinion about her and testify to us about that opinion?**

A. Yes, and I believe I spent enough time evaluating Ms. Anderson.

Limits of Data

"You mean you talked only to the patient and no one else?"

Psychological examinations are frequently questioned as to their thoroughness. Were other family members interviewed? Were medical records, work performance evaluations, school records, or police reports available?

Q. **Now, I want to ask you about the information you obtained about Ms. Anderson. You said you had medical records from her gynecologist, is that right?**

A. That's right.

Q. **Did you have medical records from her regular doctor, Dr. Leong?**

A. No.

Q. **Did you have records of her work performance from the employer?**

A. No.

Q. **Did you have a chance to talk to her boyfriend, any member of her family, or any of her friends?**

A. No, I did not.

Q. **So, although you are testifying about Ms. Anderson's behavior, feelings and worries, you did not verify any of this with outside sources, isn't that true?**

A. Yes, I didn't talk to anyone except Ms. Anderson and briefly with Dr. Bernstein.

Q. **By your own admission, aren't you saying that your evaluation was not complete because you didn't talk to anyone other than the patient?**

a. Well, I feel my evaluation was adequate ... but it's true, I didn't talk to anyone other than the patient, and only briefly with her doctor.

This response may undermine whatever evidence the expert has provided, as it readily admits to an incomplete evaluation. A preferred reply would be:

A. Although it's true that I didn't interview anyone other than the patient, I had the patient's complete medical file, I conducted several hours of interviews with her, and I analyzed the results of several hours of psychological testing performed on her. Thus, I had substantial data on which to base my opinion about her psychological state.

Situational Effects

"Did you consider how the surroundings affected your interview?"

Research suggests that circumstances related to the examination can affect the outcome of the interview (Rosenthal & Rosnow, 1991), particularly when sensitive and personal matters are involved. Thus, different information might be provided if the person were to be interviewed in a hospital, at home, or in the doctor's office. Individuals might respond differently when interviewed alone, or in the presence of family members or their attorney. Consequently, you might be subjected to the following questions about situational effects:

Q. Doctor, when did you conduct your examination of Ms. Anderson?

A. My initial consultation visit was at General Hospital, where the patient was admitted following the sexual assault. Later, I saw her in my private office on three occasions.

Q. Was there anyone present during your visits with her?

A. Well, her husband was at her bedside in the hospital, and she also asked him to be present in her first visit in my office. In the last two sessions, the patient and I were alone.

Q. Do you know why her husband was present for the first two visits?

A. He said he wanted to provide support, and she was appreciative of his presence.

Q. Doctor, aren't you aware of studies that indicate that people are affected by the presence of others and that the information you obtained is colored by having a third party present?

a. Well ... I'm not aware of such studies, but I think she would have given me the same information even if her husband was not present.

The latter response has two undesirable features. It is not advantageous to admit ignorance of important studies, and suggesting that a husband's presence has no effect on the interview may not be believed. A more acceptable response might be:

A. I realize that the presence of a spouse might influence what a person says. In this situation, with a recently traumatized person, I chose to have the patient be more at ease and comforted by her husband's presence, and I believe I obtained valuable details from the patient. Furthermore, her husband was not present during our last two sessions, and her responses were consistent in all four sessions.

Use of *DSM–IV*

"Isn't it true that DSM–IV diagnoses are not reliable?"

No clinical examination is complete without a diagnosis, usually derived from the *Diagnostic and Statistical Manual of Mental Disorders, Fourth Edition – Revised* (*DSM–IV*; American Psychiatric Association, 1994). Research evidence suggests that diagnosticians often disagree among themselves on the same group of subjects (Kreitman, 1961; Spitzer & Fleiss, 1974). Hence, the following questions may be asked:

Q. **Doctor, are you aware that studies have found a lack of reliability in psychiatric diagnoses?**

A. Yes, I am.

Q. **Didn't you reach your diagnosis based on the standard *DSM–IV*?**

A. Yes, I did.

Q. **And haven't studies of *DSM–IV* also shown some disagreement in certain psychiatric diagnoses?**

A. That's correct.

Q. **So, Doctor, aren't you saying that your diagnoses are based on methods proven to be unreliable?**

a. I can't prove to you that my diagnoses are reliable but I stand behind my diagnosis of this patient.

One cannot deny the limitations of current diagnostic nomenclature. The expert witness should, however, stress (a) the improvements made and that continue to be addressed in the *DSM* system (i.e., *DSM–IV*), and (b) the value of the total assessment of the individual and not merely the patient's diagnostic label. A better response would be:

A. *DSM–IV* represents continued improvement over past diagnostic systems, with more clearly defined, objective criteria and categories derived from empirical literature. In any event, one should keep in mind that the clinical examination not only provides a diagnostic label, but its full value is in offering a detailed description of the entire personality and behavioral patterns of the individual.

Precision of Diagnosis

"How can there be two different diagnoses for the same person?"

Psychiatric diagnoses are sometimes thought of as less precise than medical diagnoses, such as a bone fracture. What one mental health professional diagnoses as anxiety, another might label as panic. Because of the apparently ambiguous nature of psychiatric diagnoses, the attorney might attempt to cast doubt on the expert witness' conclusions.

> **Q. Besides the diagnosis of PTSD, what alternative diagnoses did you consider?**
> A. In Ms. Anderson's case, I considered other possibilities, such as an adjustment disorder, an anxiety disorder, a depressive disorder, or possibly a phobic disorder.
> **Q. Is it likely that another therapist could have arrived at a different diagnosis than you did, such as an adjustment disorder?**
> A. That's possible.
> **Q. And another examiner could have diagnosed her as an anxiety disorder, and yet another doctor could diagnose a depressive disorder?**
> A. Yes, that's possible.
> **Q. In other words, four different mental health experts could come up with four different diagnoses for Ms. Anderson?**
> a. That's right.

This response is not sufficient and may lead the court to believe that mental health professionals arrive at very different conclusions regarding a patient. Such a perception would have damaging effects on the expert's testimony. Consider this reply:

> A. Four experts may use different words to describe the patient, but they would agree that the person has suffered significant emotional problems as a result of a traumatic event. The labels differ because they may place emphasis on different aspects of the person's emotional reactions. Studies have shown that clinical judgments among clinicians are usually similar.

Malingering and Faking

"Can you tell when someone is lying?"

Other criticisms of a clinical examination center on the honesty of the examinee and possible malingering or faking of symptoms (Rogers, 1984). These questions could be asked:

> **Q. When you met with Ms. Anderson, you asked a lot of questions about the alleged assault, and you also asked her about her childhood, education, work experience, health, and social background, is that correct?**

A. Yes.

Q. How do you know that she was answering correctly?

A. I did have medical records from her referring physician, Dr. Bernstein, to corroborate some of the information, and it was my impression that Ms. Anderson had fairly accurate memory of past events and that she was honest in her replies to my questions, so I was confident that she was answering correctly.

Q. You're not trying to tell us that you can always tell when a person is lying, are you?

A. No.

Q. Then, you don't know for sure if the answers Ms. Anderson gave you were accurate or honest, isn't that true?

A. Yes.

A favorite line of questioning concerns possible lying or faking during an evaluation.

Q. What do research studies tell us about the frequency of lying among persons accused of a criminal offense?

a. I'm not familiar with any specific data about lying among criminal defendants.

Simply to admit ignorance about any area of research is likely to weaken the expert's credibility. Experts are not expected to know all of the existing studies about lying or malingering but should be prepared to explain how a person's honesty is assessed:

A. I can't cite specific percentages of lying among defendants, but in this case, I evaluated the defendant's previous behavioral patterns and personality makeup. I made a special effort to corroborate what he told me with what is recorded in police files, as well as what other witnesses have stated. Because of the possibility of lying in criminal cases, I take every precaution to note the honesty of persons I evaluate. In my opinion, the defendant has been truthful in what he has related to me about the incident.

Studies examining the ability of clinicians to detect malingering reveal high rates of error, when attempting to identify those feigning brain injury and psychosis (Faust & Ziskin, 1988).

An attorney may also ask:

Q. Isn't there a likelihood that the patient lied to you and you didn't know that she lied?

a. Yes, but ...

There is always the possibility that one is fooled by a person, but a competent witness can provide a better response:

A. There is always the potential for lying or exaggerating in any situation like this; for this reason I am very careful to obtain solid, reliable and objective data, and I am confident that lying was not a factor in this case.

Avoiding Conflicting Findings

"Are you saying that there's not a shred of evidence inconsistent with your conclusions?"

In an effort to present the most convincing testimony, some expert witnesses are tempted to disregard or minimize clinical or test findings that run counter to their conclusions. Intentionally neglecting conflicting data and alternative observations is inappropriate, if not unethical, and should be avoided.

Q. **Doctor, you have stated that Mrs. Fernandez shows no evidence of psychological distress, is that correct?**

A. Yes.

Q. **In your 4- to 5-hour examination, did you find any indication of psychological distress from the sexual trauma?**

A. No, I didn't.

Q. **You mean, there is not a scintilla of distress from the sexual trauma?**

a. Mrs. Fernandez has been able to work full time as an accounts clerk at her usual level of productivity and has continued to have an active social life. I believe she is without any psychological distress from the assault.

It is perhaps true that the patient exhibits no major psychological impairment, but it is suspicious if one finds no sequelae to a sexual assault. Such an absolute denial of psychological symptoms runs the risk of being accused of deliberate misrepresentation to the court (Rogers, 1987). A more credible response would acknowledge some residuals of the traumatic event.

A. Mrs. Fernandez has an occasional dream about the assault, which affects her sleep, and she is cautious about where she goes at night. However, she does not have any psychological impairment and does not need any psychotherapeutic assistance at this time.

MISCELLANEOUS Q & A

In addition to the questions and answers just given, there are several different ways to challenge the clinical examination. The following is an assortment of questions pertaining to the interview method.

Supportive Literature

Q. Can you tell us what research literature supports what you just said?
a. Off-hand I can't recite any authors or articles, but I can find references if you want.

The expert should be prepared to identify basic textbooks or journal articles that are relevant to the matter being discussed. A more convincing response would be:

A. Regarding sexual trauma, research has been done by _____ and reported in _____. The textbook _____ by _____ is also very informative.

Authoritative Textbooks

Q. Would you consider the textbook by _____ to be authoritative?
a. It's a well-known text. Yes, I would consider it authoritative.

One should be very careful when asked about the authoritativeness of a book or writer. To acknowledge that a text is authoritative may imply agreement with viewpoints in the book that are inconsistent with one's expert testimony. Acknowledgment by an expert that a text, periodical or pamphlet is reliable authority may allow statements from those sources to be admitted into evidence. A more desirable response would be:

A. It's a very informative book, but I don't consider it authoritative because there are probably some conclusions with which I do not necessarily agree. (Be prepared to explain at least one of the conclusions with which you disagree.)

Controversy

Q. Isn't there some controversy as to how sexual trauma should be evaluated?
a. Yes. There's controversy in this area of psychology as there is in many areas of psychology.

To deny controversy is to compromise one's credibility, but simply to admit controversy about an assessment tool is insufficient. The expert should offer cogent reasons why certain evaluation procedures were selected over others. It is better to say:

A. Yes, that's true. This is why I was careful is selecting assessment techniques that have been found in a body of research to be reliable and valid in evaluating sexual trauma.

Criticisms

Q. **You admit that the assessment tool you used has been criticized by other psychologists. How can we be confident in its results?**
a. I use this tool all the time, and I find it to be trustworthy and helpful.

Although your positive experience with the assessment tool is reassuring, it is more convincing to report its reliability and validity data, as published in professional journals.

A. Although the assessment tool has been criticized, many studies have found the tool to be a reliable and valid method in assessing sexual trauma in women, such as Ms. Anderson.

Other Information

Q. **Could there be any other source of relevant information that you did not have that might change your opinion?**
a. No, I don't think so. I was quite thorough in my evaluation of the patient.

There is temptation to say "no" to the questions because a "yes" answer implies that you overlooked relevant information regarding the case. However, a "no" answer appears naive and defensive, because there is always the possibility of data that were not available for review. A more thoughtful response would be:

A. Yes, there could be medical records or job evaluations that I haven't seen that could affect my opinion. I would welcome such relevant documents. The more I know about this person the better.

Faking Good

Q. **Isn't it obvious that a defendant who is accused of sexual assault would present only a positive picture of himself?**
a. Yes, but I had a long interview with him and I believe he was honest in his replies.

Criminal defendants are desperately eager to gain the approval of the examiner. To deny the possibility of a guarded and defensive examinee would appear to be naive in view of the critical nature of the evaluation. A more credible response would be:

A. I realize that a criminal defendant may do his best to portray himself as a normal person. Thus, I would rely not only on a personal interview but also obtain information from multiple sources, including police arrest records, employment records and psychological tests.

Cultural Differences

Q. Have you ever evaluated a (foreign national) before?
a. No, but I think there's enough communality among cultures to draw useful conclusions.

When evaluating ethnic minority individuals or foreigners, there is considerable potential for misunderstanding due to language barriers and cultural differences. Efforts to overcome these obstacles should be included.

A. No, but to assure that he could understand me I assessed his command of English with a vocabulary test. Furthermore, when I administered the MMPI–2, I employed relevant cultural norms for a more appropriate baseline.

CLOSING ARGUMENTS

Whereas the *voir dire* challenges are relatively brief and not particularly difficult, the cross-examination can be stressful, especially for the inexperienced witness. Unlike the attorney who welcomed the direct testimony, the opposing counsel is expected to launch a sharp assault on the witness' opinions to emphasize any weaknesses and possibly discredit the testimony. The witness who has performed a valid assessment, while recognizing its limitations, will be able to cope with the most challenging questions.

This chapter focused on the testimony pertaining to the mental health examination of the client, along with a myriad of issues that arise from the clinical process. The patient's evaluation can be questioned with respect to

1. Interview reliability.
2. Standardization and norms.
3. Validity of assessment tools.
4. Duration of examination.
5. Limits of data.

6. Situational effects.
7. Use of *DSM–IV*.
8. Precision of diagnosis.
9. Malingering and faking.
10. Avoiding conflicting findings.

A clinical examination is not above reproach. However, you can admit to its imperfections without totally capitulating to the challenges on its usefulness in the court. Questions about its scientific accuracy, its thoroughness, and the possibility of lying can be managed with knowledge of the empirical bases of clinical examinations and efforts, albeit limited, to assess lying and malingering. Properly prepared, you can respond with confidence and authority.

CHAPTER 4

PSYCHOLOGICAL TESTING

"True or false: Psychological tests are grossly overrated"

Psychologists who are called on to testify in court often utilize psychological tests to buttress their diagnosis and clinical opinions. Psychological test results can be powerfully persuasive instruments in the courtroom because of society's long-standing affection and respect for these measurement tools. Psychological tests have, throughout this century, played a vital role in education, industrial personnel practice, mental health fields, and clinical medicine and, thus, there has been virtually no resistance to their introduction into judicial proceedings (Dahlstrom, 1993; Matarazzo, 1990).

The direct examination will elicit, at the bare minimum, the names of the psychological tests administered, the test findings, and the conclusions reached as a result of the tests. A more detailed inquiry may ask for the purpose of each test, what the test measures, the scores from each test, and the significance of each of the test scores. Because of the sheer quantity and complexity of psychological test scores, an effective testimony would favor the less detailed inquiry so that the typical judge or juror can have a clear understanding of the test results rather than be befuddled by the morass of technical data.

The following is a sample direct examination of a psychologist who performed psychological testing on an 11-year-old boy who, one year previous, had a head injury and was experiencing some learning difficulties in school:

Q. After your interview of Daniel, what psychological testing was performed?

A. The test battery included the Wechsler Intelligence for Children, Third Revision, or WISC-III, the Wide Range Achievement Test-3 [WRAT-3], the Halstead–Reitan Neuropsychological Battery for Older Children, and the Children's Personality Questionnaire.

Q. **Could you describe the purpose of each test and the conclusions you reached with each test?**

A. Yes, I can. But for the sake of time and clarity, may I suggest that I give an overview of the test battery, the test results, and my conclusions? There are so many tests and test scores that a description of each will consume considerable court time.

Q. **That will be fine. If I have specific questions or need clarification, I'll ask more from you. Now, please tell us about the tests you performed on Daniel.**

A. Okay. The battery of tests I administered was designed to evaluate Daniel's cognitive or mental abilities, by assessing his general intelligence, his brain functioning, and his psychological status. I performed this examination because of Daniel's declining school grades, to find out if the head injury he had several months ago led to brain dysfunction, and to find out if there were other reasons for his poor academic performance this past semester.

Q. **And what did you find out?**

A. First, the test for general intelligence found Daniel to be performing below average, at about the 15th percentile level in verbal abilities and at about the 30th percentile level in eye–hand coordination skills. Second, he performed poorly on a few of the neuropsychological tests, but it was not indicative of significant brain dysfunction. Third, as far as his school learning is concerned, he obtained very low reading and spelling scores, performing more than 2 years below his classmates, while doing adequately in arithmetic. Finally, from an emotional standpoint, he seems to be stable, with a degree of enthusiasm and vigorousness being fully acceptable within his age group.

Q. **Doctor, do you have a diagnosis for Daniel?**

A. Yes. The diagnosis is developmental reading disorder. This means that he has a reading ability that is below the expected level, given his schooling and intellectual abilities.

Q. **Is the reading disorder related to the head injury he sustained a year ago?**

A. No. I believe the boy's reading disorder is congenital in nature. A review of his school records indicated that his reading problems preceded the head injury. In addition, the boy's father may also have had a learning disability and he did not complete high school. Thus, the disorder may be a familial trait.

Q. **Is there any brain damage from the head injury he received a year ago?**

A. I don't think so, based on the neuropsychological test results.

CHALLENGING PSYCHOLOGICAL TESTS

Although psychological tests are embraced in the courtroom because of their scientific and quantitative characteristics, these instruments are fallible and the cross-examination will attempt to draw out as much of their limitations as possible. The expert should be prepared to discuss the following:

- technical terminology
- scientific precision
- empirical foundation
- role of psychological tests
- examiner influence
- test invalidity
- scoring errors
- inconsistent single item
- computerized test results
- ethnic minority factors
- faking and malingering

Technical Terminology

"Excuse me, what do you mean by standard error of measurement?"

Psychological testing, as a subspecialty area of psychology, consists of several esoteric concepts and terminology that are foreign to most laypersons. These terms need to be clarified, and the expert in psychological testing has to be prepared to answer questions such as:

What does test reliability mean?
Would you explain concurrent and constructive validity?
What is an IQ?
Can you tell us what a standard score means?
What kind of items are in the MMPI-2 Scale 3?
What is the correlation between the WISC-III and the WRAT-3?
Would you explain how the Rorschach inkblots work?
On what normative sample was the Beck Depression Scale based?
How many ethnic minorities were included in the development of this test?

Psychologists are not expected to have nitty-gritty technical details at their fingertips (e.g., the intercorrelations between WISC-III subtests), but an expert in psychological testing is expected to explain major concepts and terminology in everyday language understandable to the layperson. Avoid obfuscating by employing technical jargon. The following is scientifically accurate but fails to explicate anything:

Q. What is an IQ?

a. An IQ is a standard score, with a mean of 100 and a standard deviation of 15 or 16, depending on whether the WISC-III or the Stanford–Binet, Fourth Edition, is administered.

Consider this less precise but immensely easier to understand response:

A. An IQ is an intelligence test score that tells us how a person compares with other of similar age. For example, an IQ of 100 is an average score, which means that the person does as well on the test as 50 % of his or her age group.

Questions about psychological terms offer a window of opportunity for witnesses to showcase their professional expertise, and maximum advantage should be taken to be authoritative without being pedantic and obtuse.

Scientific Precision

"Are the MMPI and MRI equally accurate?"

Attorneys will frequently try to defuse strong psychological testimony by comparing psychometric techniques to high-tech biometric methodology. Loaded questions might follow, such as:

Q. Isn't it true that psychological tests can't compare with the precision and accuracy of scientific medical tests, like the MRI?

a. You can't compare medical and psychological tests. It's very different when you measure physical matter and when you assess mental processes. It's not a fair question.

This defensive and evasive answer does not address a relevant issue (i.e., the scientific quality of psychological tests). Another weak and ineffectual reply would be:

a. That's true, but psychology has come a long way to improve on the accuracy of psychometric tests, and we continue to work on improving the scientific quality of our test equipment.

This "Yes, but ..." response is better than the previous reply, as it agrees with the obvious truth that certain medical tests, like the MRI, are highly precise instruments. However, the response is vague and unconvincing. Consider the following answer that places medical and psychological methods in fuller perspective and draws the focus back to the case at hand.

A. Although certain medical tests, like the MRI, give a clear picture of the body, they provide no information about the important psychological aspects of this patient, which are central to this legal case. Psychological tests, such as those used in this case, have been demonstrated to be reliable and valid measures of brain functions and reading disorders, and are essential components in the total assessment of this child's condition.

Empirical Foundation

"What's the scientific proof for your opinion?"

A psychologist who testifies as to the presence of a mental disorder by pointing toward certain cutoff scores or a pattern of scores on a particular test often may have these interpretations accepted without challenge. However, an astute cross-examiner may demand that the psychological expert fully explain the theoretical and empirical bases for the diagnostic statement.

> **Q. Doctor, you testified that the wide discrepancy between the low Verbal IQ and high Performance IQ was indicative of the patient's developmental reading disorder. Do you have any scientific basis for reaching these conclusions?**
> a. Yes, in my graduate classes and during my clinical internship, I was trained to interpret these scores in this manner.

This reply does not answer the attorney's question, and neither does the following:

> a. I have many years of experience with IQ tests and am confident of my diagnosis of this boy.

The attorney's serious inquiry into the scientific rationale of the test score interpretation demands a more in-depth explanation of IQ score comparisons.

> A. Numerous studies have been conducted on the Wechsler IQ scores. Researchers have found that a 12-point difference between the Verbal and Performance IQs occurs less than five times out of a hundred. In addition, other investigators have found that learning disabled children who have a reading disorder have Verbal IQs much lower than Performance IQs. An extensive body of research in clinical child neuropsychology, such as the work of Dr. Byron Rourke at the University of Windsor, is the basis of some of my conclusions.

Although it is unwise to pontificate repeatedly in one's testimony, when faced with incisive questions, you should rise to the occasion and share the breadth of knowledge commensurate with your educational background and clinical experience. This display of professional sophistication can leave a positive impression in court as well as discourage the cross-examining attorney from venturing to cast doubt on your scientific credentials. Once you demonstrate your expertise and begin to favorably impress the court, the experienced attorney will back off to avoid having you cause further damage to his or her case.

Role of Psychological Tests

"Aren't you contradicting your own test scores?"

Because of the respected reputation of the psychological tests, or any scientific test for that matter, it is sometimes assumed that test scores are the major bases for the diagnosis and conclusions. Thus, if the cross-examining attorney, by citing critical literature, can generate sufficient doubt about the test results, the diagnosis and core of the testimony can be disputed. The following series of questions may ensue:

Q. **Was the 12-point difference between the Verbal IQ and the Perform-ance IQ an important basis for your diagnosing the patient as learning disabled?**
A. Yes. A 12-point difference between the Verbal IQ and the Performance IQ occurs in less than 5 % of the population and is typically associated with learning disabilities.
Q. **Doctor, isn't there a margin of error in the Verbal and Performance IQ scores?**
A. That's correct.
Q. **And what is that margin of error?**
A. For the Verbal and Performance IQs, I believe the margin of error, or what we refer to as the standard error of measurement, is about 3 or 4.
Q. **Doctor, does that mean that on another occasion this boy could have scored plus or minus 3 or 4 IQ points differently on this test?**
A. Yes.
Q. **So, because of the margin of error in this test, it's within psychologi-cal probability that the Verbal IQ could have been 3 points more and the Performance IQ 3 points less than the present testing. Is that correct?**
A. Yes, that is correct.
Q. **In other words, instead of a 12-point difference between the Verbal IQ and the Performance IQ, this boy could have only a 6-point difference between these two IQs?**
A. Yes.
Q. **Would a 6-point difference between the Verbal IQ and the Perform-ance IQ lead you to suspect a learning disability in this boy?**
a. Probably not.

This is a fairly sophisticated line of questioning from an experienced trial attorney or one who may be assisted by another expert psychologist. If the expert witness makes no further comment, the testimony related to a learning disability diagnosis have been seriously damaged. It is not difficult to survive this volley of skilled questioning if you remain calm and remember that the diagnosis is not based simply on present test scores, but that the total assessment incorporates school records, previous test results, interview with the patient, and other relevant sources of information.

The expert psychologist can better respond with a fuller reply:

A. A 6-point difference between the Verbal and Performance IQ by itself would not suggest a learning disability. However, in this particular case, I did not base the diagnosis solely on the Verbal and Performance IQ differences. As is my usual approach in evaluations on learning problems, I reviewed the patient's past medical history, his school transcripts, current teacher reports, and previous psychoeducational test results, as well as interviewing him and his parents. All of this information was important in reaching the diagnosis of developmental reading disorder.

Placing the test scores in proper perspective, the expert witness has explained that a wealth of data was available and analyzed to effect a comprehensive assessment of the patient. The expert can then be prepared for the possibility of a persistent attorney scrutinizing each and every source of information, (e.g., medical history), and inquiring how each source contributed to the diagnostic conclusions, again searching for possible flaws and inconsistencies in the data obtained.

Examiner Influence

"You mean she would have the exact same scores no matter who tested her?"

Psychological tests have been known to be influenced by characteristics of the examiner. Ziskin (1981) pointed out that the examiner's theoretical orientation and personal, social, and political attitudes may have an effect on testing procedures. Thus, you may be asked:

Q. **Isn't it true that the data collected in testing can be affected by the type of examiner administering the tests?**
A. I'm not sure what you mean.
Q. **Doctor, isn't it true that the patient being tested by an examiner with a different theoretical orientation, a different personality, and different attitudes than yourself might produce different test results?**
a. Yes, that is true.

A simple agreement that test data are influenced by examiner differences would lead the court to believe incorrectly that psychological tests are highly unreliable and that test scores would differ widely from examiner to examiner. Although examiner influence exists, it is important to explain that these influences are kept to a minimum by standardized testing procedures, which limit the possibility of individual variation. A test's high reliability coefficient implies that examiner differences are relatively insignificant. A better response to the challenging question would be:

A. No, it would be incorrect to believe that these results are greatly affected by the personality of the examiner. Examiner effects are minimized by thorough training in standardized test instructions, test procedures, scoring methods, and interpretation of scores. Only tests that have been proven to be sufficiently reliable were used in the examination of this patient.

Past Test Invalidity

"And how good was the Blacky Test?"

Attorneys may attempt to cast doubt on psychological tests by citing research that has found certain test conclusions to be invalid. This artful technique, described by McConnell (1969) as the "historic hysteric" gambit, involves an attack on one's expertise by converging on a past failing in the profession. The questioning takes the following form:

Q. **Doctor, are you familiar with the test called the Bender Visual Motor Gestalt Test, better known as the Bender Gestalt?**

A Yes.

Q. **What kind of test is the Bender Gestalt?**

A. It is a test involving the copying of nine different geometric designs. It requires perceptual skills as well as fine motor coordination, and is frequently used to assess brain functions.

Q. **Doctor, do you realize that the Bender Gestalt was used for many years as a measure of personality traits, such as aggressiveness and dependency?**

A. Yes, but studies have shown that the Bender Gestalt is ineffective as a test of personality traits.

Q. **Thank you, Doctor. If these conclusions believed to be true for many years have been later found to be invalid, how do we know that the conclusions you are reaching from your tests will not some day be found to be invalid?**

a. We can only be certain about what we now know about our tests. No one can be sure what future research will discover.

This apology will not allay the court's anxiety raised by the previous question. The expert witness must be prepared to admit honestly the limits of scientific disciplines, which by their very nature rely on ongoing testing of hypotheses and continual discovery of new findings. In short, what is "fact" at one point in time may become "fiction" at some later time. Consider this reply:

A. Misuse of the Bender Gestalt emerged when test users prematurely drew conclusions supported by theory or by clinical lore, but not substantiated by empirical findings. The experience with the Bender Gestalt test cautions psychologists to be extremely careful in the selection and interpretation of the tests. Responsible psychological examiners are required to utilize psychological tests whose validity and usefulness have been demonstrated in a body of research as well as in clinical practice.

Scoring Errors

"Two and two doesn't equal three, does it, Doctor?"

When psychologist tests are administered, it is easy for attorneys to review raw test data and discover errors in scoring and computations. These errors will be highlighted during court testimony and may shed unfavorable light on what are otherwise persuasive objective data. The following questions may ensue:

Q. **Doctor, is it important to accurately score the answers in the WISC-III?**

A. Yes.

Q. **Were you careful in scoring Daniel's WISC-III?**

A. Yes, I believe so.

Q. **What measures did you take to insure the accuracy of the WISC III test scores?**

A. My technician has been trained well to administer and score this test. I make a cursory examination of the test scores, but I don't take any special measures to check or recompute the test scores.

Q. **Are you aware that one of the Arithmetic test items was incorrectly credited when it was a wrong answer?**

A. No, I wasn't aware of that.

Q. **And did you know that the Vocabulary score was inaccurately calculated?**

A. No.

Q. **Don't these errors raise doubts in your mind as to the accuracy of the WISC-III scores and their interpretations?**

a. In a way, it does.

Psychological test records that are to be included in a court proceeding should be carefully reviewed so as to recognize any clerical errors in scoring. Such errors make it easy for the attorney to emphasize the sloppiness or unprofessional quality of your work. You have no choice except to acknowledge the errors and to emphasize, if applicable, that the computational errors were relatively minor and have no substantial impact on the diagnostic conclusions. Consider this response.

A. There is no excuse for the clerical errors you noted. Fortunately, the changes involved only 2 or 3 points on the test and would not alter the diagnosis reached by the overall test findings.

Inconsistent Single Item

"Can he be dyslexic if he can spell dyslexic?"

Psychologists recognize the significance of global test scores, such as an IQ, which represents a summary of a series of subtest scores. Psychologists are aware that a summary score is valued for the quantity of data it represents; for example, the Verbal IQ is based on the performance of six subtests, each of which involves numerous task items. Attorneys and laypeople, on the other hand, may not be certain about the significance of a global score, and they understand better what a passing or failing performance means on a single test item (e.g., a vocabulary definition or arithmetic problem). When a patient performs on a single item in a manner that is not commensurate with what the total score indicates, the attorney might draw attention to this apparent inconsistency, as a way to disparage the test findings. The questions from the attorney could be as follows:

Q. **Doctor, do 11-year-old boys usually know the definition of the word** *umbrella*?

A. Yes, that is a simple word that most 6-or 7-year-olds know.

Q. **Can an 11-year-old boy define** *bicycle*?

A. Yes. I believe so.

Q. **What about** *contagious*? **Do you think the average 11-year-old boy can define** *contagious*?

A. I'm not sure. I think not. That's a hard word for the average 11-year-old child.

Q. **And if an 11-year-old boy had a verbal weakness and a reading disorder, wouldn't you agree that he would have difficulty defining** *contagious*?

A. I would agree.

Q. **In this case, Daniel was able to define** *contagious*. **He said, "Something you catch. Like germs." Wouldn't his answer raise doubts that he has a verbal weakness or a reading disorder?**

a. Well, it might throw some doubt on the diagnosis.

The latter response is submitted by a psychologist who has forgotten that a diagnosis is rarely determined or ruled out by a single test item. The confidence in a diagnosis is bolstered by several test responses (e.g., several erroneous answers or several high quality responses) that would then be reflected in the total test score. A more appropriate reply would be:

A. Daniel's ability to define one difficult word does not alter the overall impression that he has poor verbal development, which was determined by numerous words that he could not adequately define. Psychologists rely heavily on the cumulative test score and not a single test item, and in Daniel's case his Vocabulary scaled score of 7 was definitely below average.

The targeting of a single apparently incongruous item by a sharp cross-examiner can occur not only with intelligence testing but on personality and behavior assessment scales as well. For example, a person who answers "True" to an MMPI-2 statement such as "I am not feeling much pressure or stress these days" may, in fact, be feeling stressed and having stress symptoms, and may have the diagnosis of adjustment disorder based on the total MMPI-2 profile configuration. Your role is to edify the court about the broad database for the diagnostic conclusions and the unreliability of a single test response.

A. It is important to keep in mind that the diagnostic impression of an adjustment disorder reached by the MMPI-2 results was based on the patient's response to 567 test items. The single answer which seems to be inconsistent with the diagnosis could have been the result of misreading or misinterpreting that particular item. In any event, the patient's many responses on this test pointed clearly to the presence of psychological impairment due to current situational stressors.

Before going to court, the psychologist would be wise to identify the test responses and scores that may not be in synchrony with the overall test findings. When aware of the incompatibilities in the test protocol, you will not feel caught off guard and can respond in the rational manner just described.

Computerized Test Reports

"Who is more accurate, you or the computer?"

The advent of a computerized interpretation system for psychological tests has led many practitioners to rely on an automated testing process as an efficient way to evaluate patients. Computerized versions of intelligence tests and objective personality inventories, such as the MMPI-2, are widely employed by psychologists, psychiatrists, and other mental health professionals, and the automated interpretation reports are often the object of scrutiny by the attorney (Ziskin, 1995).

Q. Did you utilize a computerized version of the MMPI-2?
A. Yes, I did.
Q. Are the statements in the test interpretation report of the MMPI-2 supported by psychological research?
A. Yes.
Q. That means that the interpretation statements are empirically validated, is that right?
A. Yes, that is right.

Q. In the present case, does this statement, "He may view himself as highly virtuous," apply to this particular patient?

A. No, it doesn't.

Q. How about this statement, "He seems to manage conflict by excessive denial and repression." Does this statement apply?

A. No, I don't think so.

Q. Didn't you say that the interpretation statements are valid?

A. Yes, I did. But not all of the interpretation statements apply to this patient.

Q. So, then, you pick and choose whatever statements you like and relate them to this patient, is that right?

a. Well, you could say that.

A simple agreement suggests some arbitrariness and subjective bias in the use of this interpretation system. It is better to explain how computerized test reports offer hypotheses about the patient and are employed in conjunction with a personal interview, direct observation of the patient, and other supportive documentation, such as work records (Graham, 1993).

A. The statements from a computerized test report are never accepted *in toto*. The report offers probability statements about the patient that need to be clinically correlated with actual behavior and objective observations of the patient. Thus, in light of what I know about this person from clinical examination and other information I obtained, I do not believe that the statements you singled out apply to him.

Ethnic Minority Factors

"Do you have norms for someone from Bangladesh?"

Psychological tests have been criticized when inappropriately administered to persons from socioculturally divergent backgrounds (Anastasi, 1988). Certain psychometric devices, such as intelligence tests, have been known to have a middle-class bias with normative standards that are not relevant for ethnic minorities, such as Native American and African, Hispanic, and Asian Americans. Thus, if an examinee's roots are outside the American mainstream you could be asked the following questions:

Q. Doctor, aren't you aware of studies that found IQ tests, such as the one you used, place ethnic minority members at an unfair disadvantage?

Q. Did you use normative standards that are not appropriate for a minority person?

Q. Isn't it true that the State of California does not permit the use of IQ tests for the special class placement of school children because of test bias against minorities?

a. Yes, I'm aware that IQ tests may be at times inappropriate to use with ethnic minority members, but I have no other choice than to use these tests and norms, because they are the only ones available to me in evaluating school children.

This response does nothing to counter the serious charge that intelligence tests are inadequate measures when used with members of an ethnic minority. There are legitimate reasons to use intelligence tests for evaluating ethnic minority persons (Sattler, 1992), and these arguments need to be proffered in one's reply.

A. Yes, I am aware that IQ tests can be inappropriately applied with ethnic minority persons. Although national norms do not precisely fit all ethnic minorities, intelligence test scores nonetheless are useful objective measures of mental abilities, which provide an index of present and future school performance. It is far better to have some objective testing of intelligence, with vital educational information, including those reflecting the apparently unequal opportunities available to minority members, rather than resort to previous evaluation methods which are essentially subjective judgments that are even more vulnerable to bias and prejudice.

Another effective reply would be:

A. Because of the well-known limitations of intelligence tests when used with ethnic minority individuals, I was careful in selecting multiple tests, some requiring the mastery of the English language along with some nonlanguage tests that rely principally on nonverbal problem solving. Furthermore, I reacquainted myself with the research findings about how persons from the patient's ethnic background perform on the tests I chose, so that I could interpret the test data appropriately.

Faking and Malingering

"Can someone fake on a malignering text?"

Based on the work of Rogers (1984) and others, mental health experts are informed that psychometric methods to detect lying and exaggerating about symptoms have limited effectiveness. Thus, you are likely to be queried about the ability of psychological tests to assess faking by examinees.

Q. Are you familiar with the psychological research that have found that standardized tests are not accurate in identifying those who are faking good or bad?

It is not prudent to state:

a. I'm a clinician and I'm not aware of those research results.

Nor is it wise to simply answer:

a. Yes, I'm aware of those studies.

It is critical for those who utilize psychological tests to know that the research literature has shown that instrument, like the MMPI-2, have shown some value, albeit limited, in assessing patient dissimulation. Thus, a more desirable response would be:

A. Psychological researchers have found that no single test can reliably detect faking of emotional problems, but there is some value in utilizing certain tests and special scales designed to assess a dishonest response. Thus, researchers such as Richard Rogers recommended that varied approaches in evaluating faking be employed by practitioners. This is what I did in my assessment of this patient.

CRITICIZING PSYCHOLOGICAL TESTS

A clever attorney may lead the expert into volunteering severe criticisms about psychological tests by asking questions about the limits of the psychometric approach. Brodsky (1991) referred to this powerful technique as collaborative criticism, when witnesses inadvertently help the cross-examiner inflict the worst damage on their own testimony. A sample tempting question might be:

Q. **Doctor, tell us some of the important ways in which personality tests fail in their aim to accurately measure a person's emotional state.**

Answers that are evasive or deny the shortcomings of psychological tests will appear to be unreasonably defensive about one's profession, such as the following replies:

a. No test is perfect, but I can tell you many good things about the tests I used.
a. I can't think of any better psychological tests than the ones I used with this patient.

A more acceptable response would address the imperfections inherent in any psychometric instrument, and explain how these factors can be overcome.

A. Personality tests are affected adversely by several factors, including the mood or test-taking attitude of the patient, sociocultural influences, and possible administration errors, to name a few. To be used appropriately, personality test interpretation should take into account these influential factors so that the assessment of the individual is fair and objective.

Another way to be enticed in to dangerous self-criticism is to be asked about an hypothetically ideal test or test battery to evaluate the patient.

Q. Ideally, if you had the time and resources, which additional tests could you have included for a more complete assessment of this patient?

a. Let me see. I could have used an alternative intelligence test for comparison purposes. Also special anxiety and depression scales would have helped. I could go on ...

One cannot be expected to administer an ideal battery of tests. A psychologist is expected to follow customary and practical testing approaches, which are based on previous research and experience, rather than a hypothetical ideal. A wiser reply is:

A. For an ideal examination, with more time and resources, one could test *ad infinitem*. Given the realities of this case, I am confident that the tests I administered were more than sufficient to answer the diagnostic questions being asked.

MISCELLANEOUS Q & A

The following is an assortment of questions regarding psychological testing.

Unstandardized Procedure

Q. Were you trained to allow patients to complete the MMPI-2 at home?
a. I don't think it makes any difference. She said she would adhere to my standard instructions.
A. No. I allowed this patient to complete the MMPI-2 at her apartment where she lives alone, because she could not remain at my office any longer. Because this was an unstandardized administration of the MMPI-2, I did not give the results the weight I usually do.

Test Reliability

Q. The test score shows that the patient was of average intelligence that day, but wouldn't his score be different on another day?
a. Yes. It could depend on things like his mood that day.
A. Yes, although the test reliability score indicates that his IQ would not vary markedly, plus or minus 3 points.

Normal Pattern

Q. Aren't there many normal people who have a 15-point difference between their Verbal and Performance IQs?

a. Well, that's true.

A. Yes. However, given his college education and his experience in a highly verbal occupation in sales, I believe his lower Verbal IQ is unexpected and probably related to his recent head injury.

Relevance of Single Score

Q. What does the extremely high score on the MMPI Scale 4 mean?

a. Such a score tends to be seen in persons who may be antisocial or are in conflict with authorities.

A. A high score on an single MMPI scale is difficult to interpret without looking at the scores on the other scales. Test interpretation is done by taking the entire profile configuration into consideration.

Schizophrenia

Q. The defendant scored high on the Schizophrenia Scale. What does schizophrenia mean?

a. Schizophrenia is a serious mental illness characterized by psychotic symptoms such as delusions and hallucinations.

A. Scale 8 was originally called the Schizophrenia Scale, but research has indicated that Scale 8 identifies a heterogeneous group of disorders, with difficulties in thinking, mood, and behavior, and is not limited to diagnosing schizophrenia.

Rorschach Criticism

Q. Aren't there published studies that raise doubt about the accuracy of the Rorschach?

a. Yes, but I don't put too much stock in them. I find the Rorschach to be a valuable psychological test.

A. Yes, and there are also many published studies supporting the usefulness of the Rorschach. We need to be aware of all of these studies when using this test.

No Testing Done

Q. Why didn't you have psychological tests administered to the defendant?

a. I don't administer psychological tests and do well without them. Besides, you can fake your way through these tests.

A. Psychological tests can be helpful, especially when the diagnosis is not clearly defined. In this case, there was abundant evidence to support that diagnosis of major depression and I didn't think psychological testing was needed.

Legal Opinion

Q. Do the psychological test results indicate that the client is not competent to sign a legal document?

a. That's right. The client is mentally retarded and is incompetent to sign a legal document.

A. The test results indicate that the client is mentally retarded and unable to understand the contents of a legal document. Stating that he is incompetent is a legal opinion, which only the court can render.

CLOSING ARGUMENTS

This chapter covered the numerous questions that emerge when psychological tests are employed, including the use of technical jargon, the scientific bases and accuracy of tests, computerized reports, and faking on tests.

When a psychologist is well-trained and experienced in psychological testing, he or she can bring to the courtroom valuable information that can be immensely helpful to the trier of fact. The expert in psychological testing must be prepared to clearly explain technical data and to report the empirical bases of these interpretations. The expert must be cognizant not only of the scientific merits of psychological tests but also must be fully aware of the notable limits of psychometric findings. It is likely that today's trial lawyers are increasingly test-sophisticated and prepared to vigorously challenge the professional witness.

CHAPTER 5

PSYCHOTHERAPY

*"As the therapist, aren't you too involved to provide
an unbiased testimony?"*

Many expert witnesses are hired by attorneys specifically to render an opinion about a criminal case, a litigant, or a child custody issue, having had no previous professional contact with the involved party. However, there are also many mental health practitioners who are subpoenaed to testify in court about a person who has been in psychotherapy with them. Attorneys at times refer to the former as an *expert witness* and the latter as the *treating doctor* although in court these distinctions are blurred because the treating doctor, by virtue of having relevant specialized knowledge that is unknown to the average juror, qualifies as an expert.

The expert witness/consultant has the advantage of appearing to be an objective, independent evaluator. Furthermore, the expert witness is usually supplied with a comprehensive set of documents, including past medical and psychiatric records, job evaluations, arrest records, and the like, much of which is not in the possession of the treating doctor because persistent initiatives to obtain such documents do not usually occur in the clinical setting.

The treating doctor, in contrast, has the advantage of knowing the individual in depth, having multiple therapy contacts over an extended period of time, as compared to the usual single-visit assessment by the expert witness/consultant. In terms of liabilities, the expert witness can be depicted as biased and favoring the side who has employed him or her (as the so-called "hired gun"), whereas the treating doctor could be perceived as the biased advocate of the patient.

Although most clinicians would not voluntarily seek out the experience of being scrutinized in the courtroom, when their patients are involved in legal proceedings in which emotional factors have a substantial bearing, they have little choice but to comply with a court order mandating their appearance to testify. Patients who file a lawsuit alleging psychological injury or mental incompetence waive their traditional doctor–patient privacy privilege and therapists are permitted to testify about previously confidential treatment sessions.

DIRECT EXAMINATION OF THE PSYCHOTHERAPIST

The direct examination of the therapist is conducted by the attorney who has summoned the professional to court and who desires the testimony of the treating doctor. Consequently, the attorney's questions are expected to be straightforward attempts to facilitate the therapist's input, such as the following:

Q. **After you diagnosed Mr. Edwards as having a major depression, what did you do for him?**

A. I recommended a treatment program aimed at improving his condition, which included depressed moods, periodic crying, irritability, lethargy, and poor sleep.

Q. **How many treatment sessions did Mr. Edwards have?**

A. My records indicate that we have had a total of 14 psychotherapy sessions.

Q. **Could you tell us what happened during your treatment of him?**

A. Initially, the patient had mood swings and was complaining of low energy and insomnia. I, therefore, referred him to a psychiatrist, Dr. Freeman, who prescribed an antidepressant medication, Trazodone, which seemed to be very helpful. Meanwhile, I saw Mr. Edwards once every 2 weeks for psychotherapy, during which time he learned to look at his problems in a more constructive manner and alter his daily living patterns.

Q. **Did Mr. Edwards make any progress in treatment with you?**

A. Yes. The combination of psychotherapy and antidepressant medicines began to lift the patient's low morale and labile moods. He was sleeping better and had more energy. After about 8 weeks of treatment, he began looking for a new job and in about 3 weeks, he was able to find a job as a sales representative for food products, which he now performs on a full-time basis.

Q. **Are you still seeing Mr. Edwards?**

A. Yes. He has been able to discontinue his medications in the past month, and we are anticipating terminating his psychological treatments in about 6 or 7 weeks.

Q. **What is your current diagnosis and prognosis for Mr. Edwards?**

A. The diagnosis is major depression, in remission, and the prognosis is good. I do not expect him to have any permanent psychological symptoms.

Q. Do you have an opinion, based on medical (or psychological) probability, as to the cause of the emotional problems for which you treated Mr. Edwards?

A. Yes.

Q. And what is that opinion?

A. In my opinion, the depression for which Mr. Edwards has been treated was the direct result of his sudden termination from his job last year, which left him emotionally and financially devastated.

The direct examination of the professional witness is expected to be easy. The more challenging questions arise in the next phase — the cross-examination of the psychotherapist.

CROSS-EXAMINATION OF THE PSYCHOTHERAPIST

The psychotherapist can anticipate a whole range of questions from the opposing counsel, with the purpose of lessening the impact of the statements of the treating doctor. In the testimony just presented, the most significant points were the causal connection made between Mr. Edwards' job termination and the psychological sequelae that required several months of treatment. Techniques to raise doubt about the etiology of the patient's psychiatric condition are discussed in chapter 8. The remainder of this chapter consists of the frequently asked questions when a treating psychotherapist takes the stand.

In the cross-examination the opposing attorney may cover:

- controversy in psychotherapy
- past failings
- therapist bias
- medications and psychotherapy
- unconfirmed observations
- therapy notes and memory
- multicultural issues
- criticizing psychotherapy
- limits of the expert

Controversy in Psychotherapy

"Isn't psychotherapy controversial?"

Psychotherapy, like any treatment modality in medicine, is subject to criticism, especially from those who espouse disparate theoretical and methodological schools of thought (Garfield & Bergin, 1986). The cross-examining attorney will likely want to show that controversy exists in the field of psychotherapy, so that the therapist's treatment program can be questioned.

Q. Doctor, does your psychotherapy technique have a name, like psychoanalysis or Freudianism?

A. Yes. I have been trained in the treatment methods known as cognitive–behavioral therapy.

Q. Is cognitive—behavioral therapy the only method practiced by psychotherapists?

A. No, there are other approaches, such as psychodynamic psychotherapy and interpersonal psychotherapy.

Q. What about eye-movement desensitization and reprocessing or EMDR? Isn't that a somewhat new therapy method?

A. Yes.

Q. Isn't there some controversy about EMDR?

A. Yes. I believe so.

Q. Isn't there controversy among the different psychotherapists as to the best way to treat a psychiatric illness?

a. Yes.

Q. If there is controversy among the professionals, how can we laypeople know that what you've been doing—your cognitive–behavioral therapy—with Mr. Edwards is the right way for him to be treated?

a. I don't know. I can only tell you how cognitive–behavioral therapy works and that I've been pleased with the success I have with this treatment method.

It is assumed that therapists use only methods that work, so that the reply just given is a nonanswer. The juror will be concerned about disagreements between practitioners of different treatment approaches, and their concerns need to be addressed more thoroughly. Consider the following:

Q. Isn't there controversy among the different psychotherapists as to the best way to treat a psychiatric illness?

A. There are differences among professionals in our field, just as among professionals in other fields of medicine and health care.

Q. If there is a controversy among the professionals, how can we lay people possibly know that what you've been doing with Mr. Edwards is the right way for him to be treated?

A. Years of research in psychotherapy outcome have shown that psychotherapy works, but there is no single best way to conduct treatment for all psychiatric conditions. For depressive disorders, such as Mr. Edwards, cognitive–behavioral therapy has been found to be highly effective, and I believe he has responded well to cognitive–behavioral therapy, with a reduction in his mood swings, depressive thoughts, and withdrawn behavior.

A mental health professional need not feel intimidated or defensive simply because there are disagreements in one's discipline. The reality is that controversy exists in all sectors of scientific endeavor, including medical and surgical treatments, and psychiatric and psychological therapies are no exception. An expert witness would do especially well by being prepared to explain psychotherapy methods in understandable everyday terms, to cite research findings that support the efficacy of its approaches, and to admit the limitations of its techniques.

Past Failings

"If previous therapy techniques have fallen into disfavor, don't you think your techniques will also fall into disfavor someday?"

One of the ways to raise doubt about the credibility of the expert and psychotherapy is to single out treatment methods from the past that have fallen into ill repute. This "historic hysteric" gambit described in chapter 4 consists of discrediting the professional by citing past sins in the profession. The following questions may be asked:

Q. Doctor, are you familiar with the name, Arthur Janov?

A. Yes, I am.

Q. Tell us what you know about Dr. Janov?

A. He is a psychiatrist who developed a psychotherapy technique, known as primal therapy. According to Dr. Janov, a patient's psychological problems are rooted in very early traumas, and therapy involves the releasing of deep hurt, resulting in writhing and screaming. This is a very sketchy explanation but it describes the basics of Janov's technique.

Q. What is the current opinion about Janov's primal scream therapy?

A. Although it enjoyed some popularity in the 1970s, primal therapy and other confrontational techniques were found to produce undesirable side effects, such as increased anxiety, because of its intense emotional release methods. Today, there appear to be fewer practitioners of the Janov therapy.

Q. So, you are saying that a psychotherapy technique that was once thought to be very helpful is now considered an undesirable treatment choice, is that correct?

A. Yes.

Q. Then, Doctor, doesn't it follow that the psychotherapy method you are employing with Mr. Edwards may some day also be considered undesirable?

a. I don't know. It's possible, but I don't think cognitive–behavioral therapy can be compared with primal therapy.

The expert witness is not required to defend all of the failings of the past, but there may be value in briefly explaining why a certain treatment method such as primal scream therapy is no longer widely used.

A. Dr. Janov developed a method with some theoretical appeal but probably failed to adequately test its methodology under strict scientific controls. In contrast, cognitive–behavioral therapy has been subjected to a large body of investigations, and there is much reason to be confident in this form of psychotherapy.

Therapist Bias

"As the therapist, aren't you biased toward your own patient?"

The psychotherapist who has had a relatively long-term treatment with a patient may be questioned as to his or her ability to remain objective in legal proceedings that are important to the patient. In such instances, the therapist's biases may be implied by the following questions:

Q. **Doctor, how long have you known Mr. Edwards?**
A. Our first session was a year and a half ago, shortly after his job termination.
Q. **And you've had 14 psychotherapy sessions with him, is that correct?**
A. Yes.
Q. **Would you say that you have a good relationship with Mr. Edwards?**
A. Yes. I believe I do.
Q. **Is that what some psychotherapists refer to as a** *positive transference*?
A. That's correct.
Q. **During the course of your treatment, Mr. Edwards has had several different problems, such as with his employers, his insurance company, and even his medical doctors, is that correct?**
A. Yes.
Q. **And you've helped him by being sympathetic and supportive, and at times you've served as an advocate for him, isn't that true?**
A. That's true.
Q. **And today, as you sit here testifying for Mr. Edwards, aren't you advocating for him once again?**
A. In a way, yes.
Q. **So, isn't it likely that, as his advocate, you may skew your answers in court so as to help him?**
a. Well, I am his therapist and I want to help him, but I would not lie in court for him.

There is no way to deny the fact that you are Mr. Edwards' doctor, and that you continue to be his supporter. It is also difficult to avoid the court's perception that you may be tilting your testimony in favor of your patient. You can, however, affirm the advantages of a therapist's testimony because of the abundance of information and observation you have accumulated through the course of psychotherapy.

A. I am aware of my role as Mr. Edwards' therapist. I am also aware of my responsibility to testify honestly and fairly in court. Thus, I have tried to include in my testimony not only my many personal observations of Mr. Edwards but also documentation of his past work history, his previous medical records, and other achievements and citations he has earned, so that I could be as objective as possible.

Medications and Psychotherapy

"Why do you prescribe medicines that produce such dangerous side effects?"

In the course of psychotherapy, psychiatrists often incorporate psychoactive medications. There is an abundance of research indicating that the combination of pharmacotherapy and psychotherapy enhances the treatment of depressive disorders and schizophrenia (Klerman, 1986). Because medicines produce a variety of adverse reactions, attorneys can easily bring out the negative aspects of psychiatric medications as a way to discredit the expert.

Q. **Doctor, in your treatment of depression, do you often rely on medication?**

A. Yes, I often prescribe antidepressant medications.

Q. **Isn't it true that antidepressant medications create unpleasant side effects?**

A. That's true. That is why in Mr. Edward's case I chose to prescribe a medicine like Trazodone, which produces fewer adverse reactions, like dry mouth.

Q. **Well, Trazodone can cause side effects too, can't it?**

A. Yes.

Q. **In fact, doesn't Trazodone sometimes cause a drop in blood pressure?**

A. Yes.

Q. **Doesn't Trazodone sometimes impair mental functions and driving ability?**

A. Yes.

Q. **And isn't there a special warning that Trazodone can lead to abnormal persistent erections in males, which in some cases requires surgery, resulting in permanent impotence?**

A. Yes.

Q. **Is Trazodone a 100% cure for depression?**

A. No, it isn't.

Q. **Then isn't it risky to prescribe Trazodone, which isn't a 100% cure, with its known dangers?**

a. I don't think it's risky. I have found Trazodone to be a very helpful medication.

Rather than citing merely personal experiences, psychiatrists should edify the court as to the research evidence that supports the benefits of any medicine use in clinical practice. A stronger reply would be:

A. Before any medicine is permitted to be used, its benefits and side effects undergo years of careful investigation by the Food and Drug Administration. The adverse reactions you described are indeed associated with the use of Trazodone, but they occur in a small percentage of patients who take the medicine. Furthermore, doctors who prescribe Trazodone give clear warnings before hand so that, for example, the patient who experiences erectional problems is instructed to discontinue the medicine immediately and see the doctor to avoid any serious consequence.

Another helpful response could be:

A. Some medication can have unpleasant side effects. So can psychotherapy, when probing and uncovering defenses, lead to increased anxiety and emotions. Studies indicate that the combination of psychoactive medications and psychotherapy have proven to be highly therapeutic when administered by a trained professional.

A less likely and more sophisticated critique of the psychopharmacological approach would focus on the undesirable psychological side effects when drugs are administered to the psychotherapy patient. A skilled attorney aware of some of the subtle issues involved when medications are prescribed to therapy patients may ask the following:

Q. **Doctor, can you tell us some of the negative psychological reactions when medications are prescribed to psychotherapy patients?**

A. Well, for some patients, the prescribing of medicine many impose an authoritarian role on the part of the therapist, and the patient may become more passive and dependent, relying on the healing powers of medicine rather than actively working on resolving personal problems.

Q. **You've heard it said that when medicines reduce the symptoms of anxiety and tensions, the patient might be less motivated for psychotherapy, haven't you?**

A. Yes, I have.

Q. **And you've also heard of symptom substitution, that is, the forming of other symptoms when medications rapidly reduce anxiety, haven't you?**

A. Yes.

Q. **If medicines can cause patients to be passive, dependent, less motivated for psychotherapy and develop new symptoms, isn't is unwise to prescribe them?**

A. In some cases, yes. But in other cases, like that of Mr. Edwards, no, because of the benefits obtained from their use. Beyond that, I haven't observed any indication of Mr. Edwards becoming less motivated or developing new symptoms as a result of his prescribed medication.

The responsible professional yields to the incisive probing about the demerits of psychotropic medications. As before, the psychiatrist needs to recall the scientific foundations of psychopharmacology and its valuable role in mental health care.

A. There are some psychological risks in prescribing psychiatric medications, as you well noted. Because of this, a doctor must be careful when including medications in the treatment regimen. Psychiatrists are encouraged by the strong evidence that supports the positive contributions of medicines, like Trazodone, in the treatment of emotional problems. As a physician, I must weigh both the benefits of medications against the known risks when prescribing medication to a patient.

Unconfirmed Observations

"But you don't have any objective evidence to support that opinion, do you?"

In the course of psychotherapy, the clinician forms opinions based on a wealth of information from the patient as well as from family members. In court, the therapist may share the many observations and findings made in treatment sessions. Although some of the therapist's conclusions are based on solid objective evidence, for other opinions the factual supportive data may be lacking. The attorney may attempt to reveal the tenuous grounds on which an opinion was reached.

Q. **Doctor, you testified that the patient has difficulty controlling his temper and that he sometimes yelled at his wife, is that correct?**

A. Yes, that's correct.

Q. **Did the patient tell you that he yelled at his wife?**

A. No.

Q. **Didn't you obtain that information from the patient's wife?**

A. Yes.

Q. **And that information was important in your assessment of the patient's temper, isn't that true?**

A. Yes.

Q. **Did you give him a test measuring his anger level?**

A. No.

Q. **Doctor, do you know for sure that the patient actually yelled at his wife?**

A. No, I'm not sure.

Q. **So, you based your diagnosis on something you're not sure about?**

a. Well, I trust that the patient's wife told me the truth.

It is irresponsible to base an important conclusion on hearsay evidence. A therapist who obtains external confirmation on what is revealed in sessions will present more convincing testimony.

A. No, I didn't base the diagnosis on the wife's comments alone. In our sessions, I noted that the patient became irritated quickly when we discussed the problems he was having at work. Also, the receptionist in our office informed me that the patient raised his voice to her on a couple of occasions when he couldn't get through to me on the telephone. In other words, there were varied substantiating information that served as the basis of my opinion that the patient had some difficulty in anger control.

Therapy Notes and Memory

"Are you testifying that you can remember everything that's been said in the therapy?"

Legal proceedings often occur many months after psychotherapy has ended. The psychotherapist will be asked about specific details and events, and it is likely that neither thorough therapy notes nor a flawless memory can provide the exact information being requested. Questions you can expect will be as specific as the following:

Did the patient have sleep problems when you saw him in October?
How many hours of sleep was he averaging at that time?
Was he taking any nighttime sedatives?
What medicine was he taking and what was the dosage?
Could his sleep problems be the cause of his fatigue and irritability in October?

As conscientious as one might be in maintaining detailed psychotherapy records, it may be impossible to record or remember all of the relevant data pertaining to a patient's psychological condition. The responsible therapist has noted the most important details pertaining to the patient's mental health, including medications and dosage levels, but practical considerations prevent the documenting of every fact shared in a treatment session. Nonetheless, the probing attorney may take maximal advantage of any gaps seen in the therapist's record keeping.

> **Q. Doctor, isn't sleep an important component of a person's mental health?**
>
> A. Yes, it is.
>
> **Q. Wasn't insomnia one of Mr. Edwards' problems?**
>
> A. Yes.
>
> **Q. In October, how well was Mr. Edwards sleeping?**
>
> A. May I refer to my clinic notes?
>
> **Q. Sure.**
>
> A. Uhmm. My notes don't indicate how much he was sleeping at that time.
>
> **Q. If you don't have any notes about his sleeping problems, do you have any independent recollection as to how well he was sleeping in October?**
>
> A. I don't think I can recall accurately how much sleep he was getting.
>
> **Q. Doctor, aren't you trained to keep complete notes of your psychotherapy sessions?**
>
> A. Yes.
>
> **Q. If you have excluded from your records an important fact, like his sleep patterns, isn't it likely that you have forgotten other important facts about his psychological life?**
>
> a. Well ... I suppose that's possible.

Questions about the completeness of psychotherapy notes can be anxiety-provoking, because no one has impeccably complete therapy records. However, clinicians do not have to be embarrassed to admit that treatment notes are not all inclusive and that one cannot remember all of the details that occurred during the treatment process. The therapist can calmly admit the following:

> A. Although it is true that the therapy notes do not contain all of the details in the patient's life, my practice is to record the major factors involved in his treatment. I am not able to recall how many hours Mr. Edwards was sleeping in October, but I am confident that he was at that time continuing to be depressed, as reflected in my clinical notes that state that he was periodically weepy and preoccupied with his work problems.

Multicultural Issues

"How can you have empathy with a person from a totally different background?"

If the racial or sociocultural makeup of the psychotherapist is at variance with the background of the patient, the attorney may attempt to question the effectiveness of the treatment process. The cultural responsiveness hypothesis (Sue, Fujino, Hu, Takeuchi, & Zane, 1991) asserts that psychotherapy benefits are greater when the therapist and patient are similar in ethnic and language background. The following questions may therefore follow:

> Q. **Are you aware of studies that have shown that patients who are similar in terms of ethnic background to the therapist have lower rates of treatment dropouts and greater length of treatment?**
>
> A. Yes, I am.
>
> Q. **Are you aware of studies that have shown that patients who did not speak English as their first language did better in psychotherapy when matched with a therapist of similar language background?**
>
> A. Yes.
>
> Q. **Then, Doctor, don't you think it would have been better to refer the patient, who is Hispanic, to a Hispanic therapist rather than treat him yourself?**
>
> a. Well, that could be true, but I believe I was able to provide appropriate treatment for this patient.

It may be ideal to match psychotherapist and patient with respect to various demographic (gender, age, socioeconomic level) and cultural variables, but this idealistic match is often unrealistic or impractical. A better response can be:

> A. Although there are benefits in matching psychotherapists and patients on the basis of culture and primary language, we must remember that ethnicity is not the only determinant of therapy effectiveness. A therapist's sensitivity and ability to establish rapport are also essential, regardless of the sociocultural similarities of the patient and the therapist.

Another credible response is:

> A. It may have been ideal for the patient to have had a Hispanic therapist. I attempted to provide the best treatment for him by acquainting myself with the cultural values and beliefs of his ethnic background, and tried to assure that he and I were able to communicate well with each other.

Criticizing Psychotherapy

"So, tell us, what's wrong with psychotherapy?"

An infrequently used but clever courtroom technique is to have the experts criticize their own craft. This method, labeled *collaborative criticism* by Brodsky (1991), was referred to in chapter 4, and involves the following approach:

> **Q. Doctor, you keep abreast of the research on psychotherapy, don't you?**
> A. Yes.
> **Q. Could you tell the jury what you know are some of the limitations or shortcomings in psychotherapy?**
> A. Well, psychotherapy is not a cure-all. Even under the best of conditions, not everyone responds positively to treatment. A 60%–70% success rate is generally expected for those in therapy.
> **Q. Who doesn't benefit from psychotherapy?**
> A. Traditional psychotherapy may not be effective for those with verbal limitations or language barriers. Some disorders, such as substance abuse or psychotic disorders, may not respond to outpatient psychotherapy alone. There are many different psychiatric conditions that are not responsive to psychotherapy.
> **Q. So, aren't you saying that psychotherapy is very limited in dealing with many psychiatric conditions?**
> a. Yes.

It is the expert's responsibility to explain the limitations of one's professional methods. In fact, to evade this line of questioning is to appear defensive and disingenuous. However, the expert witness needs to be as candid about the strengths as well as the weaknesses of psychotherapy and, most importantly, the value of psychological treatment in the case at hand.

> A. It is true that psychotherapy has its limitations, and it is also true that psychotherapy can be highly effective in alleviating stress symptoms, as in Mr. Edwards' case.

Limits of the Expert

"You provided psychotherapy, but you didn't perform a thorough forensic investigation, did you?"

All mental health professionals, when asked to testify in court, are theoretically "experts," in that they provide specialized knowledge based on their training and experience that is beyond the ken of the average juror. As psychotherapists, the clinician has detailed technical information about the patient's diagnosis, treatment, and prognosis. However, because psychotherapists typically do not conduct a thorough investigation of the specific causal factors in a particular case (e.g., premorbid personality, preinjury school and work performance, details of the accident or incident, etc.), clinicians must be sensitive to the limits of their expertise. Consider the following questions:

Q. **Doctor, your patient, Mrs. Hogan, suffers from anxiety, is that correct?**

A. Yes.

Q. **And you based your diagnosis on her general nervousness, her difficulty falling asleep, and her stomach problems, is that correct?**

A. Yes.

Q. **You further concluded that the bomb explosion at her workplace was the reason for her psychological condition, is that true?**

A. Yes.

Q. **Are you aware of comments made by her supervisor at work and her coworkers that Mrs. Hogan is a generally nervous person?**

A. No.

Q. **Did you know that a few years ago, long before the bomb incident, she was prescribed sleeping pills by her family doctor?**

A. No, I didn't know that.

Q. **And did Mrs. Hogan ever tell you that she has been buying nonprescription medications, like Gelusil and Tums, for many years because of her sensitive stomach?**

A. No, she didn't tell me that.

Q. **Doctor, if you knew that Mrs. Hogan was thought to be a nervous person at work, had need for sleeping pills in the past, and has bought drugstore products for stomach problems for many years, would that change your opinion as to the cause of her current anxiety problems?**

a. No. As I wrote in my report, the bomb explosion was very traumatizing to Mrs. Hogan and she has been much more anxious than she's ever been.

Although it may be true that the patient's anxiety condition has worsened since the explosion, the therapist-witness has minimized or ignored obvious nonaccident-related contributing factors, and thus jeopardized his or her credibility and potential contribution to this case. The psychotherapist should not have offered any absolute opinion about the causative connection between the bomb incident and subsequent anxiety reactions. The prudent response to the last question could be:

A. I was not fully informed about Mrs. Hogan's previous behavior and health status. Until I can review all available evidence about her preinjury functioning, I should withdraw any conclusions about the specific causes of her current anxiety disorder.

MISCELLANEOUS Q & A

A variety of questions pertaining to psychotherapy are provided here.

Specialist

Q. **Because the patient's primary problem is alcoholism, don't you think he should have been treated by a certified substance abuse counselor?**

a. That would have been ideal, but he asked me to be his therapist and I think I've been doing a good job.

A. A psychologist (psychiatrist) is trained to treat mental disorders, including substance abuse and dependency. I have treated many alcoholics in the past and am capable of treating this patient as well.

Other Psychotherapies

Q. **Did you ever look into the possibility that the patient would have responded better to a different style of psychotherapy than the one you provided?**

a. No. I never gave it a thought. I believed that he would improve with my help.

A. Yes. However, I felt that he would do well if he received the combined behavioral and cognitive approach I employ with conditions like his.

Patient Gender

Q. **Was it a concern to you that the patient, a female victim of sexual assault, might not respond as well to treatment by you, a male therapist?**

a. No. My gender wasn't of any concern. She never said anything about being uncomfortable having a male therapist.

A. It was something I brought up in our first session, and she said she trusted me and wanted to remain in therapy with me. I know of no studies that state that male therapists cannot help female victims.

Inpatient Care

Q. **Doesn't it stand to reason that he would do better in a hospital to cure his alcoholism?**

a. Yes. But it's too expensive and he can't afford to be hospitalized.

A. It may seem that way, but studies have shown that alcohol problems, as in this case, can be managed as effectively in a day hospital program as in long-term hospitalization.

Defining Distress

Q. Can you explain what you mean when you say the patient is still suffering emotional distress?

a. It's really very subjective. We don't have any benchmark measurements, no exact quantification. It means he can't handle what's happening in his life.

A. The patient is still having problems falling asleep, and he doesn't eat well and has lost about 20 pounds in the last 4 months. He doesn't cry anymore, but he still isolates himself and rarely leaves his home.

Length of Treatment

Q. Don't authorities recommend long-term psychotherapy for a case like this?

a. I'm a believer in short-term therapy. Besides, in this age of managed health care, I have no choice but to do short-term treatments.

A. Yes, in general long-term psychotherapy could lead to more lasting results. In this particular case, however, I see extraordinary resilience in this patient as well as reliable support systems to assure continued maintenance of his emotional stability.

Prognosis

Q. How much longer will the patient remain in treatment with you?

a. That's impossible to say. No one has a crystal ball. It depends on so many factors that I can't predict.

A. In my experience with conditions such as hers, treatment may be needed for another year. If she can find a job where she feels secure and anticipates no further intimidation, treatment may be terminated in less than a year.

Deferring to Expert

Q. Because you, as the treating doctor, did not investigate causal factors in detail as did the independent expert witness, you would defer to her expertise, wouldn't you?

a. Well … yes, I would.

A. I'm not certain how the expert reached her opinions, so I would not necessarily defer to her. In our therapy sessions, I have all along been looking at the source of my patient's emotional difficulties.

CLOSING ARGUMENT

In today's litigious climate, a mental health practitioner is likely at one time or another to treat a person who is involved in a lawsuit and thus be requested to testify about the nature and course of the psychotherapy for the litigant. This chapter reviewed the issues that arise when a psychotherapist is summoned to court.

The psychotherapist who is subpoenaed to appear in court to testify about a patient in treatment will likely be a reluctant witness, who has been taken away from the comforts of a familiar office setting to the ominous atmosphere of the courtroom. You need not feel intimidated if appropriately prescribed treatment strategies have been rendered, if sufficient therapy records have been maintained, and if you keep current on the research literature pertaining to psychotherapy issues. You need to keep in mind that you have the major advantage of possessing the most in-depth professional knowledge of the patient and are, indeed, an expert witness.

CHAPTER 6

CRIMINAL LAW

*"How can you be certain that the defendant was insane
at the time of the offense 3 months ago?"*

In criminal law procedures, mental health professionals have several entrees as expert witnesses. Most often, they participate in hearings that consider the accused's mental state at the time of the criminal offense, as part of the well-known insanity plea. Criminal experts address several other important mental health issues such as the fitness to stand trial, dangerousness, and malingering. This chapter focuses primarily on the insanity defense and other general issues arising in criminal court. Subsequent chapters provide more attention to mental competency and dangerousness (chapter 10) and faking and malingering (chapter 11).

Direct Examination: Witness Qualification

"Is this your first time in criminal court?"

In addition to the usual questions to qualify a doctor as an expert witness (see chapter 2), the expert in a criminal trial can expect to answer the following more pertinent questions:

In your practice, do you have a special interest in forensic psychiatry (psychology)?
Have you done any research or teaching in the field of criminal psychiatry (psychology)?

Have you ever been appointed to a panel evaluating an insanity plea?
Have you ever worked for the prosecutor's office in a criminal trial?
How often have you been appointed by the court, how often have you worked for the prosecutor, and how often have you been hired by the defense in criminal trials?

With regard to the last question, you may not have exact numbers at your fingertips, but it is helpful for the court to know in what capacities you have served in previous criminal court proceedings. Ideally, the mental health professional has done evaluations for the prosecutor as well as for the defense (i.e., without any apparent bias or preference in criminal cases). Of course, it is not essential that you have been an expert for both sides in criminal court; it is essential that you are impartial, objective and professional in your role as expert witness.

Direct Examination of Prosecution Witness

"You performed a comprehensive examination, didn't you?"

The expert witness for the prosecution will first undergo the direct examination by the prosecuting attorney, who will elicit testimony that he or she hopes will refute the defense of mental disorder, or insanity, and aid in the conviction of the accused. The questions will probably be intended to enhance the conclusions of the prosecution witness. The direct examination is therefore usually the easy part for the expert witness.

(To facilitate reading, the direct and cross-examinations presented here contain the bare essentials and are much more concise than an actual courtroom testimony.)

Q. Doctor, did you perform an evaluation of Mr. Gregory?
A. Yes, I did.
Q. At whose request did you do the evaluation?
A. At the request of the court, I became a part of a three-member panel evaluating Mr. Gregory's plea that he was not sane at the time of the killing of his neighbors.
Q. When and where did you conduct your examination?
A. I examined Mr. Gregory on March 8 at the State Hospital where he is being held until his trial.
Q. How did you conduct your examination?
A. I interviewed him for about 1 hour and I administered psychological tests, including the Wechsler Adult Intelligence Scale-Revised, the Bender Gestalt, the Draw-A-Person, the Thematic Apperception Test, and the Rorschach. In addition, I reviewed his arrest records that were at the prosecutor's office and his medical records at the State Hospital.

Q. What was the total amount of time you spent with Mr. Gregory?

A. About 4 hours.

Q. What did you learn about Mr. Gregory from your evaluation?

A. Mr. Gregory told me that the shooting incident involved neighbors with whom his family had been feuding for more than 5 years. About 3 years ago, Mr. Gregory fired a shotgun in the air because the neighbors made him angry after they teased his mother. On the day of the multiple killings, the neighbors were arguing again with his mother, and he decided that he had had enough of the arguments, went for his rifle, jumped out of his bedroom window, and fired several times at the neighbor's house, not knowing whom he shot. He then ran away, but later returned and was apprehended by the police.

Q. What did the psychological tests show?

A. The psychological testing revealed no evidence of a psychotic disorder, an impulse disturbance, or a paranoid personality. The results, in short, showed no mental disorder.

Q. In your opinion, do you believe that Mr. Gregory knew right from wrong at the time of his offense?

A. Yes.

Q. Can you tell us, based on reasonable psychological certainty, what you concluded from your examination?

A. In my opinion, on the day of the killing of his neighbors Mr. Gregory appreciated the wrongfulness of his actions and he had the ability to control his behavior in accordance with the law.

Cross-Examination of Prosecution Witness

*"Do you know for sure that the defendant didn't have
a dissociative reaction?"*

After the direct examination by the prosecutor is completed, it is the defense attorney's turn to challenge and possibly nullify the testimony of the prosecution witness. The defense attorney wants to neutralize opinions attesting to the defendant's sanity and amplify evidence about his mental illness.

Q. Doctor, did you know that Mr. Gregory, who hasn't had a job in 2 years, wants to move to Canada, live as a hermit, and raise wolves?

A. Yes, I read about that in his files.

Q. Did you read about his writing to a Romanian Olympic skating star, saying he planned to visit her in Romania?

A. Yes.

Q. Did you know he owned 9 guns and liked to shoot 200 to 300 shells at 1 time, sometimes as many as 400 shells at a time?

A. Yes.

Q. **Did you know that he sometimes shot his revolver, loading and shooting it until his ammunition was gone and he got blisters on his fingers?**

A. Yes.

Q. **And did you read about his expecting his neighbors' relatives to kill him, and threatening to escape from the hospital to shoot everyone in sight to get back at the state?**

A. Yes.

Q. **Now, doesn't his desire to raise wolves, his wish to visit a skating star in Romania, and his threat to shoot everyone in sight—aren't these signs of abnormal psychological problems?**

A. I do not doubt that Mr. Gregory has psychological problems. However, I do believe that he appreciated the wrongfulness of his actions and that he can control his behavior.

Q. **Can you say he can control his behavior when he starts shooting, doesn't stop even when his mother is screaming for him to stop, and doesn't stop till his ammunition is gone?**

A. Mr. Gregory was very angry and scared on the day of the shooting, but he did not lose contact with reality and knew what he was doing when he shot his neighbors.

Q. **Dr. Hawk has testified that Mr. Gregory is not psychotic but had a dissociative state and for a few minutes he didn't know what he was doing. Can you prove this did not happen, in the exact way that Dr. Hawk described?**

a. No, I cannot prove that Mr. Gregory did not have a dissociative state.

The latter response gives some credence to the opposing point of view. If the witness does not believe that a dissociative state occurred, a better response might be for the expert to restate his or her conclusions.

A. I can neither prove nor disprove Dr. Hawk's theory. On the basis of my thorough evaluation of this case, I believe Mr. Gregory knew what he was doing when he shot his neighbors.

More Cross-Examination of Prosecution Witness

"If a person doesn't know what he's doing, isn't that consistent with a dissociative disorder?"

Q. **Doctor, would you agree that a schizoid personality is a serious mental illness?**

A. It may or may not be, depending on the individual's symptoms.

Q. So, you look at the symptoms the person has to determine whether that person has a schizoid personality disorder and, if he or she does have that disorder, whether it is a serious mental illness, is that right?

A. Yes.

Q. According to *DSM–IV*, aren't there 7 typical symptoms for a schizoid personality disorder?

A. That's right. There are 7 criteria of symptoms for that diagnosis.

Q. Isn't it fair to say that the patient displayed at least 4 of the 7 symptoms at one time or another in the past year?

A. Yes.

Q. Isn't it true that a person who has a schizoid personality disorder has less ability to cope with conflicts than a person with no psychological problems?

A. Yes.

Q. Could you tell us what a dissociative disorder is?

A. You could describe it as an altered state of consciousness in which there is an unawareness of the environment and of one's behavior.

Q. When does a dissociative reaction take place?

A. It usually occurs when a person is upset or is in a state of emotional duress.

Q. Could you say that some people have a dissociative reaction when they can't cope with their problems?

A. Yes.

Q. If a schizoid personality disorder can't cope with his problems, could he have a dissociative reaction?

A. He could.

Q. So, if someone with a schizoid personality disorder, like the defendant, wasn't aware of his environment and didn't know what he was doing, you'd describe that as a dissociative disorder, wouldn't you?

a. I think I would.

The defense attorney has deftly portrayed, with the inadvertent help of the prosecution expert, that the defendant has a serious mental illness, and most importantly had a dissociative reaction and was not aware of his shooting of his neighbors. If the expert's opinion was that the defendant had a schizoid personality disorder but was capable of knowing right from wrong and adhering to the law, the expert has unwittingly altered his or her opinion significantly. It is important not to lose sight of what conclusions were reached after hours of study and discernment, and to be consistent with one's own assessment of the case rather than acquiesce to clever and unrelenting questions. The following reasserts the expert's original position.

A. I do not believe that Mr. Gregory did not know what he was doing on the day of the killings. I am reasonably certain that the defendant has some kind of personality disorder, but he was able to know right from wrong and able to conduct himself according to the law.

Direct Examination of Defense Witness

"Aren't you saying that the accused didn't know what he was doing at the time of the offense?"

The direct examination of the expert witness for the defense consists of questioning by the defense attorney, who will try to highlight testimony that indicates that the defendant was not legally responsible for the criminal act of which he is accused.

Q. Doctor, have you had a chance to examine the defendant, Mr. Gregory?

A. Yes, I have.

Q. How did you become involved in this matter?

A. I was appointed by the court to the 3-member commission to examine Mr. Gregory, who I understand had pleaded insanity regarding the shooting of his neighbors.

Q. When and where did you examine Mr. Gregory?

A. I saw him at the State Hospital on March 10 and 12 of this year.

Q. Could you tell the jury how you performed your examination?

A. Yes. I interviewed him for 3 hours on March 10 and 2 more hours on March 12. I also read his chart at the hospital and his criminal arrest records.

Q. Did you perform any psychological tests?

A. No. That was done by the psychologist member of the commission.

Q. Tell us what your examination revealed.

A. During my interview of the defendant I was impressed by his marked unawareness of killing or even injuring anyone. He had no plan to shoot them. His only intention had been to stay away from the neighbors. During the episode he felt as if something made him move ("Like somebody picks you up and moves you"). He saw the son's mouth moving but he heard nothing as he aimed his rifle. But he said, "Something spoke in my mind, but you cannot hear ... weird!" Squeezing the trigger never crossed his mind, and when the people dropped, he still did not know what he did. He then ran away from the scene.

Q. Did you reach a diagnosis regarding Mr. Gregory?

A. Yes.

Q. What is that diagnosis?

A. My diagnosis is dissociative episode in a schizoid personality.

Q. **Based on reasonable psychiatric (psychological) certainty, what is your opinion regarding Mr. Gregory's mental state at the time of the offense?**

A. I believe that Mr. Gregory felt estrangement from his own body and surroundings and also had no control over his actions. In my opinion, he was not able at the time of the offense to distinguish right from wrong or to control his behavior.

Cross-Examination of Defense Witness

"If he didn't do anything wrong, why did he act so guilty?"

After the direct examination, the defense witness will undergo a cross-examination by the prosecuting attorney, whose aim is to challenge the opinions about the defendant's lack of criminal responsibility.

Q. **Doctor, you're aware that there was a long-time feud between Mr. Gregory's family and their neighbors, aren't you?**

A. Yes. They had a feud for about 5 or 6 years.

Q. **And you're aware of the police record that includes a charge by the neighbor, Mr. Hogan, that Mr. Gregory had punched him in the face once, made threatening remarks, and shot a rifle into the air 3 times, aren't you?**

A. Yes, I am.

Q. **On the day of the shootings, there was another argument between Mr. Gregory and Mr. Hogan, with Mr. Hogan's son prodding the defendant to come out and fight, isn't that true?**

A. Yes.

Q. **And Mr. Gregory responded by jumping out of a window with a shotgun, loading it, aiming it at the son and shooting twice. Is that correct?**

A. Yes.

Q. **And then Mr. Gregory shot Mr. Hogan once, and then Mrs. Hogan once, isn't that true?**

A. Yes, that's true.

Q. **Did Mr. Gregory tell you he didn't know what he was doing?**

A. Not exactly. I concluded from what he was describing about the incident that he was only half conscious of what he was doing when he was fighting with the neighbors.

Q. **Did he tell you that he had no control over his actions?**

A. No. I realized that he was having a fuguelike and disoriented state, with his feelings cut off from his thinking. I concluded that he had no control over his actions.

Q. **When a man has a long-time feud with his neighbors, gets into another argument, is challenged to come out and fight, and then grabs a shotgun, loads it, aims it, and fires it at the neighbors and no one else, doesn't that tell you he knew what he was doing?**

A. Not necessarily. As I said, Mr. Gregory was not aware that he was injuring anyone or killing anyone. He was at that point not conscious of what he was doing.

Q. **Well, he didn't point a broom at Mr. Gregory, did he?**

A. That's true.

Q. **And he didn't point the gun at a tree or the dog, did he?**

A. No, he didn't.

Q. **If he didn't know he injured or killed anyone, why did he run away?**

a. I think he knew that something was wrong. He said that the word *run* entered his head, and he ran.

An accused's behavior after the alleged crime is often dissected to reveal his or her state of mind at the time of the offense. In this case, it is difficult to explain away the defendant's running away from the scene of the shootings. Consider this reply:

A. Mr. Gregory was only half conscious of what was happening. He knew something was wrong and felt he had to get away.

More Cross-Examination of Defense Witness

"Was your evaluation thorough enough to reach a valid conclusion?"

Q. **To reach a valid diagnosis about a person, do you need accurate information about the person's background?**

A. Yes.

Q. **Have you substantiated all of the statements the defendant made in your examination?**

A. Not all of the statements.

Q. **Doctor, actually you've only read the reports provided to you and you've never checked out the accuracy of the reports, isn't that true?**

A. Yes. I didn't do an independent investigation. I relied on the consistency of what he said and what is in the records.

Q. **Suppose you were told that one of Mr. Gregory's neighbors testified under oath that the defendant told her several times that he would kill the Hogan family some day. Would that in any way change your opinion as to whether the defendant told you the whole truth about what happened?**

A. It might. I'd have to decide whether the neighbor or Mr. Gregory had the more accurate memory. So, I think I'd say I don't know.

Q. **Assuming the neighbor had the more accurate memory, wouldn't that contradict your position?**

A. It would. However, in these kinds of emotional battles between neighbors, it is difficult to remember accurately everything that happened or was said.

Q. **Isn't it true that a defendant would give a version that would help rather than hurt his position of pleading insanity?**

A. Yes, I suppose that's possible.

Q. **If Mr. Gregory said he wanted to kill his neighbors, wouldn't it affect your opinion about his state of mind?**

A. No. These verbal threats often occur in bitter arguments between people. But it doesn't necessarily mean that they will carry out their threats.

Q. **Isn't Mr. Gregory capable of planning and premeditating?**

A. Yes.

Q. **Doesn't the statement, "I'll kill them someday" imply premeditation?**

A. It could be seen that way. In his case, I believe he felt great rage, had a dissociative reaction and didn't know that he was shooting at his neighbors.

Q. **When you say he had a dissociative reaction, that's really speculation on your part, isn't it?**

A. No. My opinion, based on years of examining homicides, is based on more than speculation.

Q. **Isn't it reasonable to simply say that Mr. Gregory shot his neighbors because he was angry at them?**

a. You could say that.

The latter, apparently innocent statement could negate the defense witness' position that had been affirmed several times. This capitulation may occur because the witness is fatigued and may not realize the contradictory statement in the casual response, "You could say that." To be consistent with one's testimony, the more appropriate reply is:

A. It is overly simplistic to say the Mr. Gregory shot his neighbors because he was angry. I believe the shooting took place out of blind rage without his knowing what he was doing.

GENERAL CHALLENGES

Several issues are commonly presented to the expert witness in criminal court as well as in other judicial situations. The mental health professional may encounter the following challenges:

- scientific conclusions
- thoroughness of examination
- disagreement among experts
- deferring to other experts
- "hired gun" fees
- beyond your data and expertise

Scientific Conclusions

"Your years of experience helped you reach your conclusion, right?"

Experts are asked to reach a precise opinion about a very specific incident, such as the mental state at the time of a criminal act. Attorneys will try to show that the expert's conclusions are weak, arbitrary, and not based on solid scientific findings.

Q. Doctor, you testified that the defendant was insane and in a dissociative state on the night of December 23, is that right?

A. Yes.

Q. And you stated that he was not responsible for his actions, correct?

A. Yes, that's correct.

Q. Did you conclude that he was insane because of the viciousness of his assault on the victim?

A. That was part of my reasoning.

Q. Did you conclude that he was insane because of the way he was ranting and raving at the time of his attack?

A. Yes, that was also part of my conclusion.

Q. Was there a lot of evidence that he was out of touch with reality?

A. No, not a lot of evidence. There were witnesses who tried to yell and stop him but he seemed not to hear them and was oblivious to their pleas.

Q. You've been doing work as a forensic expert for several years, haven't you?

A. Yes.

Q. You have years of experience in evaluating a case like this, right?

A. Right.

Q. So, even though there wasn't a lot of evidence, your experience helped you reach your conclusion that he was out of touch with reality, right?

A. Yes.

Q. In a situation like this, with little evidence, your conclusions must be based on your experience rather than scientific proof, is that correct?

a. Yes.

An expert's testimony is admissible even when based primarily on one's experience. However, a psychiatrist and a psychologist are expected to testify according to their scientific training and knowledge. The response just given may hinder the expert's credibility because he or she has stated that experience, rather than scientific proof, served as the basis of his or her opinions. Consider this reply:

A. My professional experience as well as my training help me to understand that dissociative states are brief episodes for which there is little direct evidence. I reached my conclusions based on Mr. Gregory's description of the event as well as his previous inadequate coping with the neighbors and his long-standing personality disorder.

Thoroughness of Examination

"What's your excuse for not talking to his family?"

The evaluation of a criminal defendant is significantly different from the ordinary clinical examination of a person seeking psychotherapy from a mental health professional. The individual involved in a forensic assessment is accused of a criminal act and, thus, has major consequences at stake when being evaluated. In some cases, the defendant feels that he or she has been coerced by his or her attorney, or ordered by the court to undergo the examination and, therefore, he or she may be highly emotionally charged, angry, anxious, or defiant. Hence, interviewing problems such as total disclosure, exaggerating, and lying must be seriously considered. Accordingly, the mental health expert has to thoroughly assess possible manipulativeness, honest memory gaps, and even amnesic states, and must obtain supportive evidence by checking with external sources of information, such as police records, eyewitnesses, and family history. A cross-examination will often challenge the thoroughness of the forensic evaluation in the following way:

Q. **Doctor, can you tell us how you conducted your examination of the defendant, Mr. Greg ory?**
A. Yes. I interviewed him for 3 hours on March 10 and 2 more hours on March 12. I also read his hospital chart and his criminal arrest records.
Q. **According to your written report, your diagnosis of schizoid person- ality disorder was reached in large part because of his tendency to be a loner, isn't that correct?**
A. Yes.
Q. **Other than Mr. Gregory telling you that he was a loner, did you interview family members to corroborate his statement?**
A. No, I did not.
Q. **You indicated that he was of average intelligence. Did you perform any psychological test to verify that opinion?**

A. No, I did not. I left that up to the psychologist member of the panel of experts.

Q. Were you aware that he was on the honor roll throughout his high school days?

A. No. I didn't see any of his school records.

Q. Did you review the police records of previous complaints by the neighbors against Mr. Gregory, in which he fired his shotgun in the air?

A. No.

Q. Mr. Gregory told you that he was unaware of his shooting his neighbors and seems to have forgotten many aspects of the incident, is that correct?

A. Yes.

Q. Are you aware that his mother testified yesterday that he told her many details of the shootings—the same details that he told you that he didn't remember?

A. No. I never spoke to Mr. Gregory's mother.

Q. Doctor, because you never interviewed Mr. Gregory's family to verify that he was a loner, you didn't review his school records nor the police records of previous complaints against Mr. Gregory, and because Mr. Gregory has much more recollection about the incident than he told you, isn't it fair to say that you do not have complete information about this man?

a. I guess you could say that.

If indeed the expert witness failed, as in this example, to obtain major pieces of evidence to support his or her opinions, then his or her testimony will probably not convince anyone in court. There is no excuse for such an incomplete examination, which is a disservice to the court. On the other hand, if the missing information about the family, the school, and police records is not germane to the issues at hand, the expert could state:

A. No. I did not interview Mr. Gregory's family nor did I see any school or previous police records. But, I am satisfied with the information I obtained through my 5-hour examination of him and the review of the hospital records and police files in this particular case.

Disagreements Among Experts

"You aren't more accurate than a Freudian, are you?"

The existence of various schools of psychology suggests to some that there are considerable disagreement and variability in judgments in insanity evaluations. Attorneys may attempt to amplify this point with the following questions:

Q. To what school or theory of psychotherapy do you subscribe?

A. In general, my therapy approach is based on cognitive—behavioral psychology.

Q. Do you practice psychoanalysis?

A. No, I don't.

Q. Do you subscribe to humanistic psychology?

A. I don't consider myself a humanistic psychologist, but there are many aspects of humanistic psychology practiced by most therapists.

Q. Are you a behavioral therapist?

A. Not exactly. I utilize some behavioral techniques, but I would not say that I am a behavioral therapist.

Q. Are psychoanalysis, humanistic psychology, and behavioral psychology valid ways to understand psychiatric disorders and criminal behavior?

A. Yes.

Q. If there are several ways to understand criminal behavior, then we can't tell which opinion is more correct, isn't that true?

a. I suppose that could be true.

Conceding to the latter question could seriously impair the expert's testimony, which now supports the contention that psychological opinions regarding insanity are highly variable and unreliable. Instead, the expert needs to remind the court that studies of insanity evaluations indicate that the degree of agreement of professional opinions is quite substantial among those with forensic training (Melton, Petrila, Poythress, & Slobogin, 1987).

A. Although there are different schools of thought in psychiatry and psychology, the opinions reached by experts on the insanity issue are not widely different. Studies have shown high levels of agreement reached by clinicians from different schools who performed mental evaluations.

Deferring to Other Experts

"Isn't the other expert more expert than you?"

One way to negate an expert's testimony is to suggest that the expert offering an adverse opinion has more experience and knowledge in the matter at hand. The ultimate purpose of this strategy, which is regularly used, would be to ask the witness to defer to the other expert.

Q. Isn't it true that two experts can look at the same set of facts and reach different conclusions?

A. Yes.

Q. **When two experts reach different conclusions based on the same set of facts, it's important to know the expert's degree of experience in the area in which the expert is offering an opinion, isn't that true?**

A. Yes.

Q. **In other words, an expert who has greater knowledge through training or experience in a particular subject area would likely be more qualified to offer an expert opinion than someone whose training and experience are not in that subject, wouldn't you agree?**

A. Yes.

Q. **And an expert's accuracy and judgment are related to training and experience in a particular subject, isn't that true?**

A. That's true.

Q. **For instance, if an expert has done a lot of work with a particular problem, then that person's opinion probably would have greater validity than a person who hasn't had as much experience with that problem, isn't that true?**

a. It depends on what kind of work, but I think that's true.

Being too agreeable with this kind of questioning may reinforce the cross-examining attorney's assertion that the attorney's witness, who happens to have a national reputation with the clinical problem involved in the case, offers opinions that are more qualified and valid. A better reply might be:

A. A person's experience is valuable, but the accuracy of an opinion depends on many factors, such as how thoroughly the expert investigated the facts in a case.

"Hired Gun" Fees

"You mean that the written report cost $4,500 to type?"

Discussion of expert fees are aimed at implying that an opinion has been bought—the "hired gun" gambit—and that a witness is merely a mercenary taking advantage of a business opportunity rather than a sensitive mental health professional.

Q. **When an expert conducts an evaluation for a fixed fee, it's prudent to be efficient in conducting the evaluation, isn't that correct?**

A. That's correct. If you use too much time, the fixed amount may not be adequate compensation.

Q. **In contrast, if you are doing an evaluation on a hourly fee, efficiency and speed are not as essential, isn't that correct?**

A. Yes.

Q. Now, your fee arrangement, in this case with district attorney, is on an hourly basis, isn't that true?

A. Yes.

Q. For every additional hour that you spend on this case, you'll be paid at an hourly rate for that hour, isn't that correct?

A. Yes.

Q. Were there any limitations on the number of hours that you are putting in on this case?

A. No limitation was mentioned.

Q. And what is the hourly rate that you are charging the DA's Office for your opinion as an expert?

A. My rate for forensic work is $200 per hour.

Q. What is your usual hourly rate for an office visit?

A. $150 per hour.

Q. Why is it that you charge more for your courtroom work than for your treatment of patients?

A. Forensic psychiatry (psychology) is more intense, requires more expertise, and can be stressful. That's why I charge more for expert work.

Q. Do you know how many hours you have spent on this case to date?

A. I don't know exactly.

Q. What would be your best estimate of the number of hours that you will be billing the DA's office for this case?

A. I think it will be about 30 to 40 hours altogether.

Q. Is part of the 30 to 40 hours the time you took to prepare your report?

A. Yes, it is.

Q. And that report is 45 pages long, is it not?

A. Yes.

Q. And it's correct to say that the first 35 pages are verbatim or practically verbatim quotations from documents that were provided to you, isn't that true?

A. Yes.

Q. Then, your opinion is expressed in the last 10 pages, isn't that true?

A. Yes.

Q. So, you are being paid a handsome fee not only for your opinion but also for rehashing the documents that were provided to you, isn't that true?

a. I believe my fee is fair and in keeping with what is customary in this community.

The expert who is being paid on an hourly basis can do little about this litany of questions aimed at portraying the witness as a gun for hire. It is best not to be argumentative or evasive, and to simply admit the financial arrangement that is an accepted practice in forensic work. As for the last response, one could also say:

A. I am being paid for my services and time for evaluating the defendant and for providing an unbiased professional opinion. I am not being paid to provide a specific opinion merely to benefit the defendant.

Beyond Your Data and Expertise

"Is that a matter of fact or merely your theory?"

With the status of expert witness, some mental health professionals inadvertently offer conclusory opinions, when in fact they are engaging in speculations that go well beyond their data or even their expertise. Instead of providing objective clinical descriptions of thoughts, emotions, and behavior, the witness may be led by the attorney to offer theories as if they were known facts about a criminal defendant's behavior.

Q. Doctor, does Mr. Tortorella have any medical problem?
A. Yes. He has a long-standing seizure disorder or epilepsy.
Q. What kind of behavior problems would an epileptic show?
A. Epileptics are prone to mood disorders. A number have personality disorders, with heightened emotions, hyposexuality, and sometimes religiosity. Most disturbing would be a psychiatric condition called interictal psychotic states.
Q. Can you describe an interictal psychotic state?
A. These psychotic states resemble schizophrenia and are manifested by paranoid delusions and auditory hallucinations in the presence of a clear consciousness.
Q. So, Doctor, a person in this state can be conscious and yet behave in an unexpected paranoid psychotic manner, is that what you're saying?
A. Yes.
Q. Did Mr. Tortorella know what he was doing when he went on his shooting rampage?
A. He was conscious, but he could not control what he was doing. It was totally out of character.
Q. What is your opinion about Mr. Tortorella's epilepsy and the shooting incidents with which he is charged?
A. I believe that Mr. Tortorella suffered interictal psychotic states in which he believed he was being attacked by hostile government agents, and shot anybody coming to his home.
Q. On what evidence did you base your opinion?
a. On my 3-hour clinical examination of him and his history of epileptic illness.

A history of epilepsy does not readily imply the propensity toward violent behavior. In fact, only in very rare cases can violence be attributed to a seizure disorder (Kaplan & Sadock, 1991). A response that is consistent with the empirical research will consider the extreme rarity of violence as a seizure phenomenon.

A. Mr. Tortorella was evidently psychotic, as he was delusional and shouting irrational accusations about the people whom he thought were hostile federal agents. Whether or not his psychosis was seizure related is difficult to establish, as such interictal violent states are quite rare.

MISCELLANEOUS Q & A

The following is an assortment of challenging questions for criminal expert witnesses.

Deceiving Doctors

Q. **Haven't there been studies that have shown that psychiatrists (psychologists) have been fooled by people faking their mental illness?**
a. Yes. It's very difficult to tell when somebody is saying they're mentally ill when they're not, or when they are not well when they say they are.
A. Yes. Psychiatrists (psychologists) have to consider the possibility of malingering, especially in a criminal case when a person is facing a potentially long prison term. Thus, I took careful precautions to interview the defendant at length and corroborate his statements with police records and witnesses.

Believing Patients

Q. **Do you believe everything your patients tell you?**
a. I have to trust my patient's word. Without trust there is no therapy.
A. I usually do, but when there are criminal charges against them, it is essential to try to corroborate what is said with outside sources.

Incomplete Examination

Q. **If your examination of the defendant was incomplete, wouldn't it be reasonable to disregard your testimony?**
a. It would be reasonable.

A. It depends on what is missing in my examination. If it was relatively minor, I don't think my testimony should be disregarded.

DSM Changes

Q. **If every new edition of *DSM* eliminates certain conditions and adds new ones onto the list of mental disorders, how do we know if this defendant's mental illness won't some day be eliminated and not be considered a disorder?**

a. I can't tell you what will happen in the future, but I know now that this man is mentally ill and not responsible for his actions.

A. It is true that certain behaviors, such as homosexuality, are no longer considered mental illnesses in *DSM—IV*. However, psychotic conditions, such as that of this defendant, are among the most serious psychiatric disorders. The defendant's condition may change in terms of its name, but I cannot imagine that his condition will ever be considered normal human behavior.

Premeditation

Q. **He was able to purchase a gun, register it, and buy bullets. Doesn't that show that he can plan and premeditate?**

a. He did buy a gun and bullets, but that doesn't mean he planned to kill his neighbors.

A. A mentally ill person is not totally unable to have a plan of action, such as buying groceries for food. But when he is in an intensely emotional situation, such as being threatened by neighbors, a person like this defendant can be so overwhelmed by his mental illness that he loses control over his actions.

Normal Rorschach

Q. **You said that his Rorschach response "a monarch butterfly" is a popular response and an indication of his psychological normalcy. Isn't it true that a certain percentage of psychotic patients also give normal, popular Rorschach responses?**

a. That's true.

A. Psychotic patients do not give as many popular responses as the defendant did. Moreover, the defendant in this case gave none of the unusual distorted perceptions that psychotics typically report. I made my diagnosis not on one response but a pattern of test responses which reflected his psychological normalcy.

Effects of Jail

Q. Since you examined the defendant after he was in jail for over 3 months, couldn't his poor state of mind reflect the effects of imprisonment rather than it being his usual state of mind?

a. I don't think his being in jail caused him to be so disturbed.

A. I think his being in jail for three months affected him, but his depressed mood was a relatively small part of the total picture. This is a man who has been seriously mentally ill for several months, with paranoid delusions that were present long before his imprisonment.

Schizophrenic

Q. Although the defendant is schizophrenic, when she gave her father the poisoned drink, she understood that poison would kill him, didn't she?

a. Yes, she did.

A. She understood that the poison would kill him, and it was also her understanding that she was following the will of God in killing a servant of Satan.

CLOSING ARGUMENTS

Because of its history and its continued exposure in the popular media, the insanity defense is familiar to everyone in the criminal courtroom—not only to experienced attorneys and judges but to lay members of the jury as well. Thus, you have to be well prepared to present clear and well-documented testimony in order to have any convincing effect on relatively sophisticated triers of fact.

This chapter on criminal law underscored the difficulty for both the prosecution and the defense witnesses in establishing the accused's state of mind at the time of the crime. In addition, the criminal expert frequently faces challenges, such as those listed in this chapter.

Criminal court deliberations consider extremely serious matters that affect a person's life and freedom, as well as the safety of the community. You must be mindful of the importance of your role when performing your critical examination of the accused.

CHAPTER 7

CHILD CUSTODY DISPUTES

"Doctor, what is the very best custodial arrangement for these children?"

Mental health professionals enter into child custody disputes in various ways. A psychotherapist may be treating a parent or a child involved in divorce proceedings with contested custody for the children. On occasion, a child expert is hired by a parent or family law attorney specifically to evaluate the custody issue and to testify in family court on behalf of one of the parents. Finally, a mental health professional can be appointed by the court or hired by a guardian *ad litem* (for the lawsuit) to provide expert opinion regarding custody arrangements that are in the best interests of the children. The latter role may be the most desirable for the expert because of the advantage of having equal access to both parents, with the capacity to obtain a more complete assessment of the family constellation and dynamics.

Direct Examination

Q. Doctor, could you tell us how you became involved in these divorce proceedings?
A. I was appointed by the family court judge to conduct an evaluation of Mr. and Mrs. Johnson and their 3 children. Specifically, I was asked to determine the best custodial arrangement for the 3 children after their parents are divorced.
Q. How did you conduct your evaluation?
A. I interviewed each parent for 1 hour in my office and 1 hour at their respective residences. I also administered the Minnesota Multiphasic Personality Inventory-2 to each parent at my office. I interviewed each

child for 1 hour in my office, and I observed the three children at the home of each parent, with the parent present. I had brief telephone interviews with Mr. Johnson's sister and Mrs. Johnson's mother, both of whom live in this city, and telephone conversations with the teachers of the three children.

Q. You submitted a 20-page report. Can you briefly summarize your findings for the court?

A. Yes. I found Mr. Johnson to be a solid breadwinner, working successfully as a manager of a print shop. He's been conscientious about caring for the three children when he can, such as playing with them on weekends. I found Mrs. Johnson to be very close to her children. Because she works part time, she has been available to spend more time with them than their father. The three children have a healthy relationship with both parents. Depending on who asks them or who they are with, the children have at different times expressed preferences for being with either parent. Although Mr. Johnson is more financially capable, it is my opinion that the legal and physical custody should be jointly shared by both parents.

Q. Do you have any reservations about Mr. and Mrs. Johnson being able to resolve visitation and other childrearing issues amicably?

A. Although they are currently at odds about the marriage and their relationship, I have the confidence that both are mature adults who have their children's interests at heart and can remedy any differences in a reasonable manner.

Q. Mrs. Johnson has testified that she is being treated for depression by a psychiatrist. Will her mental condition present any problems for the children?

A. Mrs. Johnson had no previous psychiatric problem until the sudden breakup of her marriage. I believe that when the family situation settles down and she is assured of being with her children on a regular basis, she will return to her usual normal emotional functioning.

Q. Could Mr. Johnson manage the care of the three children while working full time?

A. Fortunately his managerial position allows him the flexibility to meet any needs or emergencies of the children.

Q. Then you are recommending joint legal and physical custody for the Johnson children, is that correct?

A. Yes.

Cross-Examination by Mother's Attorney

"But isn't the mother clearly the primary parent of these children?"

Child experts uphold certain principles and opinions that have widespread support in the community and among their colleagues, such as visitation patterns for very young children (Musetto, 1985). Although some of these ideas find support in research literature, others persist without apparent empirical foundation. It behooves the expert in family court to keep current on the studies of divorce and its effects on children.

    Q. Doctor, you are in favor of joint custody in this case, isn't that so?
    A. Yes.
    Q. Aren't you aware that these three children have spent much more time with their mother than with their father?
    A. Mr. and Mrs. Johnson agreed that the mother would work part time, and spend more time in child care. So my answer is "yes."
    Q. Do you realize that the children prefer that their mother help them with their homework?
    A. Yes.
    Q. Do you know that they go to church and other places with their mother but not as often with their father?
    A. Yes, I do.
    Q. Have you heard of the term, *the primary caretaker*?
    A. Yes.
    Q. Don't you agree that the mother in this case is the primary caretaker and the psychological parent?
    a. You could say that.

The concept of a *primary caretaker* or *psychological parent* lacks empirical support and is subject to debate (Melton et al., 1987). Although a child may prefer one parent over the other, studies find that children develop attachments to both parents as well as other caregivers.

    A. Research shows that a child develops multiple attachments to caretakers, and the notion of a primary psychological parent is not supported by empirical evidence. Although the Johnson children seem to favor their mother in several ways, I believe they have an important relationship with their father, and I support its continuity with joint custody.

Cross-Examination by Father's Attorney

"Aren't you ignoring the important financial security that the father can provide?"

The determination of the most desirable child custody arrangements considers multiple variables (Clingempeel & Respucci, 1982). Although some considerations seem to be basic, such as the economic support for the children, there is no single factor that determines the outcome of contested child custody proceedings.

Q. Doctor, you favor joint custody. Are you aware of how much Mr. Johnson earns annually?

A. Yes. He told me that he earned $45,000 last year.

Q. And are you aware of how much Mrs. Johnson earned last year?

A. Yes. She earned about $8,000 from her part-time job.

Q. Does Mrs. Johnson have a full-time job at this time?

A. No. She is looking for more hours to work, but she still has only her half-time clerical job.

Q. How will she be supporting herself and her responsibilities to the three children?

A. I believe she's currently requesting state assistance, financially and with food stamps.

Q. Isn't it true that Mr. Johnson is more capable of meeting the physical needs of the children?

A. That's true.

Q. Isn't it true that Mr. Johnson can provide more educational support, such as private school?

A. Yes.

Q. Isn't it also true that Mr. Johnson can provide a safer home setting in a nice neighborhood?

A. Yes.

Q. And on top of all that, doesn't Mr. Johnson have a close relationship with his children?

A. He does.

Q. Doctor, given his close relationship with his children and his ability to provide more educational support and a safer home setting, shouldn't he be given primary custody of the children?

a. I think Mrs. Johnson can give enough support and the children won't be deprived,so I'm in favor of joint custody.

The physical needs and comfort of the children are important considerations in custody evaluations, but they are not overriding factors. The continued close relationship with both parents is also an essential concern. Consider this reply:

A. The children will undoubtedly enjoy the material comforts provided by their father. However, the success of custody dispositions depends on many factors, such as the ongoing close ties with both parents as well as the extended family.

Challenges in Custody Disputes

As in all areas of forensic testifying, the mental health expert in family court can anticipate vigorous cross-examination by attorneys who are at odds with the recommendations being proffered. The child expert should be prepared to address the following issues:

- incomplete information
- unsubstantiated statements
- inconsistent data
- situational effects
- evaluating only one parent
- insignificant differences
- primary rationale
- current ideals
- specialists

Incomplete Information

"Didn't you know the living conditions with the mother are appalling?"

Child custody disputes demand the assessment of multiple relevant factors. The expert considers not only the obvious parent–child relationships and the personalities of each family member, but the evaluation also considers financial matters, living conditions, relatives and support groups, and educational opportunities. If any of these elements has been overlooked, the attorney will probably explore this oversight in cross-examination.

Q. Doctor, you've been the therapist for Mrs. Johnson for several months, haven't you?

A. Yes, I have.

Q. You testified that after you examined the 3 children and their parents in your office, you concluded that the children's custody should be given to their mother, isn't that true?

A. Yes.

Q. And the reason for your opinion is because of the children's apparent bonding with their mother, correct?

A. Yes.

Q. Did you know that at Mrs. Johnson's one-bedroom apartment there are only two beds for the three children and the mother?

A. No. I didn't know that.

Q. Did you know that the apartment building is in an older part of town where there are many homeless people?

A. No.

Q. Did you know that the children will be walking seven city blocks and crossing several busy streets on their way to and from school?

A. No.

Q. Did you realize that after school, when Mrs. Johnson works full time, the children will be at home for 2 hours without adult supervision?
A. I didn't realize that.
Q. Wouldn't you admit that you did not know some important aspects of the living conditions with their mother when you recommended that the custody of the children should go to her?
a. I would have to admit that. Yes.

The mental health professional may have done a thorough evaluation of this family and their interrelationships, which are vital factors in determining child custody, but the child expert may have overlooked some important features of the living conditions for the children. There may not be any adequate way to justify the noteworthy gaps in the database for this case. A better response to the preceding question could be:

A. The living conditions you described are definite shortcomings if the mother obtains custody of the children. Nonetheless, I believe that the three children have an exceptionally close relationship with their mother that should not be set aside unless there are extremely critical reasons.

Unsubstantiated Statements

"What evidence do you have for making that statement?"

In the course of testifying, the mental health expert expresses many opinions, with an assumption that those opinions are based on observed facts or scientific principles. Unfortunately, a witness sometimes renders opinions that go beyond any documented data or research-based findings. In such instances, the witness can expect to be aggressively challenged.

Q. Doctor, you've been hired by Mr. Johnson to testify in this case, is that right?
A. Yes.
Q. You indicated in your report that you favor the father's educational plans for the children. Could you be more specific on what you mean by that?
A. The father plans to keep the children in private schools near his home, which I believe would mean a superior education for them.
Q. Are you saying that private schools are superior to public schools?
A. Yes. Private schools provide a stronger academic curriculum and they produce better behaved children because they demand stricter obedience to rules.
Q. Doctor, are your statements about private schools based on your own personal opinions or on proven psychological facts?

A. These are my professional opinions, not my personal opinions.

Q. **Do you have any scientific evidence to support your professional opinions?**

A. I believe there are numerous reports of test scores that show that private school students do better academically than public school students.

Q. **Is that because the private schools are better or because the private school students come from families that are better educated and provide more academic help at home?**

A. That's a good question. I'm not sure there's a good answer for that one.

Q. **Do you have any proof that private school students in this city are better behaved because they are strictly required to obey the rules?**

A. No. I guess that's my own assessment of the situation, but I believe it's a widely known fact.

Q. **So, are you saying that the general public knows about private schools in this city producing better behaved children because the schools require stricter obedience to rules?**

A. Yes, that's right.

Q. **Is the general public also aware that private schools in this city are superior to public schools?**

a. I believe so.

By providing no professional or scientific foundation for his or her opinions, this witness has essentially voided his or her contribution to the proceedings. Moreover, with the latter two responses, he or she has testified that the general public or average layperson can assess the private versus public school issues (i.e., no expert opinion is warranted). Instead of this self-damaging testimony, consider the following:

A. As far as I know, there are no hard data to prove that the private schools in this city produce more capable students than public schools. My opinion is based on studies of private and public schools in other similar areas of our country, as well as my years of experience with local public and private school children and my many visits to these institutions.

Inconsistent Data

"How can you reconcile her answer to that test question?"

When an expert's evaluation has been critical of a parent's personality or behavior, the cross-examining attorney will search for evidence to the contrary. An often used tactic is to identify single test items, say, from an MMPI-2 record, that seemingly contradict the expert's opinion about the parent.

Q. You have reservations about my client's capacity to be a good mother because you found her to be depressed, isn't that true?

A. Yes.

Q. Did the psychological test results of the MMPI-2 play an important role in reaching that opinion?

A. Yes.

Q. The conclusions from the MMPI-2 are based on many true and false statements, isn't that correct?

A. Yes.

Q. For the statement, "My daily life is full of things that keep me interested," my client answered "True." Is that a sign of depression?

A. No.

Q. For the statement, "I don't seem to care what happens to me," my client answered "False." That doesn't sound like a depressed person, does it?

A. No, it doesn't.

Q. And for the statement, "I usually feel that life is worthwhile," my client answered "True." Again, does that show that she is depressed?

A. No.

Q. I won't go through several more examples like that, but are her responses to these statements consistent or inconsistent with the diagnosis of depression?

a. They are inconsistent.

Without any further qualifying statements by the expert, the court is led to believe that there is notable doubt or ambiguity about the expert's findings pertaining to the mother's depression. The witness could in redirect examination be asked to explain the apparent contradictory findings, or the witness may immediately reply:

A. The diagnostic impression from an MMPI-2 is based on the total score from each of the 10 clinical scales and not from individual items. There are more than 30 items in the Depression scale. If a depressed person doesn't endorse all of the Depression items, it simply means that the person is not extremely depressed. It doesn't mean that she isn't depressed at all.

Situational Effects

"Wouldn't anyone be depressed if they had to go through what she's been through?"

Parents being evaluated during contested child custody examinations invariably are in one of the most stressful and unpleasant periods of their lives. Hence, it would not be unusual for one or both parents to be exhibiting noticeable psychological impairment that may have a major impact on the decision as to who gets the children. Evaluators must be prepared to address the issue of divorce-related psychopathology versus predivorce mental and emotional traits.

Q. Doctor, you have stated that the mother's depression was a major reason for your favoring the father's obtaining the legal custody of the children, am I right?

A. Yes.

Q. What were some of the factors that led you to conclude that the mother was depressed?

A. When I interviewed her she was obviously somber and her affect was blunted. Her depressed state was quite apparent, with her eventually sobbing in my office.

Q. Was her behavior during the interview an important part of your evaluation?

A. Yes.

Q. But, it's not unusual to feel sad and be tearful during emotional interviews about divorce, is it?

A. I suppose not.

Q. So you based an important part of your evaluation on normal reactions to an interview about divorce, isn't that true?

A. Well, I also based my opinion on other findings I obtained.

Q. Could you tell us what other findings you obtained about the mother?

A. The mother herself told me, and I was able to corroborate her statements with her sister who lives nearby, that she — Mrs. Johnson—has for a long time been sad and worrisome, not eating or sleeping well, and prone to frequent crying.

Q. How long has the mother shown these signs of depression?

A. For several months.

Q. Do you know how long she has been separated from her husband and seeing her children every other week?

A. I believe it's been about a year.

Q. Do you have any evidence that indicates that the mother was a depressed person before her marital breakup?

A. Her husband told me that she's always been negative and had low self-esteem.

Q. Did anyone in her family tell you that she was negative and with low self-esteem?

A. No.

Q. Isn't it likely that the breakup of her 10-year marriage, the inability to see her young children every day and the financial burdens she's been facing are the reasons for her depression?

A. Yes.

Q. Isn't it also likely that under more normal circumstances, the mother would not exhibit any of the depressive reactions you described?

a. Yes.

If the mental health expert has no objective data to indicate that the mother had depressive symptoms in the past—it is precarious to rely only on the husband's viewpoints—the expert must concede that the depression noted during the custody evaluations could be the product of the acute changes taking place in the mother's life and may be temporary reactions. Only if there is corroborated evidence of depression prior to the dissolution of the marriage can the expert be assured of a chronic condition.

A. I was aware that the mother's depression was exacerbated by the upheaval of her 10-year marriage. However, there was abundant information from a thorough social work study and from neighbors that she has been despondent for many years.

Evaluating Only One Parent

"So, what's your opinion of your patient's spouse?"

Sometimes a mental health expert who testifies in court only knows one parent very well—the patient he or she has examined—while not knowing well or even meeting the other parent. Because the patient has spoken so much about the spouse, it is tempting to offer an opinion about that person, even if the expert did not conduct any formal examination of the spouse. This, of course, is an unacceptable practice; one must limit opinions to persons who have been directly examined (American Psychological Association, 1994). No comparisons can be made as to who is the better custodian unless both parents have been sufficiently evaluated.

Q. You examined the father, but not the mother, isn't that true?
A. Yes.
Q. Could you tell us how many times you have seen Mr. Johnson?
A. I have seen Mr. Johnson 6 times in my office. During 2 of these sessions, I spoke to his children alone and once I observed them interacting with their father.
Q. What conclusions did you reach regarding Mr. Johnson?
A. Mr. Johnson is a well-respected manager of a small print shop. He works about 50 hours a week, but he makes time to pick up his children from the afterschool care program, and plays with them whenever he can. Through my evaluation of him and his children, I concluded that he has a very positive and close relationship with them.

Q. Do you think he can be a good parent for the three children?
A. Yes, I do.
Q. Did the children tell you who they preferred to live with after the divorce?
A. Yes. They told me they wanted to live with their father.
Q. Did they tell you why they wanted to live with their father?
A. They said he was nice to them, played with them more than their mother, and he bought them toys. He also has a nicer house.
Q. Couldn't you infer from the children's statements that Mr. Johnson is the better parent for them than their mother?
a. I think you could.

The latter statement is untenable because the witness has not evaluated the mother and is in no position to make comparisons between the two parents. More than likely, the opposing attorney will object to that response and request that it be stricken from the records. The only acceptable response is:

A. I cannot make comparisons between the two parents because I have not evaluated Mrs. Johnson.

Insignificant Differences

"Are the differences between the two parents statistically significant?"

In contested child custody cases, mental health experts are asked to determine which parent would be the better custodian for the child. In some instances, one person may emerge as the preferred parent, in the presence of small, if not insignificant, differences between the two parents (Ziskin & Faust, 1988). The witness in these cases may be asked the following questions:

Q. After your thorough assessment of this family situation, how did you come to conclude that the mother was the better parent for the child?
A. I found that throughout the child's life his mother had been the primary caretaker, conscientiously assuring that his physical and emotional needs were met. She assisted him with his homework and drove him to his soccer team practice and games. She and her son communicate very well with each other.
Q. Did his father contribute to his care?
A. Yes.
Q. Did his father also assist with his homework?
A. Yes, although perhaps not as often as his mother.
Q. Wasn't his father an assistant coach for the son's soccer team?
A. Yes.

Q. **Wasn't his father also a den leader with the boy's Cub Scout pack?**
A. Yes.

Q. **Now, the father and the boy—they communicate a lot with each other, don't they?**
A. Yes, but the boy feels closer to his mother and tells her more about his feelings.

Q. **Couldn't you consider that father is a conscientious caretaker as well?**
A. Well, yes.

Q. **So, would you say that the difference between the two parents are great or small?**
a. I'd say small, but definitely in favor of the mother.

A child expert must adhere to the objective data that have been obtained. When the difference between parents are, in fact, relatively small, it is inappropriate to testify otherwise. The task is to be as descriptive and specific as possible about the strengths and liabilities of each parent.

A. While I favor the mother, I would say that the difference between these two parents is relatively small.

Primary Rationale

"Is that the main reason you're recommending giving custody to the mother?"

The "best interests of the child" has been for many years the guiding principle when determining the optimal custody arrangements for children (Goldstein, Freud, & Solnit, 1973). If it appears that custodial preferences are decided because of other motives, such as the needs of either parent, the expert can face the following challenges:

Q. **Doctor, you've been Mrs. Johnson's psychotherapist for several months, haven't you?**
A. Yes.

Q. **You've been helping her because she's been upset by the sudden breakup of her marriage and by the threat of losing custody of the three children to their father, is that correct?**
A. Yes.

Q. **Today you are testifying that you are in favor of Mrs. Johnson obtaining custody of the children, correct?**
A. Yes.

Q. **And if Mrs. Johnson is awarded custody of the children, wouldn't it greatly benefit her mental outlook and psychological state?**

A. Yes, it would.

Q. **As her therapist, isn't is your duty to do what is in her best interests psychologically?**

A. Yes.

Q. **And your helping her gain custody is one of the ways to help her psychologically, isn't that true?**

a. It's true.

If it is true that the therapist favors custody for the mother primarily to help his or her patient psychologically, then the decision has been made for ulterior reasons. Family court is principally concerned with the welfare of the minor children, not what helps one parent or the other. If the therapist indeed was advocating for the children's best interest, the response should have been:

A. Giving custody of the children would undoubtedly diminish Mrs. Johnson's worries considerably. However, my preference for her obtaining custody of the children is based on my interviews with them and observing them interact with their mother. There is an obvious close bond between the children and their mother.

Current Ideals

"Now, Isn't that idea out of date?"

Opinions regarding ideal child custody arrangements are subjected to societal values. For example, in the past mothers were automatically designated as the custodial parent when very young children were involved, a decision based on the "tender years" doctrine (Weitzman &Dixon, 1979). Such rules of thumb have evolved over the years, and the child expert must be alert to contemporary beliefs of divorce professionals and be able to explain any determination that deviates from mainstream thinking.

Q. **At one time in the past, wasn't it the rule to prefer mothers over fathers when it came to deciding legal custody?**

A. Yes.

Q. **Mothers were presumed to be essential in cases involving very young children, isn't that true?**

A. Yes.

Q. **And in the past, in order to give the custody to a father, wasn't there a need to demonstrate that the mother was incompetent?**

A. Yes.

Q. **But we have since learned that mothers aren't necessarily the more skilled or important parent, and that fathers have an equally valid claim to custody, isn't that right?**

A. Yes.

Q. **In other words, haven't our beliefs about the best custodial arrange-ment gone through big changes over the years?**

A. Yes.

Q. **At the present time, child experts believe that, whenever possible, joint custody by both parents of the children is the preferred custo-dial arrangement, isn't that true?**

A. Yes.

Q. **Isn't it more reasonable, then, to apply the present day practice of joint custody in this case?**

a. No, I don't agree.

Awarding joint custody whenever possible stands as a present-day ideal (Musetto, 1985). An expert needs to provide convincing explanations for selecting an alternative custodial arrangement.

A. No. I felt that the children's custody should go to the mother because of their obvious closeness to her, the mother's superior skills in parenting and communication, as well as the older children's expressed preference to live with their mother.

Specialists

"Would you consider yourself a specialist?"

The mental health professions have advanced in various aspects of their discipline, so that experts can now substantiate their skills with specialty certifications in different areas, such as child neuropsychology and substance abuse. When opinions are expressed on specified clinical issues, the witness may be asked about his or her qualifications to testify on that particular topic.

Q. **Isn't it true that you are favoring the custody of the child being awarded to the father because of the mother's alleged abuse of alcohol?**

A. That's correct.

Q. **How much alcohol does the mother consume on a daily basis?**

A. She doesn't drink daily, but on weekends she consumes at least a quart of vodka and is often intoxicated.

Q. **Doctor, did you administer the Michigan Alcoholism Screening Test?**

A. No.

Q. **Did you use the CAGE questionnaire?**

A. No.

Q. **Are you familiar with the 1972 Criteria for the Diagnosis of Alcohol-ism, published by the National Council on Alcoholism?**

A. No.

Q. **Doctor, you're not a certified substance abuse counselor, are you?**

A. No, I'm not.

Q. **Wouldn't it be correct to say that you are not a specialist in alcoholism?**

a. That's true.

One does not have to be certified or a board diplomate to offer expert opinions. It is important to have sufficient training, experience and knowledge in the issue being discussed, and it is better to respond in the following manner:

A. I'm not sure what you mean by a specialist, but as a clinician, I have been trained to diagnose and treat mental disorders, such as alcohol abuse and dependence. I have treated countless numbers of patients with drinking problems, such as this woman.

MISCELLANEOUS Q & A

The family court expert can encounter the following variety of inquiries.

Scientific Basis

Q. **If there is no scientific research information about the effect of different custody arrangements on children, you can't help us decide what's best for their child, can you?**

a. That's a good point. I didn't realize there was no research done on custody arrangements.

A. No, that's not true. There aren't any solid data to guide us in determining the best custody arrangements for children. To that extent, my assistance may be limited. However, I believe that mental health professionals such as myself can assist the court by offering our insights into family relationships and conflicts, which need to be understood when deciding on the best environment for the child.

Biased Information

Q. **Doctor, you interviewed the mother's sister and friends, but aren't they all biased in her favor?**

a. I guess everyone I interviewed was probably biased, including the father's supporters. But you can't mistrust everybody.

A. Because of the inherent bias that family and friends have, I was careful to look for tangible evidence rather than mere opinions, and to see consistency in what I was being told. It's important to have information from those who know the parents and not limit yourself to testing the child and observing the parents.

Therapist Bias

Q. As the mother's psychotherapist, isn't there an alliance that makes it difficult for you not to advocate for her?

a. Yes, that's true.

A. That's correct. However, I am here to tell the truth and I try to be as objective as I can in my answers here.

Memory Problem

Q. You inquired as to how the marriage was in the past, but don't we, with the passage of time, distort our memories?

a. Not really. Except for the obviously impaired, we have good recall of our past.

A. Memories are subject to some fading and change. Thus, examiners like myself have to corroborate statements with outside sources and to interview others, and we don't rely purely on one's personal memory.

Both Parents Help

Q. The child has lived with both parents and you said he's normal, so doesn't that say that both parents have done a good job of raising him?

a. You could say that.

A. I believe the child's psychological health is largely due to the father's great devotion to the child's upbringing. That's why I recommended that the child's custody go to him.

Parental Flaw

Q. All parents have some flaws, don't they?

a. Well, that's true.

A. That may be true, but when I refer to the father's anger and abusiveness, I am not talking about a flaw. This is a major behavioral problem in need of professional treatment.

Nice Parent

Q. When you say that the mother gets along better with everybody, aren't you favoring the mother just because she's a nice person?

a. That's one way of putting it.

A. No. It's more than that. A good custodial parent tries to get along with the other parent, helps the children maintain contact with grandparents and extended family, and is most willing to negotiate differences.

For the Young

Q. **Isn't it common sense to give the custody of a young child to the mother?**

a. Yes, but in this case I feel the father is quite capable of raising his young child.

A. That may be a popular belief, but there is no evidence to indicate that fathers are less capable than mothers of caring for a young child.

Parent in Therapy

Q. **Don't you think it's better to award custody to the parent who doesn't need psychiatric care?**

a. As a general rule it might be true, but I believe the mother is making great effort to overcome her depression and is now very capable of handling the children.

A. No. Being in psychotherapy doesn't preclude being a capable and loving parent. The mother's depression was a reaction to the sudden breakup of her marriage, and she is already considerably improved and able to care for the children as she always has.

Joint Custody

Q. **Isn't it a contradiction to consider joint custody when this couple can't stand to live with each other?**

a. Well, for the sake of the children, the parents have to set aside their differences and co-parent as well as they can.

A. It's true that this couple are choosing not to live together, but they are devoted to the children and both told me that they would try to work cooperatively with each other.

CLOSING ARGUMENTS

Testifying in contested custody disputes means participating in an emotionally charged setting involving parents with a history of hostilities who are engaged in a bitter battle over the custody of their children. Because of the high stakes involved, you can anticipate aggressive challenging by the attorneys. The lack of scientifically based evidence to guide you further increases the difficulties of testifying (Melton et al., 1987). Compared to criminal and civil court, the family court tends to permit some latitude in the expert's testimony so that the professional can be a helpful consultant to the hearing, but there is no less demand for you to provide objective and thoroughly considered conclusions.

This chapter discussed the relevance of the primary caretaker concept as well as financial considerations in child custody determinations. You can face many different challenges,including the nine discussed here.

A thorough assessment of the entire family situation is essential if you are to assist the family court in making critical decisions in the best interests of the child.

CHAPTER 8

PERSONAL INJURY

*"What makes you so sure that the accident caused
all the emotional problems?"*

When the present day atmosphere is characterized as a litigious society in which monetary compensation is sought for practically any maloccurrence, reference is being made to tort law. Tort pertains to a civil wrongdoing, ranging from libel to assault to professional malpractice, which is brought to the legal system for remedial action. One of the most common tort actions involves the negligent or intentional infliction of personal injury on the plaintiff by the defendant, a prime example being a motor vehicle accident.

Personal injury entails physical damage as well as emotional and mental problems for which the injured party may seek financial compensation for medical bills, wage loss and, in some instances, pain and suffering. (Legal rules pertaining to the plaintiff's right to recover for psychological symptoms vary among different jurisdictions). When emotional injury is claimed, a psychologist or psychiatrist plays a critical role in determining the presence of psychological damage and its etiology (Ewing, 1985; Melton et al., 1987).

The courtroom examination of the mental health expert in civil lawsuits is similar to what occurs in criminal trials (chapter 4). The expert witness will be asked how the clinical examination was conducted, what findings were obtained, and the causal connection, if any, between the plaintiff's psychological state and the alleged incident. After the usual qualification process, the following direct examination many ensue.

113

Direct Examination

Q. Doctor, you had the occasion to treat a person by the name of Kim Lucas, is that correct?

A. Yes.

Q. When did you first see her?

A. On June 8th of this year.

Q. Who referred Ms. Lucas to you?

A. It was her neurologist, Dr. Matthews.

Q. Could you tell us the history you took from her on June 8?

A. Okay. She said she was being referred to me because of her headaches as well as her neck and back pain problems. She had been seeing her neurologist and an orthopedist and she was taking Dilantin, Flexeril, Esgic Plus, and Motrin. She said that she had these physical problems since last September when she was involved in a motor vehicle accident, when the car she was driving was struck from behind. Would you like to hear more?

Q. Go on.

A. She said she immediately felt pain in her neck. She doesn't recall hitting her head nor losing consciousness. She was able to drive to her family physician's office where she was examined, given some pain medications, and sent home. When her headaches persisted, she was referred to a neurologist, Dr. Matthews, who ordered an EEG, CT scan and an EMG nerve conduction study, all of which were negative. Dr. Matthews recommended physical therapy, which relieved some of her neck pain. She took off from work for 2 months, but in November she slipped and fell at a drug store and began to have increased lower back pain. She is presently under the care of an orthopedist for the low back problems. Since the car accident she has had some difficulty sleeping about three or four times a week because of neck pain. She says she tends to be irritable and can't stand loud noises when she has headaches. That's it.

Q. Did you conduct any tests on Ms. Lucas in that initial visit?

A. Yes. I administered the Minnesota Multiphasic Personality Inventory-2, or MMPI-2.

Q. Could you tell us the results of that test?

A. The patient had mildly abnormal scores on Scales 1, 2, and 3 of the MMPI-2. This pattern of scores is frequently seen in individuals who have been injured and continue to have physical symptoms as well as some psychological effects from the ongoing condition. According to the test, she appeared to be somewhat tense and anxious as well as experiencing some depressive moods.

Q. Was there any kind of diagnosis you rendered at that time?

A. Yes. There are two diagnoses. The first is "psychological factors affecting physical illness" and the second is "depressive disorder."

Q. Do you have a prognosis for her at this point in time, Doctor?

A. I would say it's good. I expect continued maintenance of infrequent, low-level headaches, less medication, and better moods.

Q. After your treatment is completed, do you think she'll need further psychological assistance?

A. No.

Q. Doctor, do you have any opinion as to what is causing Ms. Lucas' psychological problems?

A. I believe the patient's psychological condition is due to her physical injuries from the motor vehicle accident of last June and the slip and fall injury in November.

Q. Do you have any opinion percentage wise as to what psychological injury you would apportion to each accident?

A. It's difficult to give a precise answer, but I would attribute two thirds of her psychological impairment to the car accident and one third to the fall.

Q. How did you come to those conclusions?

A. The patient complained much more vigorously about her neck pain and headaches, which arose from the car accident, than about her low back pain that she has had since her fall. She could not work for two months after the car accident, but missed only 1 week of work after her fall. The neck pain interferes with her sleep and her headaches cause her to be irritable and angry. Compared to her slip and fall accident, the car accident seemed to be much more damaging psychologically.

Q. What treatment have you provided for Ms. Lucas' psychological condition?

A. She has been seen in psychotherapy sessions 6 times to help her deal with her frustrations and moods, and she has completed 10 biofeedback sessions. The biofeedback therapy has been successful in ameliorating her severe headaches.

Q. Have you completed your treatment of her?

A. No. Although she has improved considerably since her first visit, I expect to see her for at least 3 more months because she continues to have low back pain, some headaches and, therefore, continued difficulty adjusting to her medical condition.

Q. Thank you, Doctor. That's all I have.

Cross-Examination

"Wasn't she always a tense and irritable person?"

When the mental health professional attributes a person's psychological problems to a specific accident or incident, the opposing attorney will often attempt to identify a preaccident personality disposition and nonaccident related sources of stress. The following is a typical cross-examination approach:

> Q. **Doctor, you have been Ms. Lucas' psychiatrist for the past 6 months, is that correct?**
>
> A. Yes.
>
> Q. **You testified in direct examination that Ms. Lucas suffered headaches, was tense and irritable, and experienced depressive moods, is that right?**
>
> A. That's right.
>
> Q. **And in your opinion these physical and psychological problems were a result of the car accident of last September and the slip and fall accident of last November, is that right?**
>
> A. Yes.
>
> Q. **Doctor, did you have a chance to review the medical records of Dr. Nakano, who has been Ms. Lucas' personal doctor for many years?**
>
> A. No, I haven't.
>
> Q. **Did you know that Ms. Lucas has complained of work stress and has been given Valium periodically for tension and irritability for the past 10 years?**
>
> A. No.
>
> Q. **Did you know that Ms. Lucas has had chronic tension headaches and has taken aspirins regularly for many years?**
>
> A. No.
>
> Q. **Did you know that she has told Dr. Nakano about being moody at times long before the accidents of last year?**
>
> A. No.
>
> Q. **If you knew that Ms. Lucas has had long-standing problems with tension, irritability, headaches, and moodiness, wouldn't you have a different opinion as to whether her current psychological problems are related to the two accidents of last year?**
>
> a. I probably would.

A treating psychiatrist (or psychologist) frequently does not have any preinjury medical records and observations. Without important preinjury information, it may be presumptuous to link psychological symptoms reported in therapy to a specific causal event. The therapist could reply:

> A. It may well be that Ms. Lucas has had stress and tension in the past. Nonetheless, as far as I know, she was doing well psychologically and physically before the accidents, but since the two accidents of last year she has been unusually tense and moody and suffering severe headaches, which is why I believe that her current condition is related to the two accidents of last year.

To convince the trier-of-fact that an injury has occurred, the expert has to demonstrate that significant changes have taken place in the patient's mental status. If the witness is not fully apprised of the person's preinjury condition, it may be difficult to connect putative damages to a specific incident.

More Cross-Examination

"Does she have pain every minute of the day?"

When an expert opinion appears to be securely based on convincing data and scientific support, the opposing attorney's strategy might be to reduce the significance of the findings by emphasizing its limitations.

Q. Doctor, you have testified that Ms. Lucas has a chronic pain disorder, is that correct?

A. Yes.

Q. Does she have pain every day?

A. Yes.

Q. Does she consciously experience pain all day long?

A. Yes, off and on.

Q. So, she doesn't have constant pain, every minute of the day, correct?

A. Yes, that is correct.

Q. Does she consciously experience pain while eating breakfast?

A. I don't know. I don't think so.

Q. Does she consciously experience pain when talking with someone?

A. Not usually. Talking helps to distract a person from their pain.

Q. And you've advised her to distract herself daily with different activities, haven't you?

A. Yes, I have.

Q. According to your therapy notes, in order to distract herself from the pain you've told her to do some physical exercise, go on walks, talk to family members and friends, do some light house chores and yard work, and develop some hobbies, isn't that true?

A. Yes.

Q. In addition to that, you've also trained her in relaxation and imagery techniques to control pain, correct?

A. Yes.

Q. And she's been compliant with those instructions, isn't that right?

A. I believe so.

Q. And when she does consciously experience her pain at any occasion, does she think about it for several minutes or for several seconds?

A. Probably for several seconds.

Q. Now, given the above daily routines, just how many seconds or minutes per day do you think Ms. Lucas consciously experiences pain?

a. I haven't thought about her pain in terms of time, but I'd guess that in the course of a day she consciously experiences pain about 20 to 30 minutes.

The relentlessly reductionistic approach just described has tried to minimize the seriousness of the plaintiff's chronic pain disorder. It is similar to the "chip away" strategy described by Rogers and Mitchell (1991) in the criminal context. The questions in this case have focused on the conscious experience of pain while ignoring the widespread impact on the individual's life. The clinician often has no specific information about pain in terms of minutes, and may do better by stating:

A. I haven't thought about her pain in terms of time. I think about how her pain condition has altered her lifestyle by preventing her from returning to her usual active physical recreation, like aerobics, and fun activities with her boyfriend, like dancing. She's gained over 20 pounds this year from her inactivity, and she feels like a totally different person.

The reductionistic approach can be applied to any symptom or injury, and can be very effective when carefully employed. However, the expert witness can avoid being drawn into a microscopic focus, and remind the court of the broader perspectives of the case.

GENERAL CHALLENGES

The mental health professional in personal injury lawsuits faces several commonly used challenges to his or her testimony. The challenges presented earlier as applying in criminal cases (chapter 6) and child custody hearings (chapter 7) are also applicable in civil lawsuits, in addition to the following:

- base rates
- probability statements
- differences between experts
- incomplete data
- apportionment
- hypothetical questions
- the "hired gun"

Base Rates

"Doesn't everybody have headaches?"

When interpreting patterns of symptoms and arriving at diagnoses, psychiatrists and psychologists have been known to overlook base rates, that is, the frequency with which certain syndromes occur in the general population. Ignoring base rates can lead a diagnostician to overrate signs of pathology or to "overpathologize" (Faust, Ziskin, & Hiers, 1991). These false positive diagnoses can be misleading and will be challenged by the opposing attorney.

Q. **As I understand it, you have diagnosed Mr. O'Brien as having a postconcussion syndrome, is that right?**

A. Yes.

Q. **What are the characteristics of a postconcussion syndrome?**

A. Postconcussion patients report an array of symptoms, including headache, irritability, insomnia, fatigue, anxiety, and problems with concentration and memory.

Q. **Are headaches an important feature of the postconcussion syndrome?**

A. Yes.

Q. **Did you know that in a survey of 1,200 adults, 70% of the respondents experienced headaches?**

A. No, I'm not familiar with that survey.

Q. **Are concentration and memory problems important features of the postconcussion syndrome?**

A. Yes.

Q. **Are you aware of studies that have shown that those with and without head injury report the same amount of problems with concentration and memory?**

A. No.

Q. **Doctor, isn't it apparent that the difficulties Mr. O'Brien is reporting, like headaches and memory problems, are the same as those who haven't had any head injury?**

a. It seems that way.

If a patient has symptoms that are, indeed, no different than any normal person, then he or she may have no claim to compensation for any injury. The patient in the previous example may well be exhibiting a postconcussion syndrome, and the witness could reply in the following way:

A. Whether or not headaches and memory problems are commonly experienced, this person did not have these symptoms until immediately after the head injury. Moreover, he has the whole complex of postconcussion symptoms, including irritability, fatigue, anxiety, and dizziness. I do not think that this mix of symptoms occurs often in the average uninjured person.

"Do abnormal test scores mean the person is abnormal?"

Acknowledging base rates is also essential in the interpretation of psychological test results. Consider the following challenge:

Q. Doctor, your diagnosis of Mrs. Palma was "somatoform pain disorder," is that right?

A. Yes.

Q. And your diagnosis was supported by the MMPI-2 results, am I correct?

A. Yes.

Q. Could you tell us about the MMPI-2 results?

A. Well, the 2-point code type based on the two highest scores in the profile, Scales 1 and 3, in this case, was characteristic of a somatoform disorder. This means that the patient reported having many physical complaints, like headaches, back pain, and weakness, with these symptoms being prone to increase in times of stress. With the 1–3 code type, there is also the possibility of secondary gain or classical conversion reactions for this patient, who has a history of chronic pain.

Q. Is it your testimony, based on the MMPI-2 1–3 code type and the diagnosis of somatoform pain disorder, that emotional problems are a big reason for the patient's pain condition?

A. Yes, it is.

Q. Are you saying that all patients with the 1–3 code type are somatoform disorders?

A. I don't think all 1–3 codes mean that the person has a somatoform disorder.

Q. Isn't it true that the 1–3 code type is often found in normal individuals?

A. That's true.

Q. Hasn't research shown that the 1–3 code type is frequently found with normals undergoing an annual physical examination?

A. Yes.

Q. So, wouldn't you agree that Mrs. Palma's 1–3 code pattern could very well be a normal profile rather than a somatoform profile?

a. I would agree.

MMPI-2 high scores about the T65 level do not automatically indicate psychopathology (Graham, 1993). Familiarity with research on various populations, such as ethnic minorities and socioeconomic groups, provides test users with important base rate information, so that overinterpretation and false positive errors can be averted. Finally, diagnoses should not be made on psychological test results alone (Anastasi, 1988).

A. Mrs. Palma's 1–3 code may be a normal variant. However, my diagnosis was principally based on my interviews and observations of the patient and a review of her medical records. It was my impression that Mrs. Palma's 1–3 profile was compatible with her somatization disorder.

Probability Statement

"Doesn't 'probable' mean you're not sure?"

The mental health professional's opinions are expressed in terms of "reasonable medical (or psychological) probability," a standard that is consistent with the psychiatrist's or psychologist's academic training. Although the expert is familiar and comfortable with probability statements, this concept may be foreign to the layperson, and the opposing attorney may attempt to cast doubt on the scientific accuracy of the expert's conclusions.

> **Q. You have testified that Mr. Quintero has an anxiety disorder as a result of the electrical accident, isn't that right?**
> A. Yes.
> **Q. When you draw the connection between the accident and the anxiety disorder, is your opinion a matter of fact or a matter of probability?**
> A. It's a probability statement.
> **Q. So, you're not absolutely certain and you're giving us your estimate or probability, right?**
> a. Well, yes.

At this juncture, the other attorney may object, and assert that the expert witness is not expected to be absolutely certain and that a probability statement of "preponderance of evidence" or "more likely than not" is the legal standard for personal injury litigation. Without the aid of an objection, the expert witness could reject the implications of gross inaccuracy by responding simply:

> A. As an expert, I am trained to establish estimates of behavior, expressed in terms of probabilities. In my opinion, Mr. Quintero's anxiety disorder is, more likely than not, a direct result of the electrical accident and the burns he suffered.

"Is the IQ score an exact score or an estimation?"

The attack on probability statements can also ensue when psychological test scores are involved. Consider this case involving a person regarded as mentally retarded:

> **Q. Doctor, you said that Mr. Rogers has not suffered any brain injury and that he is mentally retarded, is that correct?**
> A. Yes.
> **Q. You based your diagnosis of mental retardation on his IQ score of 65, is that right?**
> A. Yes.

Q. **Is his score of 65 an exact score, or is there a margin of error?**

A. There's a margin of error, which we refer to as the standard error of measurement. For the IQ test, the standard error of measurement is about 3. This means that the probability is 95% that Mr. Rogers' score is 65 plus or minus 3.

Q. **Doctor, aren't you still saying the Mr. Rogers' IQ is not exactly 65 but probably 65?**

A. Yes.

Q. **So, you're saying that the IQ score is not exact or absolute, and we don't know what his real IQ is, wouldn't you agree?**

a. Yes, I would.

The cross-examining attorney has duped the expert into implying that an IQ score is merely a gross estimate or guess. In effect, the witness has impeached his or her own testimony regarding the person's mental retardation. A better response would be:

A. We don't know exactly, but we know with a high degree of probability that Mr.Rogers' IQ is between 62 and 68, which is within the Mental Defective range.

Differences Between Experts

"Do all experts agree with each other?"

Because psychological and behavioral data are not interpreted precisely the same way by different experts, the cross-examining attorney may place emphasis on the interprofessional differences. The cross-examination may not result in any major changes in conclusions, but the attorney could obtain helpful concessions.

Q. **You concluded that the plaintiff suffered a posttraumatic stress disorder on the basis of the extensive history you obtained, isn't that correct?**

A. Yes.

Q. **Would all experts reviewing the same history you obtained arrive at the same diagnosis?**

A. No, I don't think so, although our diagnoses wouldn't be that far apart.

Q. **So, there may be varying conclusions reached by mental health experts reviewing the same data you obtained, isn't that true?**

A. Yes, but I believe that my conclusions in this case are correct.

Q. **I realize that, but isn't it true that the information you relied on is subject to different interpretations?**

A. Yes, that's true.

Q. **And different conclusions may be reached by respected experts in your field using the same data, correct?**

a. Yes.

Instead of simply conceding that experts do not always agree after reviewing the same clinical data, the witness could use the opportunity to reiterate the findings and the way the conclusions were reached.

A. Although experts may differ, in my opinion, the patient's high anxiety, frequent flashbacks and nightmares mean that she suffered a significant posttraumatic stress disorder.

Incomplete Data

"Why didn't you use Tests X, Y, and Z?"

Because there are innumerable test instruments available for mental health professionals, the cross-examination may suggest that the psychological examination excluded well-known tests and is, therefore, incomplete and insufficient.

Q. **You testified that the victim was not psychologically impaired, correct?**

A. Yes.

Q. **You based your conclusions largely on the results of the psychological testing, did you not?**

A. That's correct.

Q. **You administered the MMPI-2 in reaching your conclusions, correct?**

A. Yes.

Q. **Did you administer the Millon Clinical Multi-axial Inventory-2, or MCMI-2?**

A. No, I didn't.

Q. **Did you administer the Rorschach?**

A. No.

Q. **The MCMI-2 and the Rorschach are widely used psychological tests, are they not?**

A. Yes, they are.

Q. **Isn't it true that the results from the MCMI-2 and the Rorschach could have been very helpful in reaching your conclusions?**

a. That's true.

Q. **Isn't it also true that if you had more time with the patient you could have obtained more information that would help to know the patient better?**

a. Yes.

Agreeing to the last two questions raises the possibility that the expert's conclusions were reached without a complete examination. If the expert has done a thorough and valid evaluation, a better response would be:

A. Additional information is undeniably helpful, but I believe I conducted a thorough examination and did not need any more data to form my opinion.

Or

A. The MCMI-2 and Rorschach are alternatives that might well have yielded results leading to the same conclusions.

Apportionment

"Isn't at least half of his problems due to his preexisting personality disorder?"

In personal injury litigation, the expert witness is often asked to apportion the plaintiff's emotional injury to different etiologic factors, because the defendant wishes to pay for no more than the specific damages for which he or she is responsible. Mental health professionals in the course of their usual clinical work have some awareness of the varying influences on a person's mental condition, such as family and work pressures. However, clinicans do not consciously calculate proportionate weights of each contributing factor and they may find the process to be awkward and difficult. Note the following series of questions.

Q. In the course of your psychotherapy with Mr. Towne, you became aware of many different problems in his life, isn't that correct?
A. That's correct.
Q. You testified that his job as a car salesman has always been full of pressure, right?
A. Yes.
Q. And he and his wife saw a marriage counselor for 2 years, isn't that true?
A. Yes.
Q. You also mentioned that he had passive–aggressive personality traits, correct?
A. Yes.
Q. And those are longstanding personality features, right?
A. Yes.

Q. In other words, isn't it true that Mr. Towne's present psychological condition that affects his work performance is due to many factors and not only due to the slip and fall accident?

A. That's true.

Q. Could you give me an estimate of each contributing factor, for the purpose of apportionment?

A. You mean in terms of percentages?

Q. Yes. Could you give me an estimate of what percent of Mr. Towne's psychological disability is due to the slip and fall accident and how much is due to preexisiting nonaccident factors?

a. I found that 20% of his symptoms is due to preexisting passive aggressive personality traits and job stress, and 80% to the recent slip and fall accident.

It is not sufficient to merely offer percentages when apportioning an injury. An expert's conclusions need to be supported by relevant specified facts. In apportioning injury the description and explanation of the cause and effects of the alleged injuries are the major contributions of the expert witness.

A. Prior to the slip and fall accident, the patient suffered headaches and missed work about 10 days a year. Since his accident and subsequent neck pain and migraines, he has missed more than 40 days in the past year. Thus, I attribute 20% of his disability to his preexisting nonaccident condition, and 80% to the slip and fall accident.

Hypothetical Questions

"If the patient had done better since the accident, would you state that the accident caused the improvements?"

Attorneys frequently employ hypothetical questions to elicit opinions favorable to their side of the argument. Even if there are objections to the hypothetical questions (e.g., assuming inaccurate facts), the witness may be required to answer the question as posed by the attorney.

Q. Doctor, I want to ask you a question based on the following: assume that Mr. Towne had his slip and fall accident 2 years ago, but has continued his second part-time job selling clothes. Further assume that he has continued his ballroom dance classes 3 times a week, as he's done for the past 3 years. Finally, assume that his work performance evaluation was "good," just as it has been for the past 5 years. Given these assumptions, is it likely or unlikely that Mr. Towne has

suffered any psychological effects from his slip and fall accident 2 years ago?

a. It's unlikely that he suffered any psychological effects from the accident.

The hypothetical usually has some basis in fact, which the questioning attorney can support. However, simply to agree with the hypothetical question can seriously contradict your previous testimony. Because you are not certain as to the accuracy of the assumed elements in the hypothetical question, it is better to offer an appropriate disclaimer and/or modify the hypothetical to conform with your opinion.

A. Assuming what you say is true, it would appear unlikely that Mr. Towne suffered major psychological injury from the accident.

If the hypothetical question seems too broad or provides insufficient facts, the expert can state that there is too little information for an opinion to be formulated (Hambacher, 1994). The witness may then be asked to indicate what assumed information is needed, such as more facts about the patient's daily functioning, for the question to be answerable.

The "Hired Gun"

"If you were hired, that makes you a hired gun, right?"

When psychologists and psychiatrists appear primarily as experts for injured plaintiffs or work exclusively for insurance companies and defense law firms, the potential to be biased for one side or the other may be called into question. The practice of specializing as a "plaintiff's expert" or a "defense expert" should be avoided (Blau, 1984). Those who appear nearly entirely for one side may encounter the following challenges:

Q. Doctor, have you been retained as an expert witness for the plaintiff by the law office of Mr. Crafty?

A. Yes.

Q. How often have you been hired by Mr. Crafty's law firm?

A. About 6 or 7 times.

Q. How often have you been retained as an expert witness for plaintiffs in other personal injury cases?

A. That's hard to say. Maybe 30 times.

Q. Have you ever been hired as an expert by the defense in any personal injury case?

A. I can't say I have.

Q. **With your experience as a plaintiff's expert, wouldn't you say that you have a special skill in offering the plaintiff's views on his or her injuries?**

A. Yes, that's a fair statement.

Q. **Wouldn't you also say that, with your experience as a plaintiff's expert, you have more empathy for the plaintiff's views?**

A. I guess I would.

Q. **Wouldn't your experience and great empathy for the plaintiff make it difficult for you not to be biased for the plaintiff?**

A. Of course, I'm not biased. I am a professional and I try to remain objective in all my evaluations.

The professional who works strictly for one side cannot avoid the appearance of bias, no matter how adamantly he or she claims to be an objective professional. Some attorneys may even ask how much income has been earned annually as an expert for one side. The best protection against this line of questioning is to avoid the practice altogether, so that the doctor can say in court:

A. I have been retained about 30 times for a plaintiff's attorney, but I have also been hired many times as an expert by defense attorneys.

MISCELLANEOUS Q & A

Other questions you might encounter in personal injury cases include the following.

Treatment Doctor

Q. **Wouldn't you agree that a doctor who has treated and observed the patient on a regular basis from the time of the accident until now has an opinion that is more accurate than an opinion based on the one session you had with the patient?**

a. I would agree.

A. That's not necessarily true. Although I had only one session with the patient, I had the benefit of obtaining a large number of medical documents from previous physicians who have treated the patient in the past. Thus, I believe I was able to perform a thorough evaluation of the patient, and I am unable to say how thorough or accurate the treating doctor's examinations have been.

Limited Knowledge

Q. **Are you familiar with the very recent article by Dr. _____ published in (obscure journal) about the postconcussion syndrome?**

a. Of course not! I never heard of *(obscure journal)*.

A. I've read many articles on the postconcussion syndrome, but not that one. I'd be happy to review it if you'd like.

Lack of Certainty

Q. **When you said that the patient's emotional injury is "probably" due to the accident, does "probably" mean a high degree of certainty?**

a. No. Probably means probably. I can't be clearer than that.

A. "Probably" means it is more likely than not that the patient's injury is due to the accident.

Criticizing a Test

Q. **Doctor, aren't there colleagues of yours who criticize the MMPI-2 and never use that test to evaluate a patient?**

a. Sure. That's because they don't have any training or experience in using the test.

A. Yes. The MMPI-2, like any other test, is not infallible. That is why I use other sources of information, such as case history and a clinical examination, and I don't rely entirely on one test.

Showing Bias

Q. **Isn't it true that your experience in personal injury cases has primarily been testifying for the plaintiff?**

a. Yes, but I'm a doctor and I work for patients, not lawyers.

A. It's true, but whenever defense attorneys request my expertise I've been willing to help.

Being Misquoted

Q. **You testified about predisposing personality factors. Does that mean that the broken family and difficult childhood she had contributed to her present condition and poor recovery from her trauma?**

a. Yes.

A. I testified that predisposing personality factors were small. I do not think they contributed very much to her present condition.

Authoritative Texts

If a text is considered to be authoritative, its contents may have a binding effect, and any deviation could be considered invalid.

Q. Doctor, wouldn't you agree that DSM–IV is the most widely used and authoritative text in classifying psychiatric disorders?

a. Yes, I agree.

A. DSM–IV is widely used and is one authority, but there are some in the scientific community who believe that DSM–IV is neither the only, nor the best, system to classify psychiatric disorders.

Computerized Test Results

Q. If you don't agree with all of the interpretive statements in the computerized report, how do you decide if your interpretation is more valid than the printout?

a. I trust my clinical judgment. I have years of experience in interpreting test results, and I have confidence in my ability to read test data accurately.

A. The computer interpretations provide helpful hypotheses, many of which are quite valid. If I don't agree with the computerized results, it is because I have other more persuasive data, such as medical history and recent behavioral observations.

Lying

Q. Isn't is a fact that a doctor can't tell if a person is really in pain?

a. That's true. There is no way to objectively measure pain.

A. Pain is a subjective matter and is difficult to quantify objectively. Thus, a pain condition requires a thorough multifaceted evaluation, especially when litigation and financial compensation are involved, so that the presence of exaggerating or faking can be assessed.

After the Settlement

Q. Isn't it true that patients get better after their lawsuit is settled?

a. I believe that's true.

A. No, that's a myth that continues to be upheld by some professionals. Several research articles have indicated that injured persons continue to have pain symptoms and are disabled long after their legal cases have been settled.

Dealing with Hypotheticals

Q. Doctor, if we assume that the patient had a second car accident, wouldn't you change your opinion about the present effects of the first car accident?

a. If the patient had a second car accident, I think I have to change my opinion about the effects of the first car accident.

A. Assuming a second car accident is not enough to change my opinion. If the second car accident caused substantial injuries, I would re-evaluate my opinions about the first accident.

Disagreeing With Medical Doctors

Q. A neurologist, a neurosurgeon, and an orthopedic surgeon have all testified that there is no objective physical finding to explain the patient's pain condition. Doesn't that contradict your testimony?

a. Yes. But I happen not to agree with their opinions.

A. Pain is a subjective complaint and cannot be measured directly. A close review of the accident report, clinical examinations, effects of medicine and therapy, and reports from coworkers and family members led me to conclude that the patient has a significant pain condition.

Degree of Condition

Q. You have characterized her pain syndrome as mild, isn't that correct?

a. That's correct.

A. Compared to other severe pain syndromes that are completely disabling, her condition is mild. This is not to imply that the effects of her pain condition are mild. Her pain syndrome has severely curtailed her ability to function as she used to, 50 hours a week as a prominent executive.

CLOSING ARGUMENTS

Society's current trend to sue for any negative event has vastly increased the role of mental health professionals in the courtroom. In addition to everyday traffic accidents and slip and falls, other events such as airline mishaps, building fires and bomb explosions immediately produce hundreds of victims who are emotionally traumatized, and who seek not only psychological treatment but also pursue financial compensation for their alleged emotional injuries.

This chapter on personal injury or tort litigation emphasized the need for the mental health expert to perform an assessment that is far more extensive than the ordinary clinical examination. The expert must be knowledgeable about the plaintiff's preinjury psychological functioning and any nonaccident emotional stressors. Among the general challenges discussed were the base rate of symptom patterns, the meaning of probability statements, differences that occur among clinical experts, incomplete examinations, apportioning the injury, hypothetical questions, and the "hired gun" image.

Psychiatrists and psychologists have complex responsibilities of being skilled psychotherapists as well as effective forensic witnesses when their patients' lawsuits call for their professional documentation. In the event that the civil litigation involves impressive monetary stakes, say in six or seven figures, expert witnesses can expect to encounter intense opposition from highly paid, experienced and aggressive counsel. The personal injury arena is not for the faint-of-heart, but it can be a challenging and rewarding experience for the well-prepared professional.

CHAPTER 9

MENTAL COMPETENCY AND DANGEROUSNESS

Mental health professionals are frequently consulted when questions arise as to whether a person is mentally competent. In the medical setting, psychiatrists and psychologists are called on to determine if a patient is competent to consent to or refuse essential medical treatment. In forensic situations, psychiatrists and psychologists are asked whether a person is mentally fit to stand trial or to sign legal documents, such as a will. The first half of this chapter addresses these issues, which are the most commonly asked questions pertaining to mental competence. The second half focuses on the prediction of violence, which is a premium challenge you face when evaluating dangerous offenders.

MENTAL COMPETENCY

Competency to Stand Trial

"Does he know the trouble he's in?"

A person is said to be mentally competent to stand trial if he or she can reasonably understand the legal proceedings and can consult with his or her attorney. When there are doubts about a defendant's competency to stand trial, the court will order an examination by a qualified clinician. Empirical research indicates that competency evaluations are typically highly reliable (Melton et al., 1987). Competency examinations are usually performed in a forensic psychiatric hospital, sometimes in a jail setting, and at times in an outpatient office. Although a written report often suffices, in many instances a formal hearing is held to assess the clinical evidence pertaining to the competency issue. You will be asked who requested the evaluation, whether the defendant understood the purpose of the evaluation, and how the evaluation was performed.

Direct Examination by Prosecuting Attorney

Q. Doctor, have you had an opportunity to examine the defendant, Mr. Stephens?

A. Yes, I have.

Q. What was the purpose of your examination?

A. I was requested by the court to evaluate Mr. Stephens' mental competency, specifically his fitness to stand trial.

Q. Why was the request for the examination made?

A. According to the referral letter, Mr. Stephens began to exhibit strange behavior last month in jail, where he has been incarcerated for the past 4 months. He was often seen talking or laughing to himself, and his attorney found him difficult to understand at times because of his apparently illogical comments.

Q. Did Mr. Stephens understand the purpose of the examination?

A. Yes, he did.

Q. All right. Could you tell us about your examination and your findings?

A. I saw Mr. Stephens at the State Forensic Psychiatric Center where he had been admitted for 2 weeks. He was cooperative throughout the entire evaluation, which took about an hour and a half. He had a tendency to be overideational and he exhibited a definite thought disorder, with loose associations and nonsequitur thinking. I was, nonetheless, able to conduct a thorough competency evaluation. I found that reality testing was adequate and he had the capacity to relate and cooperate with legal counsel. He occasionally mumbled to himself and laughed for no known reason, but he was able to suppress these behaviors on request. Mr. Stephens was able to understand the criminal trial process, including the role of the attorneys, the judge, and the jury. He knew what the oath to tell the truth means and what guilty and innocent pleas mean. Mr. Stephens was aware of the charges made against him and the possible sentences or penalties he faces. Although he is psychiatrically impaired, Mr. Stephens has the capacity to understand the legal proceedings and to cooperate with his lawyer.

The mental health expert should refrain from stating conclusions about the competency to stand trial, which is a legal rather than a clinical matter. Your role is to provide a detailed assessment of the defendant so that the court can decide whether or not he or she is competent to cope with the criminal trial process. Only in certain jurisdictions can a mental health expert give an opinion on the ultimate issue (i.e., competency to stand trial).

Cross-Examination by Defense Attorney

"You mean all you did was interview the defendant?"

A competency evaluation can be adequately completed within the confines of a concise clinical interview (Grisso, 1988a; Rogers & Mitchell, 1991). You can be sufficiently thorough by evaluating the essential components of the competency to stand trial issue (viz., the capacity to understand the legal proceedings and to relate cooperatively and communicate with one's attorney). Opposing attorneys who may not fully understand the criteria for competency investigation and who expect a comprehensive diagnostic examination may ask the following questions:

Q. **You did a one-and-a-half-hour examination of Mr. Stephens, is that right?**
A. Yes.
Q. **Did you perform a mental status examination?**
A. Yes, I did.
Q. **Did you obtain a complete history from the defendant?**
A. I don't know what you mean by "complete." I asked Mr. Stephens about the criminal charges he faces and about any previous arrests or convictions, which he denied having. I didn't elicit a lot of detail about his childhood, education, work or marital background, if that is what you mean.
Q. **That is exactly what I mean. Doctor, did you take time to observe him on the ward of the hospital?**
A. No, I didn't.
Q. **What about psychological tests? Did you administer any psychological tests?**
A. No.
Q. **Did you at least administer the Competency Assessment Inventory or CAI?**
A. I asked several questions that are included in the CAI, but I didn't conduct the full CAI interview.
Q. **Why didn't you obtain a complete history, observe him on the ward, or administer psychological tests?**
a. I didn't think it was necessary and I had limited time to finish this assignment.

The "limited time" excuse is no excuse, but the necessity of a complete history, hospital observations, and psychological testing can be effectively refuted by the expert, because such information, however interesting, is not necessarily germane to the issue of mental competency. Consider this response:

A. The interview I performed encompassed the essentials of a competency examination. The information I provided regarding the defendant's capacity to comprehend the legal proceedings and to relate to the attorney is the most pertinent for the court to determine Mr. Stephens' competency to stand trial.

More Cross-Examination

"How can a psychotic person be competent to stand trial?"

Some attorneys may confuse the presence of a psychotic disorder with the issue of mental competence. An incompetent person need not be psychotic; a person may be incompetent due to mental retardation or dementia. A psychotic person can, in some instances, be competent, but not in others. Attorneys who mistakenly believe that all psychotics are incompetent may ask the following questions:

Q. Doctor, what is your diagnosis of Mr. Stephens?
A. The diagnosis is paranoid schizophrenia.
Q. And what does that diagnosis mean?
A. Schizophrenia is a psychotic disorder in which the person experiences delusions, hallucinations, and disturbed thoughts and emotions. Paranoid schizophrenia is a type of schizophrenia in which there is a systematic delusion and oftentimes auditory hallucinations.
Q. Does that mean that the person is distorting reality or is not in contact with reality?
A. Yes, at times.
Q. Now, you were asked to evaluate Mr. Stephens' competency to stand trial, correct?
A. Yes.
Q. Doctor, are you aware that Mr. Stephens believes he is an arm of the CIA?
A. Yes.
Q. And that he gets his orders from the CIA through television shows?
A. Yes.
Q. Isn't that, pardon the expression, crazy?
A. Yes, those thoughts are delusional and unrealistic.
Q. And you believe he is competent to stand trial?
A. The defendant is clearly psychotic, but he is able to comprehend the legal proceedings against him, has good memory for past events, and can communicate his thoughts and feelings quite adequately.

Q. Isn't it necessary for a defendant to work cooperatively with his attorney?

A. Yes.

Q. Don't you see that it is impossible for me as his attorney to work with him when he rambles on about the CIA?

a. I see what you mean.

Most attorneys have little training in assisting the seriously mentally ill. Thus, they may be uneasy or frustrated in working with a delusional or hallucinating person. However, if a defendant understands the court proceedings and is able to relate to the attorney, he or she is legally competent. The mental health experts can help the attorney with the following:

A. Mr. Stephens likes to talk about his CIA activity. But he realizes he needs your support for the criminal case against him and is able to cooperate with you in his defense.

Civil Competencies

The legal system protects the constitutional right of individuals to self-determination, such as managing their own property and choosing or rejecting medical treatment if they so wish. However, in some instances mental disability renders a person incapable of making rational decisions, and the courts may intervene to protect the welfare of a possible incompetent individual. Such cases usually require that a mental health professional evaluate the mental capacity of the impaired person. A clinician may also be consulted with respect to a person's mental competence when executing a will. As in the previous example of the criminal defendant's competency to stand trial, the person need not be competent in all areas of functioning, but must exhibit specific understanding of one's own property, of medical issues, and alternative choices, and of how his or her property is being distributed upon death.

Managing Personal Affairs

"Doesn't everyone know he acts crazy every now and then?"

When a person is believed to be too mentally disabled to manage his or her own estate or personal affairs, the court may delegate a guardian or conservator to assist in decisions regarding the property or vital medical treatment. The mental health professional who is requested to assess competency to manage one's own finances must be able to explain behavioral patterns, such as when a person behaves in apparently inconsistent ways.

Q. On the basis of your examination of Mr. Vincent, you believe he is able to manage his own affairs, right?

A. That's right.

Q. Have you been able to interview Mr. Vincent's two adult daughters?

A. No, I haven't.

Q. His daughters have testified that Mr. Vincent keeps in his freezer his pet bird that died last year. Did you know that?

A. No, I didn't.

Q. They said that he's been consulting a fortune teller, a Vietnamese woman who forecasts the future by interpreting playing cards. Did you know that?

A. No.

Q. They said that he keeps at least $20,000 in cash under his mattress. Were you aware of that?

A. Yes.

Q. They said he used to have close to $100,000 in cash at home, but he's been spending a lot at hostess bars in recent months. Did he tell you that?

A. Yes, he did.

Q. Doctor, Mr. Vincent's daughters are very concerned that their father is senile, shows poor judgment, and is financially irresponsible. Don't you agree with them?

a. I can see their point and why they're concerned about their father.

The fact that an individual exhibits personality changes and behaves in a strange or unreasonable manner is not sufficient to declare him or her mentally incompetent. It is tempting in this case to help the two concerned daughters, but the appropriate reply is:

A. We may not all agree with the prudence of Mr. Vincent's recent activities. Nonetheless, he is fully aware of his finances and the consequences of his current spending. He insists he has the right to spend his money the way he wants.

"He's not totally incompetent, is he?"

When a person is considered mentally incompetent, the layperson may conjure the image of a totally dysfunctional individual. The opposing attorney will attempt to single out behaviors that seemingly contradict the notion of incompetence.

Q. Doctor, you have testified that Mr. Xavier is mentally incompetent to make decisions about his health care, is that correct?

A. Yes.

Q. Isn't it a fact that he cooks some of his own meals every day?

A. Yes.

Q. Isn't it also true that he can manage his own self-care activities on a daily basis, such as bathing and even doing the laundry?

A. Yes, that's true.

Q. Did you know that Mr. Xavier reads the newspaper every morning to follow his favorite baseball team?

A. No, I didn't know that.

Q. Did you know that he uses the automatic machine at the bank to draw out cash?

A. Yes, I did.

Q. Doctor, wouldn't you say that a person who can take care of himself and even use the automatic bank machine is a fairly competent person?

a. I guess you can say that.

Although an individual such as Mr. Xavier is fairly capable of handling many of his or her personal affairs, he or she may lack the cognitive ability to cope with some of the more complex matters in his or her life. An example would be a person with memory impairment or progressive dementia. In this instance, the witness should reply:

A. Mr. Xavier is capable of handling certain simpler and familiar routines of his personal life. However, he forgets what his new heart medicine and anticoagulation medicine consist of, he frequently fails to take his medication on time, and he has a poor concept of his multisystem medical condition. He does not realize that without amputating his foot, his life is imminently in danger. Because of this, I believe he is not competent to make appropriate decisions about his medical treatment.

Executing a Will

"Being an alcoholic doesn't make her incompetent, does it?"

A psychiatric disorder does not, per se, indicate mental incompetency. Thus, a psychotic, a neurotic, or an alcoholic can draw up valid wills. The critical factor is whether the person, at the time of making the will, has sufficient capacity to understand the extent of his or her property and consequences of his or her will, such as in the following case:

Q. Doctor, your testimony about Mrs. Young's alcohol abuse raises serious doubts about the validity of her will, does it not?

A. I believe it does.

Q. You are aware that before her death Mrs. Young had recently retired as a schoolteacher, aren't you?

A. Yes, I am.

Q. **You know that she lived alone and was taking care of her own affairs, right?**

A. That's right.

Q. **Did you conclude that Mrs. Young was not mentally competent because of her abuse of alcohol?**

A. Yes.

Q. **Are you saying that a person who was recently a schoolteacher can be incompetent because of abusing alcohol?**

A. Yes, I am.

Q. **Aren't you aware that many people who abuse alcohol are well-functioning people?**

a. But that doesn't mean that everyone who abuses alcohol is well-functioning.

The diagnosis of alcohol abuse is not an adequate reason to declare someone incompetent. The most relevant matter is the person's state of mind at the time he or she made out the will. Consider this reply:

A. According to those who knew her well, such as her neighbors, Mrs. Young was in a constant state of drunkenness for the last several months of her life. Consequently, it is doubtful that she was sufficiently lucid when she altered her will just prior to her death.

MISCELLANEOUS Q & A

The following are a variety of challenges to mental competency testimony.

Environmental Influences

Q. **Don't you think that the trauma of being in jail for 3 months awaiting trial is enough to make a person appear mentally disturbed?**

a. That could be the case.

A. Yes. That is the reason I carefully examined his jail records as well as psychiatric reports prior to his incarceration, and I found a consistent pattern of inappropriate behaviors and delusional thoughts even before he was jailed.

Examiner Differences

Q. **You said he seemed angry and irritable when you saw him. Isn't it possible he could have reacted differently with a different examiner?**

a. Sure, that's possible.

A. Yes. His anger and irritability with me were only part of my findings of the defendant. His past history, including recent acts of belligerence on the ward, is one of the reasons I found him to be a continued threat to society with potential for violent behavior.

No Tests

Q. For your evaluation of the defendant's fitness to stand trial, did you administer psychological tests, like the Competency Screening Test?

a. No, I don't administer tests. I am satisfied with the clinical interview I always conduct with criminal defendants.

A. No. I did a thorough interview and I found that the defendant understands the charges and legal proceedings he faces, and he can cooperate with his lawyer for this trial.

Contrary Findings

Q. You mean you didn't have any information that might not fit with the diagnosis of mental incompetence?

a. No, I didn't.

A. The defendant was able, for brief periods, to interact with her attorney. But that was the exception rather than the rule, and for the most part she could not be depended on to cooperate with her lawyer.

Psychosis and Competency

Q. Doctor, you described the accused as paranoid and psychotic. Just because he is paranoid and psychotic doesn't necessarily mean that he is incompetent, right?

a. Yes, that's right.

A. His paranoia and psychosis are part of his global behavioral and emotional problem that impedes his ability to understand the legal procedures he faces.

Alzheimer's Dementia

Q. Doesn't the diagnosis of Alzheimer's and her poor memory test scores mean she's not able to manage her estate?

a. I don't think so. I'd rather give her the benefit of the doubt.

A. Her forgetfulness can be a problem, but she has always been a meticulous record keeper and, at this point, is still capable of knowing the extent of her estate and finances.

Coping With a Hypothetical

Q. Would it change your opinion about the accused's mental competence if you knew that he was behaving in a bizarre manner in jail?
a. Yes, it probably would. If he was behaving in a bizarre manner, it's a real possibility the defendant is unfit to stand trial.
A. I am not aware from my review of his jail records of any bizarre behavior. I would be glad to reevaluate this matter if I were provided with his complete records.

Dealing With Possibilities

Q. Isn't it possible that you examined the defendant on a bad day, and that she is usually more intact and functional?
a. Yes, that's a possibility.
A. It is possible that she could be better on another day, but with the amount of time I spent with her and given the abundance of observations in her files, I think that is highly improbable.

DANGEROUSNESS

"Can you doctors really predict the future?"

Testifying as to the potential dangerousness of individuals can be troublesome for mental health experts in view of the ongoing debate about the predictability of violent behavior. Studies in the 1970s and early 1980s suggested that clinicians are not able to make accurate predictions of violence (Faust & Ziskin, 1988), whereas more recent investigations imply that mental health professionals' short-term predictions of violence are substantially more accurate than chance (McNeil & Binder, 1991; Moss, 1994). In light of the empirical research, it is held that mental health professionals should refrain from offering opinions about the likelihood of dangerousness with a given individual, especially where long-term predictions are requested (American Psychiatric Association, 1974; American Psychological Association, 1978). Thus, any statements about the likelihood of serious harm may be challenged in the following manner:

Q. Doctor, is it your testimony that you predict that Mr. Zimbra will again commit an act of violence and is, therefore, dangerous to society?
A. Yes, it is.
Q. On what evidence do you base your opinion?
A. I am predicting Mr. Zimbra's future dangerousness on the basis of his previous violent behavioral patterns. Specifically, he has acted out his aggression on several total strangers in a carefully calculated way, he has

been especially brutal in his attacks on the past three victims, and he has shown no remorse after he has been apprehended.

Q. Do these characteristics that you elucidate guarantee that Mr. Zimbra will again be violent?

A. No. There is no 100% guarantee. However, it is my clinical judgment that these characteristics are associated with repeat violent offenses.

Q. Do you base your opinion on any particular study of dangerousness?

A. No.

Q. Are you familiar with the work of Drs. Ziskin and Faust on the predictability of violence?

A. Yes.

Q. And what are the findings of Drs. Ziskin and Faust?

A. They have observed over a series of studies that there is considerable error in the prediction of violence and that violent behavior cannot be accurately predicted.

Q. Do you agree with the conclusions of Drs. Ziskin and Faust?

A. Not necessarily.

Q. Are you more experienced or knowledgeable that Drs. Ziskin and Faust?

a. I don't know. Probably not in this area of forensic psychology. They are well-known authorities.

Although there may be professional colleagues with more impressive reputations, a mental health expert need not automatically defer to someone else's opinion. If the psychologist or psychiatrist has done a thorough analysis of a criminal defendant, the following response could be provided:

A. I am more knowledgeable about this particular case and I find I cannot overlook his past violence, the viciousness of his acts, and his total lack of guilt reactions. Thus, in my opinion, Mr. Zimbra represents a serious threat to society.

The court may or may not be persuaded by the response just given, which is based primarily on clinical intuition. A more substantive response by an expert would have included psychometric measures, such as the Psychopathy Checklist (Hare, 1991) or references to supportive research and opinions (e.g., McNeil & Binder, 1991; Monahan, 1984). Although mental health professionals at times cannot make accurate predictions of violence, they can still help judges and juries by explaining relevant empirical research and statistical prediction rules (Garb, 1992).

"He doesn't always obey the voices, does he?"

When auditory hallucinations are present, a serious psychiatric disorder is implied, but such symptoms may not be related to dangerous behavior. Furthermore, even when voices are commanding a person to commit a violent act, these symptoms do not *ipso facto* indicate that the individual has no control over his or her aggressive actions. Consider the following probe regarding a person's auditory hallucinations.

> **Q. You have opined that Mr. Xavier is potentially dangerous to others because of voices that tell him to use his knife to defend himself against people in uniform, is that right?**
> A. Yes.
> **Q. How long has he been hearing these voices?**
> A. For about 5 years.
> **Q. Do they tell him to do other things, in addition to using his knife?**
> A. Yes. Sometimes they tell him to scream obscenities at persons in uniform.
> **Q. And does he listen to these voices?**
> A. Sometimes.
> **Q. Are you saying that sometimes Mr. Xavier is able to ignore these voices?**
> A. Yes.
> **Q. In other words, in Mr. Xavier's case, there is no immediate and compulsive obedience to the voices he hears, right?**
> A. Yes.
> **Q. If the voices told him to stab a person in uniform, sometimes he was able to stop himself, right?**
> A. Yes.
> **Q. Why would he not listen to the voices and stop himself from stabbing a person in uniform?**
> A. I believe it's because he can realize that stabbing someone is wrong.
> **Q. Aren't you telling us that Mr. Xavier knows right from wrong, just like everyone else?**
> A. Mr. Xavier is not like anyone else because he is psychiatrically ill and hears voices, but it's true that he knows right from wrong and can stop himself from doing the wrong.

Most individuals with command hallucinations can discriminate between right and wrong and can, at times, control their behavior according to their conscience. However, depending on the severity of their psychopathology, some persons are unable to utilize their knowledge of right and wrong and they yield to the hallucinatory command. If this is the case, the expert's response should be:

> A. Mr. Xavier does know right from wrong, but because of the intensity of his auditory hallucinations he is, at times, unable to resist the voice commands and unfortunately submits to their directions. Thus, in my opinion, he remains a risk in terms of his potential to do harm.

"What do you know about a real suicide risk?"

Dangerousness to self, or suicide risk, is also of concern to the mental health professional. When a patient suicide occurs, professional liability could be alleged, especially if there is an appearance of a breach in the standard of care. In such cases, the mental health professional who appears as an expert witness to render opinions about the preventability of a suicide must demonstrate sufficient knowledge of suicidology.

Q. Doctor, can you tell us what you know about suicides?
A. Well, many more men than women commit suicide, even though many more women attempt suicide than men. Men use guns, jump from high places, or hang themselves, whereas women tend to overdose with pills.

Q. Anything else you can tell us about suicides?
A. There are more suicides as we get older, although the suicide rate is rising in young men as well. Single people commit suicide more than married persons.

Q. Any other factors related to suicides?
a. I can't think of anything else.

The mental health witness in this example, demonstrated some awareness of suicidal behavior, but missed the opportunity to make a convincing impression as a suicide expert. It may require a quick review of a standard psychiatric textbook, but if the clinician is going to submit expert knowledge for the court, then some preparation is advisable so that a more professional response can be offered.

A. There are several well-known factors associated with suicide risk. According to the standard textbook by Kaplan and Sadock, among the high-risk characteristics are males, age over 45, alcoholism, violent behavior, prior suicidal attempts, and previous psychiatric hospitalizations. Eight out of 10 persons who commit suicide give warnings of their intentions. The person who has a plan of action is particularly dangerous. Those who have been depressed for a long time, those who are unwilling to accept help, and those who are ill or suffered a recent loss are also suicide risks. Would you like to hear more?

MISCELLANEOUS Q & A

There are various challenges to testimony regarding dangerousness.

Ability to Predict

Q. Based on scientific evidence, psychiatrists can't predict that this person will definitely commit violent acts in the future, can they?

a. That's true. We can't make such predictions about future violence.

A. We don't make such long-range or general predictions like that. But I can state that this woman, when she is not taking her antipsychotic medication, has difficulty controlling her angry feelings and aggressive behavior.

Dangerous Impulses

Q. **Do we really know for sure that a person claiming to have aggressive impulses actually has aggressive impulses?**

a. No, we don't know for certain. But we can't just ignore what is said about aggressive impulses.

A. This person is dangerous not only because of what he claims in terms of aggressive impulses but because of his long-term and recent history of violent acts.

100% Certainty

Q. **Keeping in mind the potential damage that he could do, isn't there at least the smallest chance that this man could be dangerous to the public?**

a. Yes. Of course, I can't deny that.

A. The probability of this man being dangerous is extremely remote. That is why I testified that he is not at risk in injuring another person.

Long-Range Predictions

Q. **The defendant has a known history of physically assaulting his wife. Doesn't that mean he will always be a threat to her?**

a. Yes. Once a man hits his wife, he's bound to do it again in the future.

A. Because of the recent assaults on his wife, he is a significant threat to hurt her again, at least within the near future. Unfortunately psychologists and psychiatrists are not able to make long-range predictions about violent behavior. The defendant may become less dangerous after he cooperates with a psychotherapy program.

Test's Predictive Validity

Q. **Isn't it true that because there is no evidence of predictive validity in the MCMI-2 with regard to dangerousness, this test can't help us decide if the patient is dangerous or not?**

a. The MCMI-2 is a very good test, but I suppose you're right.

A. The MCMI-2 indicates that the patient is not emotionally disturbed and does not have an impulse disorder. These are important factors to know in considering this man's potential dangerousness.

Expertise

Q. What makes you say that you're an expert on predicting violent behavior?

a. I worked many years as a clinician and have a good record of treating angry persons.

A. I maintain current knowledge about violence prediction with books and journal articles. I recently attended a 1-day conference on dangerous offenders. I am a member of a forensic society that continually discusses this issue.

Opposing Views

Q. Doctor, you've told us how dangerous the accused is. Tell us what other opinions there could be about him.

a. Well, some people have said that he is a gentle and charming man, so I suppose they don't see him as dangerous as I do.

A. Others might look to periods of nonviolence in his life and extol his contributions to his community. However, the fact remains that he preaches a philosophy of rage, he's carried out his violent teachings several times, and he continues to threaten his foes.

Legal Decisions

Q. Would it be reasonable to ask that your testimony be stricken if your definition of dangerousness differs from the legal definition of dangerousness?

a. That would seem reasonable to me.

A. I don't know. That requires a legal judgment so I don't have any answer for your question.

Dangerousness to Self

Q. On what basis are you stating that the patient is no longer a danger to himself?

a. The patient told me that he no longer has suicidal thoughts and that he doesn't want to hurt himself. I am putting trust in what he says.

A. The patient has given all his medications to his wife and is obviously embarrassed by his recent overdose. He stated that he will be actively looking for employment because finances have been his major concern in the last few weeks.

Racial Bias

Q. Doesn't research indicate that persons of color, like Mr. Adams, are often wrongfully labeled as dangerous by mental health professionals?

a. I believe you're right.

A. Research has revealed more false positive errors in predicting violence among minority persons, but in Mr. Adams' case, his recent assaults on his girlfriend and the continued verbal threats are the reasons he is considered dangerous. My opinion has nothing to do with race.

CLOSING ARGUMENTS

This chapter dealt with basic civil rights issues: the right to stand trial, the right to handle one's own property, and the right to determine one's own medical treatment. The chapter also covered the critical social problem of the dangerous person, a situation in which the safety of the community and the freedom of an individual clash head-on.

The evaluation of a person's competency to stand trial needs to consider the defendant's capacity to understand the criminal proceedings and to cooperate with one's defense attorney. The examination can be thoroughly accomplished in a focused hour-and-a-half clinical interview. In both criminal and civil law proceedings, serious psychiatric disorders (e.g., psychosis) do not necessarily render a person incompetent, nor are all incompetent persons totally lacking in functional capacities (e.g., personal care activities).

The state of research evidence regarding violence potential precludes high levels of confidence in the area. Although it may be argued that a mental health professional's predictions of dangerousness are imprecise, clinicians are able to identify violence-related factors and, thus, can assist the courts in evaluations of dangerousness.

As in other areas of forensic testimony, mental health professionals will be challenged regarding the thoroughness of the examination, the effects of the environment and examiner differences, the role of psychometric instruments, and the presence of contradictory evidence. Legal proceedings pertaining to competency and dangerousness may not be as complex or time-consuming as child custody or personal injury trials, but the forensic opinions expressed in these hearings bear on fundamental human rights and need to be thoughtfully considered.

CHAPTER 10

FAKING AND MALINGERING

"Can doctors really know when someone is lying?"

Because court proceedings have outcomes that are of utmost importance to the involved parties, the likelihood of dishonesty as a way to effect favorable decisions must be seriously considered by evaluators. The criminal defendants who would prefer to be in a psychiatric facility than to be incarcerated in a jail cell may feign psychotic symptoms and appear unable to stand trial. The victim of a motor vehicle accident, in order to maximize the monetary award for putative injury, may magnify or even fabricate signs of physical disability or brain damage. In contrast, a parent who is embroiled in a child custody battle may simulate the essence of mental health and conceal any hint of psychopathology. Furthermore, some criminal defendants who are truly suffering from a mental disorder may attempt to conceal their symptoms, either because they do not want to be considered insane or because they prefer the prison environment over a psychiatric facility.

Although psychologists and psychiatrists are not expected to demonstrate high degrees of accuracy in detecting malingering, they are, nonetheless, required to make some assessment of a person's credibility. You should be familiar with the comprehensive review by Rogers (1988) on the evaluation of malingering, and be knowledgeable about methods to detect faking and dissimulation.

Direct Examination

"You're pretty sure that he's lying, aren't you?"

To declare that a person is lying or faking is a provocative judgment to make. It is an opinion that is difficult to prove objectively and such accusations of

149

fraud can have profound ramifications in court proceedings. Thus, the expert casting doubts about a person's integrity must be well fortified in presenting convincing supportive evidence.

Q. Doctor, can you explain to the court why you believe that Mr. Boyar was not honest in his complaints about his physical disability?

A. There were several factors that I considered in reaching that conclusion. First, Mr. Boyar was noticeably inconsistent in the history he gave, such as how long he was unconscious at the time of the car accident. Depending on whom he talked with, it ranged from a few minutes to several hours. He also gave different information about the number of days he didn't work and the income he made last year.

Q. Did you note any other inconsistencies in the history he gave?

A. Yes. He told several people he can only sit for about 20 minutes, but he sat in my office chair for over an hour and showed no discomfort. He didn't shift or change positions, and did not appear to have any of the back pain he's been reporting.

Q. What other things made you doubt Mr. Boyar's honesty?

A. His description of his pain and suffering seemed to be extreme and exaggerated. He said his pain was excruciating and that his life had become a nightmare, but he seemed neither that uncomfortable nor emotionally distressed during our sessions. He bought a cane but never seemed to use it, including walking down the long hallway in front of my office.

Q. Any other findings that raise doubts about his honesty?

A. His reports of severe pain, numbness, and weakness have not been substantiated by any medical tests, such as an MRI of his spine. Furthermore, the pattern of his pain, numbness, and weakness fits no understandable clinical syndrome. Finally, his lack of improvement of any kind to every form of therapy he's undergone is also suspicious to me.

Cross Examination

"Aren't there reasons other than lying to explain his statements?"

In the direct testimony the expert included several indicators of faking or exaggerating. Although this may constitute a persuasive point of view, the expert may, nevertheless, encounter a formidable cross-examination, such as the following:

Q. You stated that Mr. Boyar was inconsistent in the information he gave about the length of time he was unconscious, the number of days he didn't work, and the income he made last year, isn't that correct?

A. Yes.

Q. **If a person had a closed head injury and was unconscious for a while, wouldn't he have difficulty in remembering exact facts and pieces of information?**

A. That could happen.

Q. **You also stated, didn't you, that he seemed to be comfortable sitting in your office chair and showed no discomfort?**

A. Yes, I did.

Q. **Did you know he took his pain medication and antidepressant just before the appointment with you?**

A. No.

Q. **Could it be that he was without pain for the period you saw him because of the benefits of pain medication?**

A. Yes, that's possible.

Q. **You said he didn't use his cane. Could that also be due to the benefits of pain medication?**

A. Yes.

Q. **Mr. Boyar said his pain was excruciating and his life had become a nightmare. Do you have any proof that these are not true statements?**

A. No, I don't.

Q. **Can a condition involving pain be present without objective documentation of medical test results?**

A. Sure.

Q. **Including an MRI of the spine?**

A. Yes.

Q. **Doctor, aren't there alternative explanations to what you observed, other than accusing Mr. Boyar of being dishonest about his condition?**

a. I'm sure there are, but in my opinion Mr. Boyar seemed less than candid in his presentation of his condition.

The expert has stuck to his or her original opinion, but it would be of value to reinforce the judgment call with supporting reasons, such as:

A. As I stated earlier, Mr. Boyar's pattern of pain, numbness, and weakness fits no known medical disorder, and his total lack of improvement from every treatment he's received are very suspicious to me. Put together with the other observations made, I believe he was not honest in how he described his present medical condition.

To cope with possible malingering and deception in the forensic setting, you need to be aware of several issues, including:

- Assessing malingering
- Psychological tests

- Corroborative evidence
- Monetary compensation
- Malingering by the criminal defendant
- Malingering by the personal injury plaintiff
- Faking in child custody evaluations

Assessing Malingering

"How did you rule out malingering?"

Because the issue of honesty can surface in nearly all forensic cases, you should expect some questioning about the credibility of a criminal defendant or a plaintiff. The following are standard questions asked of the witness.

Q. Can you tell us what the word *malingering* means?

A. Malingering is the intentional production or gross exaggeration of physical or psychological symptoms, usually for the purpose of personal gain, such as avoiding criminal punishment or obtaining monetary compensation.

Q. So, a person may fake or exaggerate mental illness as a way to avoid jail, is that right?

A. Yes.

Q. You are aware that if Mr. Kroon is found guilty, he could be sentenced to jail?

A. Yes, I'm aware of that.

Q. But if he's found to be mentally incompetent, he will go to a psychiatric hospital and won't go to jail, right?

A. That's right.

Q. Wouldn't it be in his best interest for Mr. Kroon to appear as confused as possible, so as to go to a hospital rather than to jail?

A. A hospital is probably better than a jail for most people.

Q. Then, don't you think there is a good chance Mr. Kroon is malingering and not as ill as he has been presenting himself?

A. No. I don't think he's malingering.

Q. How did you rule out malingering in his case?

a. I used my clinical judgment. I have an intuitive feeling when people are lying to me. I spent over 3 hours with him and I'm sure he was telling me the truth.

Clinical intuition and lengthy examinations are helpful but probably not sufficient to convince some jurors that an adequate assessment of malingering was made. A better reply is:

A. In my examination I did not detect signs of malingering, such as rare or absurd symptoms or inconsistency in his history and symptoms. I used a structured clinical interview that helped me to rule out malingering in this case.

Psychological Tests

"Is the MMPI just like a psychological x-ray?"

The clinical assessment of possible malingering can be reinforced by the employment of psychological tests. One of the most widely used instruments for the detection of malingering is the MMPI and its recent revision, MMPI-2 (Blau, 1984; Maloney, 1985; Rogers, 1984). Those who utilize a psychological test can anticipate the following line of questioning:

Q. In your conclusions about possible malingering, did you use any psychological tests?
A. Yes. I used the Minnesota Multiphasic Personality Inventory, or MMPI for short.
Q. Did you use the original or revised MMPI?
A. I used the original MMPI.
Q. Why did you do that?
A. I prefer the original MMPI because of the greater accumulation of validation research done on this test over the past few decades, including research in the area of faking and malingering.
Q. What made you conclude that the plaintiff was faking on the MMPI?
A. First of all, his score on the *F* scale was above *T* 100, which means he endorsed on extremely high number of rare psychopathological items. This would not ordinarily be expected, except when a person is trying to look very disturbed.
Q. Anything else?
A. Yes. His *F* minus *K* index was 15, which means that the person was trying to "fake bad." And he overendorsed obvious indicators of mental illness and didn't identify subtle markers of emotional problems, which are other tendencies seen in malingering.
Q. The MMPI is not an exact instrument, like an x-ray, is it?
A. Well, the x-ray is not an exact instrument.
Q. Okay. Would you compare the MMPI with precise high-tech medical diagnostic tests?
a. When you put it that way, I guess I wouldn't say that the MMPI is an exact instrument.

It is important to state that psychological tests are fallible instruments, but it is equally important to cite scientific evidence that supports the utility of test instruments when evaluating an individual's honesty in an examination.

A. The MMPI is not a precise test, but research over the years has found this test to be useful in detecting malingering in forensic situations, such as in this case.

Corroborative Evidence

"Did you verify any of the statements he made to you?"

A time-consuming mental health examination may appear to be thorough, but if it relies primarily on the word of the examinee, the obtained information is susceptible to deception and incorrect diagnoses. Without reviewing outside documents or conferring with third parties, the clinician can inadvertently fall prey to a malingerer. Consider the following situation:

Q. **You testified that your conclusions regarding Mr. Annon were based on your interview of him and a 3-hour psychological test battery, is that correct?**

A. Yes.

Q. **Did you review other records pertaining to the defendant?**

A. I read his hospital chart briefly. It wasn't too informative.

Q. **Did you perform a complete examination of Mr. Annon?**

A. Yes. This is what I do in my office examination on a regular basis.

Q. **And from your examination of the defendant, did you conclude that he did not know what he was doing at the time he stole the car?**

A. Yes. He said he had been sniffing paint all week and had no recollection of the car theft. He can only vaguely recall the police arresting him.

Q. **So, if a person is intoxicated from sniffing paint he might not remember a lot of what he does, is that correct?**

A. Yes.

Q. **He would not be able to recall how he entered the car, how he wired the engine so it would start without a key, or where he drove the car, is that right?**

A. That's right.

Q. **Doctor, did you have a chance to review the arrest record of Mr. Annon with regard to the car theft charges?**

A. No. I didn't get a chance to go to the DA's office to read the records.

Q. **Sir, the arrest records, which have been entered into evidence, include a signed confession by Mr. Annon in which he gave precise details of how he broke into the car with his own tools, how he wired**

the engine, and where he went joy-riding with the car. Now, would
this information change your diagnosis of Mr. Annon?
a. Well, I'm afraid it does.

The clinician who is confident in his usual office practice of examining
private clients must realize that a forensic examination of a criminal defendant
requires more comprehensive investigative activity, such as reviewing the arrest
records. There is no excuse or defense for an inadequate evaluation of an
accused defendant which does disservice to the judicial proceedings.

A. Yes. The signed confession contradicts what I said about the defendant.
I apologize to the court for this serious oversight.

Monetary Compensation

"Isn't it likely that a person will lie to get more money?"

Mental health professionals are usually alert to the possibility that a plaintiff's
physical and emotional symptoms may be affected by the prospects of a sizeable
monetary award. This prevalent belief stems from the 19th-century literature
on compensation neurosis among injured railway workers in Prussia (Trimble,
1981) as well as the influential work of H. Miller (1961), who found that
subjective complaints in 200 severe head injury cases typically discontinued
after the patient received a financial settlement. However, the most recent
research on this issue indicates that injury symptoms, such as pain and emotional changes, are not associated with litigation or compensation (Melzack,
Katz & Jeans, 1985; Mendleson, 1986; Weller, 1985). In short, there is no
current empirical basis to support the contention that litigation and compensation exacerbate an injured person's symptoms or delay normal recovery. Nonetheless, attorneys continue to ask the following questions:

Q. **Doctor, are you familiar with the term** *compensation neurosis?*
A. Yes.
Q. **Please explain to the jury what that term means.**
A. Compensation neurosis refers to a psychological condition in which a
person's physical or mental health is affected by the possibility of
financial compensation for injuries sustained from a traffic or work
accident.
Q. **In other words, expecting a large sum of money from a lawsuit can
affect a person's medical condition, right?**
A. That's what it means.
Q. **Is that sometimes called** *litigation neurosis*?
A. I believe so.

Q. **Are you aware of the fact that the plaintiff, Mrs. Smith, is suing for financial compensation for her injuries from a car accident?**

A. Yes, I am.

Q. **Mrs. Smith has great worries about her finances, is that correct?**

A. Yes. I believe her medical bills and lack of income this year have created a considerable debt for her and her family.

Q. **A monetary award would greatly alleviate her worries and concerns, right?**

A. Yes, it would.

Q. **Doesn't it stand to reason that the prospects of winning this lawsuit and solving her financial problems can affect Mrs. Smith's physical condition at this time?**

A. It could.

Q. **Isn't this what is called compensation neurosis?**

a. Yes.

Although it is possible for a person's health to be affected by the anticipation of a monetary windfall, clinicians are hard pressed to prove a direct link between the plaintiff's lawsuit and her medical condition. Without other supportive data to indicate exaggerating or malingering, you should resist the allure of commonly held beliefs that have insufficient empirical foundation. A better response is:

A. I have no evidence to indicate that the expected monetary settlement is influencing Mrs. Smith's current health. In fact, I believe her symptoms are genuine, she has been consistent in her report of her problems, and she seems to be motivated to get well and return to her usual job.

Malingering by the Criminal Defendant

"Why didn't you take a complete history?"

As previously discussed in chapter 9 on the subject of mental competency, a criminal defendant's capacity to understand the criminal proceedings against him or her and assist in his or her own defense can be assessed in a relatively brief time, with a focus on the specific criteria related to understanding trial procedures. Because the evaluation is often completed in an hour (Rogers & Mitchell, 1991), lawyers may probe the thoroughness of this important examination and ask whether or not the accused's credibility was studied.

Q. **Doctor, you have testified that the defendant, Mr. De Martini, is not competent to stand trial, correct?**

A. Yes, that's correct.

Q. **You conducted your evaluation of Mr. De Martini at the county jail, did you not?**

A. Yes, I did.

Q. **Did you obtain a complete history of his childhood, education and work background?**

A. No, I did not.

Q. **Did you obtain a complete record of his criminal background?**

A. He told me about his previous arrests for vagrancy and shoplifting. I'm not sure if it's his complete criminal record.

Q. **Did you perform a mental status examination?**

A. Yes.

Q. **Did you administer a battery of psychological tests?**

A. No, I did not.

Q. **How long did you take to complete your evaluation of Mr. De Martini?**

A. About 50 minutes.

Q. **In clinical practice doesn't it take at least a few sessions before a doctor can be sure if a patient is being consistent and honest in his statements?**

A. I'm not sure, but that sounds about right.

Q. **And can you be certain the Mr. De Martini wasn't putting on an act for the 50 minutes you saw him, so that he can avoid staying in jail and standing trial?**

a. No, I can't be certain.

The witness' replies to the last two questions can raise serious doubts about the accuracy of the competency evaluation. When an examiner has sufficiently assessed the pertinent psychological issues regarding mental competency, including the accused's credibility, a better response would be:

A. I was not requested to conduct a comprehensive psychiatric examination for differential diagnosis or for rehabilitation planning. I was asked to evaluate Mr. De Martini's ability to stand trial. The defendant's psychotic condition has been a problem for the past 2 months and his behavior during my examination of him was consistent with his hospital record. I do not believe he was faking his mental illness.

Malingering by the Personal Injury Plaintiff

"That's just a judgment call, right?"

In many cases of personal injury, the alleged damages, such as pain, are not supported by objective diagnostic tests, even with the most sophisticated state-of-the-art medical technology. Thus, clinicians must often rely on their own subjective judgments when determining whether or not a person is malingering. The absence of objective measures can lead to the following inquiry:

Q. Doctor, you have opined that the plaintiff, Mr. Des Jarlais, may be intentionally exaggerating or faking his pain symptoms, isn't that true?

A. Yes.

Q. On what evidence did you base this opinion?

A. On several aspects of the way he presented himself in the examination. First of all, he seemed suspicious and defensive in his attitude toward my interviews of him. You could say he was evasive in answering some questions. I felt he was somewhat uncooperative at times when I asked him to show his strength and mobility.

Q. Were there any other signs of faking?

A. Although he seemed to have limited memory about any previous injuries or current emotional problems, he was able to describe the car accident in very minute details. Some of his symptoms, such as forgetting all the songs he had previously learned to play on his guitar, seemed very unusual to me.

Q. What other indications of faking did you notice?

A. He seemed to be blaming all of his personal problems, including the loss of his job and the breakup of his relationship with his girlfriend, on the accident. At the same time he didn't seem to take an active role in improving his condition, such as exercising regularly as recommended by his doctor. These are characteristics I would associate with malingering.

Q. Your assertion about his suspiciousness, defensiveness, evasiveness and uncooperativeness; that was your subjective opinion, isn't that right?

A. Well, that is my opinion. You could say it's subjective.

Q. Your description of his apparently blaming all of his personal problems on the accident—that was your subjective judgment, too, right?

A. Yes.

Q. Wouldn't you say that your testimony about Mr. Des Jarlais' supposed malingering is based primarily on your subjective judgment?

a. I can't argue with that.

If one's opinion is based solely on subjective data, then the expert will have difficulty being convincing about the determination of malingering. The mental health professional would be in a better position with tangible supportive evidence and responding in the following way:

A. In addition to the observations I made in the examination, I incorporated other facts, such as his prior accident claims, his participation in sports—which was inconsistent with his reported disability, and the abnormal validity scores of the MMPI.

Faking and Child Cutsody Evaluations

"Wouldn't he be foolish to tell you the whole truth about himself?"

In contrast to the criminal defendant and the civil injury plaintiff who may be trying to "fake bad" by simulating psychopathology for personal gains, the divorcing parent involved in a custody dispute may attempt to conceal emotional impairment. The effort to "fake good" and appear to be a stalwart citizen could favor the chances of winning custody of the child. As always, you must be prepared to rule out any dishonest representation of one's psychological status.

> **Q. You are testifying that Mrs. Gross is a person without any psychological problem or undesirable personality traits, is that correct?**
>
> A. Yes.
>
> **Q. Therefore, isn't it your opinion that she is likely to be a good parent for her daughter, Mona?**
>
> A. Yes.
>
> **Q. When you saw Mrs. Gross, wasn't it because her divorce attorney wanted you to help her with these custody hearings?**
>
> A. Yes.
>
> **Q. Didn't you think Mrs. Gross had many reasons to tell you things that would make her look good as a person and parent?**
>
> A. That's true.
>
> **Q. And she had many reasons not to tell you things that would make her look bad as a person and parent, isn't that also true?**
>
> A. Yes.
>
> **Q. Isn't it true that people can appear to be mentally normal to a psychologist when they actually have mental problems?**
>
> A. Yes, that's true.
>
> **Q. How did you assure that Mrs. Gross wasn't dishonest in concealing her psychological problems?**
>
> a. Well, I had a 3-hour interview with her, and I was confident she wasn't trying to hide anything.

Relying purely on an interview, even one that is 3 hours long, may not be sufficient to convince anyone that deception has not taken place. A better prepared witness would state:

> A. To assure that I had a valid evaluation of Mrs. Gross, I conducted a 3-hour long clinical interview. In addition I verified the information she gave me by interviewing three persons who know her well. Finally, I inspected her MMPI-2 validity scores, which did not indicate that she was being deceptive.

MISCELLANEOUS Q & A

The following is a variety of challenges pertaining to issues of malingering. Note the ineffective answers as compared to the more persuasive answers.

Admitting Limitations

Q. When a person says she hears voices that tell her to break the law, do you know or not know if she actually hears the voices?

a. I am confident that she is actually hearing voices. I don't think she is faking.

A. I don't know.

Detection Rates

Q. Aren't you familiar with studies that have shown that neuropsychologists are unsuccessful in detecting faking on neuropsychological tests?

a. Yes, I am. But I also believe those studies are flawed and don't amount to much. I think it's very difficult to fool an experienced neuropsychologist.

A. Yes. I am also aware of research that has shown that certain methods, like the "easy items missed and difficult items passed" pattern and the "forced-choice" technique, are approaches with demonstrated usefulness. I would refer you to the critical review by Dr. Richard Rogers and his associates that appeared in *Clinical Psychology Review* in 1993.

Conflicting Statements

Q. One parent says one thing, the other says the opposite. Whom are you going to believe?

a. I have to rely on my clinical judgment, and trust my experience in these matters.

A. When parents offer opposing statements, it is essential to obtain as much corroborating information, such as the input of children and mutual friends, as possible, in order to determine whose statement is more accurate.

Inconsistencies

Q. One of the main reasons you believe that the defendant is malingering is the inconsistency in his account of the events. Aren't there explanations for his inconsistent accounts, other than malingering?

a. I can't think of any other explanations except his need to avoid criminal punishment.

A. A person can be inconsistent if they are psychotic or brain impaired, but neither of these explanations apply to this defendant. That's why I believe he is malingering.

Uncooperativeness

Q. **During your independent examination for the defense attorney, was the plaintiff's lack of cooperation a major reason for your determining that she was malingering?**

a. Yes. According to the literature, lack of cooperation with an examination is a hallmark of malingering.

A. No. Because I was the examiner for the defense, I could understand her anxieties and defensiveness. I concluded she was malingering on other factors, such as her presentation of improbable symptoms, her concealing her previous car accident, and her inconsistent accounts of her condition to different doctors.

Pain Symptoms

Q. **Can you tell if the plaintiff's back pain is real?**

a. No. Pain is a subjective symptom that you can neither prove nor disprove.

A. I find that the plaintiff's pain symptoms are authentic because of the documented history of physical trauma, the consistency of the symptoms and its compatibility with underlying neuroanatomical structures, as well as the improvements made with certain treatments and medicines. These are some of the reasons I believe that the patient is not malingering or exaggerating her pain.

Projective Techniques

Q. **Is it your opinion that projective techniques are invulnerable to malingering?**

a. Unless you've had training in projective tests, it's impossible to know how to fake on tests like the Rorschach.

A. No test is invulnerable to malingering. Studies have shown that it is difficult to distinguish between fakers and mentally ill patients on projective tests.

Low Sensitivity Test

Q. **Aren't you aware that, despite its wide usage, the Rey 15-Item Memory Test is not very sensitive in detecting malingerers?**

a. I've seen those studies, but I personally find it helpful in identifying those faking neuropsychological deficits.

A. I realize that the Rey Test is a brief test that is not very sensitive. But I consider various aspects of faking, such as identifying poor performance on easy items, many near-misses and gross errors, which are characteristics found more frequently with malingering.

Inconsistent Data

Q. **Doesn't the normal Lie scale score means that my client isn't lying?**

a. That's what the Lie scale suggests, but other scores show that she was not honest.

A. My opinion about her malingering was based on several factors, including some of her exaggerated test scores and her noncompliance with her doctors.

Benefits of Lying

Q. **Isn't it likely that a person who stands to go to prison will want to appear insane in order to avoid punishment?**

a. If you're saying that the defendant fooled three psychiatrists into mistaking him as insane when he's not, you're wrong.

A. Yes. I have to suspect that an accused person might lie in order to stay out of jail. Forensic examinations must be done carefully, to look for inconsistencies, possible exaggerations and distortions.

Therapist's Trust

Q. **Don't you, as a therapist, tend to trust your patient's words?**

a. Yes, of course. What kind of therapist would I be if I doubted my own patients? I trust them and they trust me.

A. It is naive to totally trust a patient's word. It's important in therapy to listen to patients, but also to verify their statements whenever possible. Otherwise, we may be inadvertently reinforcing distorted perceptions and fantasies.

CLOSING ARGUMENTS

It is difficult to know the true incidence of faking and malingering in forensic settings, although studies suggest that the rate appears to be low, with a range between 3% and 8% (Cornell & Hawk, 1989; L. Miller, 1990; Rogers &

Mitchell, 1991). Nonetheless, malingering is perceived to be a serious problem for the courts (Maloney, 1985), and the responsibility to account for honesty and deception often falls on the mental health professional.

Because court hearings invariably result in outcomes of major consequence (e.g.,imprisonment, monetary compensation, child custody), the mental health examiner must be prepared to assess any attempts at deception and fraud. This chapter stressed the value of corroborative evidence, such as past arrest and health records and interviews of significant others. Attorneys sometimes employ videotapes of a plaintiff for a vivid demonstration of behavior which is inconsistent with alleged complaints (e.g., severe disability). In addition, psychological tests, like the MMPI-2, can provide insights into a person's defensiveness or symptom magnification (Ziskin & Faust, 1988), although you should be careful about false positive errors in overinterpreting conventional "fake bad" indices. In cases involving possible brain injury, neuropsychologists now employ methods to detect malingering, such as the forced-choice technique. Finally, this chapter also focused on possible efforts to conceal or minimize psychological problems, such as when parents vie for the custody of their children.

Faking and malingering are complex phenomena, consisting of degrees of purposeful deception, with total awareness of lying at one end to levels of unconscious motivation to exaggerate or manufacture symptoms on the other. Although mental health professionals cannot definitively say that a person is or is not malingering, they can provide valuable assistance to the legal justice system by presenting information that does or does not support a diagnosis of malingering (Garb, 1992).

CHAPTER 11

NEUROPSYCHOLOGICAL ASSESSMENT

"Are you telling us that you, who are not a medical doctor, can diagnose brain damage?"

In recent years, clinical neuropsychologists have increasingly been called on to testify in forensic cases, particularly involving personal injury suits that claim brain injury as one of the consequences of an accident or incident. When brain damage is alleged to be a permanent condition due to a head trauma, the financial repercussions can be monumental because the victim's usual occupation and earning power are severely affected. Because of the potential monetary stakes involved, both the plaintiff's attorney and the defense attorney are expected to maximize their legal experience and skills to vigorously question the input of the neuropsychology expert.

In the standard approach to a head injury case, clinical neuropsychologists administer a battery of tests and make inferences about the likelihood and severity of brain injury, the etiology of brain injury, and the consequences of brain injury for daily life. Their credentials and claims may be challenged in all the ways reported in the other chapters of this book. There may also be challenges unique to the neuropsychologist.

This chapter discusses the following forensic issues:

- qualifying as a neuropsychologist
- diversity of assessment approaches
- inferences from neuropsychological test results to brain injury
- isolating test data
- use of a psychometrist

164

Qualifying as a Neuropsychologist

"Can't anyone call themselves a neuropsychologist?"

There is currently some controversy about the qualifications one should have to practice clinical neuropsychology. Questions have arisen such as: "What kind of training is necessary?" and "Should there be a special license or certificate for neuropsychologists?" This controversy may be used to challenge the qualifications of the expert.

Q. Good morning, Mrs. Armstrong.
A. Good morning. I'm usually called Dr. Armstrong.
Q. I see, Dr. Armstrong, you have a PhD or a doctor of philosophy degree, isn't that right?
A. Yes, I have a PhD in clinical psychology.
Q. The PhD is not a doctoral degree in medicine, is that right?
A. Yes.
Q. Isn't it true that you have had fewer formal courses in neurology than a person with a medical or MD degree?
A. That's true.
Q. And you haven't had any specific courses in neuroanatomy, neurophysiology, and neuropathology, have you?
A. Although I haven't had such coursework, many of my psychology courses covered those areas.
Q. Nonetheless, you don't have the same education in neurology as a medical doctor, right?
A. That's right.
Q. Could you define for us what a neuropsychologist is?
A. A neuropsychologist is a psychologist who specializes in the study of brain and behavior relationships. Clinical neuropsychologists, such as myself, diagnose and treat individuals who may have brain-related behavioral problems, such as impaired learning and memory.
Q. Isn't it true that there are no formal or legal restrictions on who can call themselves a neuropsychologist?
A. Yes.
Q. Then virtually anyone can call themselves a neuropsychologist?
a. They could, but it would be wrong. A neuropsychologist is a psychologist who specializes in brain-behavior relationships, as I do.

Instead of sounding defensive, a better initial response might cite a generally accepted set of standards for clinical neuropsychologists.

A. Although there is no neuropsychology licensure, the Clinical Neuropsychology Division of the American Psychological Association has published standards for neuropsychologists, and I meet those standards.

Some attorneys are experienced in brain injury claims and may challenge
the expert's qualifications by a quiz on brain-behavior relationships, such as
the following.

**Q. Can you tell me what would happen if someone sustained damage to
the Wernicke's area?**
a. They would have a problem with language comprehension.

This somewhat inadequate response may be followed by even more questioning. However, an attorney is less likely to pursue a brain-behavior quiz, if
his or her questions enhance the status of the expert. When the expert provides
clear, erudite answers to the question, this line of questioning is likely to be
abandoned.

A. With damage to the Wernicke's area, which is located in the left cerebral
cortex, they would be likely to have impaired auditory comprehension
and fluently articulated but paraphasic speech. Reading comprehension
and meaningful writing are also likely to be severely impaired.

Diversity of Assessment Approaches

*"Doctor, wouldn't many respected neuropsychologists disagree
with your testing approach?"*

In the field of clinical neuropsychology there is a variety of approaches to
neurodiagnostic assessment. There are 2 major assessment batteries, the Halstead–Reitan battery and the Luria–Nebraska Neuropsychological battery, as
well as the flexible battery approach (Anderson, 1994). Because any of these
approaches can be critiqued from the point of view of the others, attorneys can
tap this diversity of opinion to discredit a specific assessment (Faust et al.,1991).

**Q. How would you characterize your approach to neuropsychological
assessment?**
A. I employ a flexible battery or collection of tests. This means that I use
neuropsychological tests appropriate for a particular person.
Q. Are you saying that you use a different set of tests for each person?
A. For most people I use the same basic core of tests. Depending on the
results with these tests, I may add further tests.
Q. What battery of tests did you use for Mr. Joshi?

A. I used the Wechsler Adult Intelligence Scale-Revised, Memory Assessment Scales, Sensory-Perceptual Evaluation, Wide Range Achievement
Test-3, and the Wisconsin Card Sorting Test.

Q. Has this particular battery been proven to detect brain injury?

a. Not this specific battery.

The flexible battery method might be defended at this point by referring to
the validation of individual tests as sensitive to brain dysfunction.

A. This set of tests hasn't, but individual tests in this battery have been
shown to be sensitive to brain dysfunction. I consider the results of all
of these tests in determining the likelihood of brain injury.

Due to the diversity of norms and interpretive procedures used even for
standard batteries such as the Halstead–Reitan Neuropsychological Battery, a
similar line of questioning may be directed at a standard battery assessment.

Q. Doctor, could you describe the tests you used in conducting your
assessment of Ms. Demetrian?

A. I used the Halstead–Reitan Neuropsychological Battery and a number of
additional tests.

Q. Do you recognize Dr. Ralph Reitan, the author of the Halstead–Reitan Neuropsychological Battery, as an authority on this battery?

A. Yes.

Q. Could you describe the Halstead–Reitan Neuropsychological Battery?

A. Yes. It is a collection of neuropsychological tests that are commonly
administered together. These tests are the Lateral Dominance Examination, Aphasia Screening Test, Finger Tapping Test, Grip Strength Test,
Sensory-Perceptual Examination, Tactile Form Recognition Test,
Rhythm Test, Speech–Sounds Perception Test, Trail Making Test, Tactual
Performance Test, and the Category Test. This set of tests has been
validated using patients with brain injuries.

Q. What were your findings?

A. Ms. Demetrian's performance was mildly impaired on all measures.

Q. How did you determine that her performance was mildly impaired?

A. I compared her performance levels to the performance levels expected
for individuals of the same sex, age, and education.

Q. Did you use norms to do this?

A. Yes.

Q. Which norms did you use?

A. I used the norms authored by Heaton, Grant, and Matthews.

Q. Have you come to any conclusions about whether or not Ms. Demetrian has suffered a brain injury?

A. Yes. I believe that she has experienced a mild brain injury.

Q. **Hasn't Dr. Ralph Reitan severely criticized these norms and recommended that they not be used for people who have suffered brain injuries?**

A. Yes.

Q. **How do you justify using the Heaton, Grant, and Matthews norms in claiming that Ms. Demetrian has a brain injury?**

A. These norms were developed for use in evaluating brain injured patients.

Q. **Are you saying that Dr. Ralph Reitan, whom you recognize as an authority, is mistaken about his own battery?**

In this exchange, the neuropsychologist has fallen into a serious trap. Because the expert has accepted Dr. Reitan as an authority without qualification, he or she may be confronted with anything that Dr. Reitan has said. The expert could have avoided an unqualified acceptance of an authority.

A. Although Dr. Reitan is one authority on this battery, there are also many other authorities who have extensively researched the battery.

The problem of multiple norms and interpretive systems can be addressed by demonstrating that one's conclusion would be the same using any of these norms and systems.

A. I analyzed Ms. Demetrian's performance using Dr. Reitan's Neuropsychological Deficit Scale and came to the same conclusion, that Ms. Demetrian has suffered a mild brain injury.

Inferences From Neuropsychological Test Results to Brain Injury

"Doctor, do you literally examine brains in your practice?"

The relation between psychological test performance and brain functioning is only vaguely understood by the average juror, who is more familiar with standard medical diagnostic methods, like a skull x-ray or brain wave test. Thus, the cross-examining attorney may question the validity of neuropsychological tests, with a line of questioning that attacks the most basic principles of clinical neuropsychology.

Q. **Isn't it true that, unlike a neurologist, you don't examine the brains of your patients?**

a. Yes.

This answer should be qualified by distinguishing between "direct" and "indirect" examination of the brain. Neurologists more directly study the brain through EEG and imaging technology. Neuropsychologists indirectly study the brain through the behavioral effects of brain activity.

A. I examine the brain by studying the behavioral effects of brain functioning.

Q. How can you conclude that Mr. Lynn has brain damage on the basis of your tests?

a. I infer brain damage on the basis of the behavior deficits evidenced on the tests.

Experienced clinical neuropsychologists have cautioned against inferring brain damage on the basis of test results alone (Larrabee, 1990). Numerous explanations are compatible with a given profile of test scores. Brain damage is diagnosed on the basis of information converging on this conclusion from a variety of sources: Glasgow Coma Scale (GCS) scores at the scene or in the hospital, posttraumatic amnesia, EEG, CT, MRI, or SPECT reports, the neurologist's examination report, the patient's medical history, behavioral observations, and neuropsychological test data. A better answer would be as follows:

A. I infer brain damage on the basis of Mr. Lynn's GCS of 5 on admittance to the hospital, his two week period of posttraumatic amnesia, and the pattern of test performance deficits.

Isolating Test Data

"A low score on that test could mean lots of things, right?"

A frequent strategy advanced by opposing attorneys is to undermine test findings by focusing on separate components of the test battery and citing the limitations of each component, and thereby weaken the overall conclusions. The approach may emerge in the following manner:

Q. Doctor, are there specific test scores that show that a person is brain damaged?

A. Yes.

Q. Could you identify one of these test scores that indicate brain damage?

A. Okay. Let's take the Speech–Sounds Perception Test. The patient made 10 errors on this test, which is a poor score and consistent with his left brain injury.

Q. Are there alternative factors, other than brain injury, that could cause 10 errors on the Speech–Sounds Perception Test?

A. Yes.

Q. What are some of these alternative factors?

A. The poor score could be the result of having a hearing impairment.

Q. I see. Tell us about other possible causes of the poor score on this test.

A. He could have problems with concentration due to anxiety, he could have reading problems that prevent him from identifying the correct answers on the response sheet, or he could have poor motivation to do well on the test.

Q. **So, what you're saying is that the 10 errors on the Speech–Sounds Perception Test could be the result of any one or more of several factors, and not necessarily from brain injury, is that correct?**

A. Yes.

Q. **All right. Now, let's talk about the patient's poor score on the Category Test. What alternative explanations are there, besides brain damage, that account for the poor score?**

The neuropsychology expert should be alert to this line of questioning because the process of reasoning, that is, assessing each test score in isolation, is unlike what a clinical neuropsychologist does in reaching conclusions by considering numerous data simultaneously. The same diagnostic process holds true for psychologists employing other test instruments, such as the MMPI-2 or the Rorschach. In the series of questions described earlier, the attorney can engage in a continual critique of each component of the test results and successfully discredit its real contributions. To ward off further damaging effects on the test findings, the neuropsychologist should interject the following:

A. Before we discuss the Category Test results, I must explain that the interpretation of neuropsychological test data does not consist of simple cookbook formulas, such as this score means brain damage and this score does not, which is what we seem to be doing at this point. Conclusions about brain functioning are based on complex relationships between test data, and takes into account other important information, such as the patient's medical history and the clinical appearance of the patient, rather than looking at one test score at a time. I would be happy to fully explain how I arrived at the conclusion that this man is seriously brain damaged, but it does involve a lengthy explanation and requires careful attention by the jury.

Use of a Psychometrist

"If you did not administer these tests, how can you be sure they are accurate?"

Following the techniques developed by Halstead and Reitan, many neuropsychologists employ nondoctoral technicians to administer the tests, while retaining the responsibility of test score interpretation and reaching conclusions regarding the neuropsychological functioning of the patient. The use of non-doctoral technicians, psychometrists, psychometricians, or psychological assistants may be questioned on cross-examination.

Q. Doctor, did you administer these test?
A. No, they were administered by my psychometrist, Mr. Drew.
Q. Is Mr. Drew qualified to practice psychology independently in this state?
A. No.
Q. Then these tests were administered by someone who is not qualified to practice independently?
A. Yes.
Q. Were you present during part of the testing of Mr. Blake?
A. I interviewed Mr. Blake, but was not present during the testing.
Q. Then you were not able to observe either your psychometrist's or Mr. Blake's behavior during the test?
A. That's correct.
Q. Is it possible that Mr. Drew's administration of the tests might have been faulty or that he might have in some other way improperly influenced Mr. Blake's performance?
A. Yes.
Q. You cannot be sure that this did not happen, is that correct?
A. Yes.

This line of questioning might be intercepted by elaborating on the qualifications and appropriateness of using a psychometrist in neuropsychological assessment (Report of the Division 40 Task Force on Education, Accreditation, and Credentialing, 1989, 1991).

A. Although Mr. Drew is not licensed to practice psychology independently, he is qualified to administer and score neuropsychological tests. The practice of using psychometrists is a long-standing, professionally accepted practice in clinical neuropsychology.

In response to the suggestion that the neuropsychologist cannot be sure that the testing is valid because he or she did not observe the testing, the following might be offered:

A. Mr. Drew has worked as my psychometrist for two years. By training him and observing him with other examinees, I have found him to be competent and reliable.

MISCELLANEOUS Q & A

The neuropsychology expert can anticipate a variety of challenging questions, such as the following.

Standard Testing Procedures

Q. Is there an accepted standard battery of neuropsychological tests?
a. No. There is no single approach to neuropsychological testing.
A. There are several widely used approaches to neuropsychological testing, the most common being the flexible or process battery, which I use. Whichever battery is chosen, a neuropsychologist should employ tests that have been well-validated in diagnosing brain dysfunction.

Accuracy of Diagnosis

Q. Do you know for sure that your diagnosis of brain disorder is accurate?
a. No, I don't know for sure.
A. Within reasonable psychological (or medical) probability, I am confident that my diagnosis is correct.

Brain Tissue Damage

Q. Are you saying that the patient has brain tissue damage?
a. No. Only his neurologist can say if brain tissue is damaged.
a. Yes. His test scores are clearly indicative of brain tissue damage.
A. Yes. The test results give clear evidence of brain dysfunction, with a pattern consistent with his severe head trauma and strongly indicative of brain tissue involvement.

Normals Do Poorly

Q. Isn't it true that even normal people can do poorly on a number of your tests?
a. That's true. It's difficult to pass all of these tests.
A. When several tests are administered, a normal person can be expected to do poorly on one or more of the tests. What separates a normal from a brain injured patient is the number of poor scores, the severity of the impairment, as well as the pattern of deficits seen.

Subtest Scatter

Q. Would you place some significance on subtest scores on the WAIS-R that differed by, say, 5 or 6 points?

a. Yes. If subtest scores differed by 5 points or so, I begin to think that some impairment is present.

A. No. We should keep in mind that the usual difference between the highest and lowest subtest scores is 7 ± 2, so that the subtest differences have to be much larger before we can consider it a sign of brain dysfunction.

Loss of Consciousness

Q. Is it possible for a person who does not lose consciousness after a head trauma to suffer brain damage?

a. Yes. I've heard of such cases.

A. As a psychologist, I want to adhere to probabilities rather than possibilities. Given the information I have in this case, I believe it is not probable that this person suffered any brain damage.

Effects of Brain Damage

Q. Isn't it terrible for a person to have brain damage?

a. Of course it is.

A. No one wants to have brain damage, even the minimal amount this individual has suffered. Fortunately, for the work she does as a hotel housemaid, her impairment in speech articulation and mathematical calculations will not prevent her from performing her usual job responsibilities.

Prognosis

Q. Will this child's mild brain disorder eventually heal as he gets older?

a. I'm sure he'll get better, as all children do, with time.

a. No. I expect him to have a permanent learning disability, and I do not expect him to graduate high school in regular classes.

A. I don't know. It is very difficult to make a long range prediction of what will heal and what will remain from his brain injury. I do believe he will need special educational assistance for at least 3 or 4 more years.

Detecting Malingering

Q. Isn't it true that research on neuropsychologists' abilities to identify faking or malingering generally shows poor rates of detection?

a. I'm not familiar with those studies.

a. Yes, that's true. But I am confident that this patient did not fake on her tests.

A. Yes. However, I believe it is important to assess a person's genuineness, and I did this by looking at her MMPI-2 validity test scores, her symptom validity test responses, and the consistency of her various test performances.

Misquoting Your Testimony

Q. **So, you're saying that the Wechsler tests measure something other than brain functioning, correct?**

a. That's correct.

A. That's not what I said. I said that some Wechsler subtests are not highly sensitive to brain dysfunction. Several Wechsler subtests, such as Block Design, are quite helpful in assessing brain functioning.

Poor Test Scores

Q. **Do poor test scores on neuropsychological tests usually mean brain dysfunction?**

a. Yes, they usually do.

A. Poor test scores do not automatically mean brain dysfunction. Poor test scores should be interpreted in light of other test scores, and considered with other data, such as past education and medical history, before any brain dysfunction is inferred.

Psychological Versus Medical Tests

Q. **Aren't the negative results of the CT scan, EEG, and MRI of the brain more convincing than psychological test scores in indicating that the person doesn't have brain damage?**

a. Those are strong pieces of evidence, but I will still stick with my diagnosis of organic brain syndrome.

A. Many cases of brain disorders go undetected by CT scans, EEGs, and MRIs, whereas neuropsychological tests reveal clear evidence of brain disorder. Early stages of Alzheimer's or closed head injuries, as in this patient, are good examples of such cases.

CLOSING ARGUMENTS

Clinical neuropsychologists are in high demand to participate in the forensic arena because of the advanced diagnostic techniques they employ, the abundance of quantifiable data they provide, and the sophisticated levels of scientific knowledge they have attained. Moreover, because of the potential monetary stakes involved in brain injury litigation, both parties in the lawsuit want to be as well represented as possible when evidence of brain damage is disputed.

It should be emphasized that sound neuropsychological diagnoses are best determined not only by neuropsychological test scores but by the integration of varied relevant data sources, such as past educational and work records, medical history, and psychoemotional status. The neuropsychology expert who keeps this in mind will be well-prepared when appearing in the courtroom.

CHAPTER 12

THE NONDOCTORAL WITNESS

"You're not a doctor, are you?"

When mental health issues arise in the courtroom situation, it is presumed that the expert witness will be either adoctoral trained psychologist or a psychiatrist. Indeed, in most jurisdictions the members of a sanity commissions to determine criminal responsibility are, by statute, limited to doctoral level clinicians.

But how do the courts treat a nondoctoral professional who is knowledgeable in psychological issues such as child abuse, domestic violence, and chemical dependency? Often, the practitioners most experienced in certain family problems and drug abuse are master's level psychologists, social workers, and those who are certified in marriage and family therapy or substance abuse counseling. What does the law dictate about the admissibility of these specialists who are skilled in mental health problems? Are academic degrees and titles, such as "Doctor," essential to be accepted as an expert in the courtroom?

In the landmark 1962 case of *Jenkins v. United States*, the opinions of three psychiatrists, who found no evidence of mental disease in the accused assailant, were accepted, whereas the jury was instructed to disregard the testimony of the three defense psychologists, who stated that the defendant had a mental disease when he committed the alleged crime. However, on appeal Circuit Judge David L. Bazelon ruled that psychologists are qualified as experts to diagnose mental disease and to express an opinion as to whether a stated mental disease caused a person to commit a given unlawful act. In *Jenkins*, Judge Bazelon affirmed that degrees or titles are not prerequisites to qualify a witness as an expert. Thus, a person is qualified to testify because of having knowledge that the jury does not have regarding the issue at hand.

In addition, under both the common law and the codified Federal Rules of Evidence adopted in 1975, judges have the authority to evaluate the admissibility of expert testimony. According to Rule 702, qualified experts are allowed to testify about "scientific, technical, or other specialized knowledge" if their testimony "will assist the trier of fact (the jury, or the judge in a non-jury trial) to understand the evidence or to determine a fact in issue."

These judicial rulings open the doors to doctors and nondoctors alike who possess unique knowledge and skills that can assist the jurors in understanding the evidence brought to the courtroom. However, being permitted to testify in court does not mean that the proffered opinions are automatically accepted by the jurors. Professionals, whose words may be unchallenged in their own office, can expect to face vigorous questioning by legal counsel and need to be prepared to support their conclusions with documented evidence and impeccable reasoning.

Direct Examination: Witness Qualification

"And what is your specialty?"

When the mental health professional appears to testify in court, the first step is to demonstrate the clinician's level of expertise and the right to appear in court as an expert witness. The following is a typical questioning process used to qualify an expert in the mental health field.

Q. Please state your full name.
A. My name is Demetria Blake.
Q. What is your profession, Ms. Blake?
A. I am a clinical social worker.
Q. Tell us your educational background and professional training.
A. I have a bachelor's and master's degree in social work from the state university. I have had 2 years of supervised experience at a psychiatric hospital, and I am a certified clinical social worker.
Q. Are you licensed in this state?
A. At the present time there is no state licensing for social workers.
Q. Where are you employed?
A. I am on the staff at the Child Protective Services, or CPS, a section of the State Department of Human Services.
Q. How long have you been with CPS?
A. About 6 years.
Q. In your work at CPS, do you have occasion to evaluate and counsel children and parents when there is evidence of child abuse?
A. Yes.
Q. About how many families have you evaluated and counseled over the past 6 years?

A. That's hard to say. I don't keep statistics on this. I'd say about 800 families. We all have a heavy caseload.

Q. Have you ever testified in court as an expert witness on child abuse?

A. I don't know if I was considered an expert, but I have testified several times in Family Court and in Circuit Court in cases involving child abuse.

Q. Has any court ever rejected you from testifying as a witness?

A. I don't recall. No.

Q. Have you had any special training in the evaluation and treatment of child abuse cases?

A. At CPS, we are continually required to attend courses and workshops in domestic violence, anger management, and child psychiatry. Last year I attended three such symposia related to my work in child abuse.

Your honor, I submit that this witness, Ms. Blake, is fully qualified to testify as an expert in the area of child abuse, its evaluation and its treatment.

Cross-Examination

"You only have a master's degree, right?"

It is unusual for any qualified psychologist or psychiatrist to be aggressively challenged as a witness in court. However, some attorneys may be apt to interrogate a nondoctoral mental health witness, particularly one who has opinions that are potentially damaging to the attorney's client. The following query may ensue:

Q. Ms. Blake, are you a doctor?

A. No, I'm not.

Q. You didn't go to medical school, did you?

A. No.

Q. You haven't had any psychiatric training, have you?

A. No.

Q. And you haven't been in a graduate psychology program, have you?

A. No.

Q. According to your resume, it took just 2 years to receive your master's degree in social work, correct?

A. Two and a half years, to be exact.

Q. In your social work training, you didn't have a specific course in child abuse, did you?

A. We were taught about child abuse in different courses, but not one specific course.

Q. Is your answer, "No, I did not have a specific course in child abuse"?

A. Yes, that's right.

Q. Have you conducted any research on child abuse?
A. No.
Q. Have you published any papers on child abuse?
A. No.
Q. Have you taught any classes on child abuse?
A. No.
Q. Do you subscribe to any journal on child abuse?
A. I subscribe to journals that include articles on child abuse, but I'm not aware of any journals specifically devoted to child abuse.
Q. Why isn't there a journal devoted to child abuse?
A. I don't know.

Whether a nondoctoral professional's credentials are accepted or not will be decided by the trial judge. It is up to the attorney requesting the professional's testimony to defend the witness' qualifications, and it is not the responsibility of the clinician to convince the judge of his or her credentials. The series of questions just presented may not disqualify the mental health professional as a witness, but the probing may affect the weight of the expert's testimony. Throughout this initial questioning, it is important to remain nondefensive, as the witness just described was, and to conserve one's energies for the more important testifying that follows.

Rules for the Nondoctoral Witness

Special challenges await the nondoctoral mental health professional in the courtroom. Issues about sufficient formal education and scientific training are commonly raised, and it behooves the nondoctoral witness to be familiar with the following rules of thumb:

- Don't embellish your credentials
- You don't have to be a scientist to be an expert
- Don't trivialize your expertise
- You don't have to be a psychologist to apply psychological principles
- Don't automatically defer to a doctor's opinion
- Maintain a neutral point of view
- Avoid rendering a legal opinion.

Rule 1: Don't Embellish Your Credentials

Q. Your resume indicates that you received an undergraduate degree in behavioral sciences from the state university, is that correct?
A. Yes.
Q. What was your major?
A. It was psychology as well as sociology.

Q. **So your undergraduate major was psychology?**
A. Well, I majored in sociology, with a minor in psychology.
Q. **How many credits did you have to have for a minor in psychology?**
A. That was a long time ago...I'd say 20 credits.
Q. **So with 20 credits, you had maybe 6 or 7 psychology courses as an undergraduate?**
A. Yeah, that's about right.
Q. **I noticed you have the initials, MS, after your name. What kind of training did you have after you graduated college?**
A. Primarily in counseling.
Q. **So, you have a master's degree in counseling?**
A. No, it's in educational psychology.
Q. **In educational psychology, did you have any special training in abnormal or clinical psychology?**
A. No, not clinical. I took courses in abnormal psychology.
Q. **How many abnormal psychology courses did you take?**
A. Well, most of it was centered toward educational psychology. Maybe one or two courses.
Q. **Your resume also indicated that you're an adjunct faculty member at the university, is that correct?**
A. Right.
Q. **How does one become an adjunct faculty member?**
A. Well, at our clinic, the entire professional staff is an adjunct faculty to the university.
Q. **Do you get paid by the university?**
A. Oh, no.
Q. **Do you teach a class at the university?**
A. Occasionally we go down and teach classes.
Q. **Is that a guest speaker kind of thing?**
A. Right.
Q. **So, you're not a teacher for any course at the university, right?**
A. That's right.
Q. **And how many days a year do you speak at the university?**
A. It varies. Just a couple of days a year.
Q. **And so, not to diminish what you do at the university, the title, "adjunct faculty member" is little more than a title, isn't it?**
A. Well, I provide instruction there.
Q. **But you're not teaching very much at all, right?**
A. No.
Q. **Your resume also lists 10 articles about counseling. Is that right?**
A. Yes.
Q. **In what kind of journals were the articles published?**

A. One is in _____ *Digest*, another in the *International Archives of* _____, and several in the bulletin of our hospital.

Q. How many of these 10 articles were published in your hospital bulletin?

A. I believe 8.

Q. As for the 2 journal articles, were they subjected to a refereed review?

A. I don't understand the question.

Q. Was your article reviewed by independent professionals?

A. If you're asking about psychiatrists reading my paper, I did have one of the staff psychiatrists at our hospital review and critique my article.

Q. But this was not an independent review, right?

a. Okay. I know what you're doing here. You're trying to compare me with a psychologist or psychiatrist who teaches and publishes scientific articles. I don't do that. I have to work 365 days a year, dealing with thousands and thousands of cases. That's how I know what I know. That's where my expertise is coming from.

(Rule 1A: Don't Be Defensive)

A. That's right.

This witness apparently submitted a resume that he uses for public relations and that enhances his professional image by stretching the truth. The proper thing to do is to prepare a resume specifically for court involvement, a summary that is precise, accurate, and relevant because of the close inspection it will undergo by a cross-examining attorney.

Rule 2: You Don't Have to Be a Scientist to Be an Expert

Q. I understand that you have lots of experience in counseling, but my question is whether your knowledge is being elevated to a level of scientifically accepted opinion. Isn't what you do really an art and not at all a science?

A. I'm not willing to say that it is totally an art.

Q. Are you saying it is a science?

A. I can't answer that "yes" or "no."

Q. Would you say it's not an exact science?

A. My skills are based on the accumulation of years of experience. At this point, there's a lot of intuition and gut feeling, rather than a scientific formula.

Q. Can your intuition be tested for reliability by anybody?

A. No, you can't give a statistical probability to what I do.

Q. Through your intuition, don't you draw conclusions or inferences?

A. Yes.

Q. Do your inferences have a database?

A. I have thousands of cases to refer to.

Q. Are your thousands of cases published anywhere?

A. No, it's in my memory.

Q. Can your thousands of cases be analyzed scientifically?

A. I don't think so.

Q. So, is your opinion based on either scientific certainty or scientific probability?

A. No, it isn't.

Q. If your skill involves your memory and gut feeling, if you have no published data that can be analyzed scientifically, and if your opinion is not based on scientific certainty or scientific probability, wouldn't you say that what you do is really an art and not a science?

a. I guess you could say that.

If you have the knowledge and experience that are beyond the ken of the average juror, and your testimony will assist the jury, you qualify as an expert witness. More than likely, the attorney who had requested your testimony will object to some or most of the questions just presented. Even without such support, it is not necessary to defend your skills as being scientific. Thus, to the very first question asked previously it would suffice to say:

A. I don't know how much of my work is art and how much is science. I know that I have many years of experience as a professional counselor and I am very familiar with the mental health issues involved in this case.

The cross-examining attorney may not succeed in disqualifying this mental health professional on the argument that his or her expertise is not "scientific," but these questions may serve to reduce the impact of the witness' testimony.

Rule 3: Don't Minimize Your Expertise

When the witness lacks the usual doctoral degree that other experts bring to court, the attorney will try to trivialize the input of the nondoctoral professional and try to strip the witness of the expert status with the following questions:

Q. You testified that, because Mr. Tracy has physically abused his wife several times, he is likely to abuse her again in the future, isn't that true?

A. Yes.

Q. You realize that the American Psychiatric Association has expressed the position that future dangerousness is impossible to predict, don't you?

A. Yes.

Q. **But you are predicting future dangerousness in this marriage, not because of any scientific data, but because it makes good sense, that it's common sense, isn't that true?**

A. Yes.

Q. **You don't need to be an expert to make the prediction that Mr. Tracy, because of his past spousal abuse, is likely to abuse her again, right?**

A. That's right.

Q. **Then, wouldn't you agree that the average juror can understand that a person with Mr. Tracy's past behavior is likely to be a danger to his wife again some day?**

a. I would agree.

The last response essentially voids any contribution by the expert witness whose presence in court is based on providing knowledge that is beyond the scope of the average juror. The expert does not have to concede the specialized skills that he or she has brought to court. A better reply is:

A. I don't know how knowledgeable and experienced jurors are to judge marital relationships and conflicts. With my training and clinical experience, I believe I can offer insights that would help the jury in their deliberations in this trial.

It is also helpful to cite review articles of empirical research that indicate that judgments made by mental health professionals are frequently more valid than judgments made by laypersons (Garb, 1992).

Rule 4: You Don't Have to Be a Psychologist to Apply Psychological Principles

Q. **What is your profession?**

A. I'm a marriage and family therapist.

Q. **You're not a psychologist, are you?**

A. No, I'm not.

Q. **Do you have a degree in psychology?**

A. No. My bachelor's degree is in human development, but I took several psychology courses in college.

Q. **When you testify about a person's motivation, aren't you making psychological conclusions about personality and behavior?**

A. I am talking about personality and behavior.

Q. **What's the definition of psychology?**

A. It's the study of human behavior.

Q. So, if psychology is the study of human behavior, and you testify as to what motivated this man to behave the way he did, you're drawing psychological conclusions, aren't you?
a. I don't think I can answer it "yes" or "no."

This response does not answer the question. Another inadequate response would be:

a. I'm a marriage and family therapist and I don't draw psychological conclusions.

A marriage and family therapist (as well as a psychiatric nurse practitioner, a school counselor, or a clinical social worker, among others) is permitted to apply psychological conclusions, as they are an intrinsic part of the professional counseling for which they have been trained. Similarly, ministers and teachers apply psychological theory and techniques within the scope of their professional work, without violating any regulatory statutes pertaining to the practice of psychology. A better response is:

A. Yes. Drawing psychological conclusions is part of my everyday practice of marriage and family therapy. It is not possible to counsel couples without drawing from the science of psychology.

Rule 5: Don't Automatically Defer to a Doctor's Opinion

The psychologist or psychiatrist with solid credentials and years of experience may appear at first blush to be more of an expert than a lesser trained professional. However, it is not uncommon for a nondoctoral clinician to be more experienced than a veteran doctor in a specialty area, such as domestic problems, and, therefore, have more expertise. Nonetheless, the following line of inquiry may occur:

Q. You have testified that the children would probably do better to live with their mother, correct?
A. Yes.
Q. As a psychiatric nurse practitioner, you don't possess a doctoral degree, do you?
A. No, I don't.
Q. You're not a licensed psychologist or psychiatrist, right?
A. That's right.
Q. How long have you been in practice?
A. Nearly 7 years.
Q. Are you aware that Dr. Guo, the chief of psychiatry at the state hospital, is also testifying in this case?

A. No, I wasn't aware of that.

Q. You're familiar with Dr. Guo, aren't you?

A. Yes. She's a well-known psychiatrist in this community.

Q. She's had many more years of experience in the mental health field than you, correct?

A. Yes.

Q. She has a good reputation as a psychiatrist, isn't that true?

A. I believe so.

Q. Would you not defer to the opinion of a psychiatrist who has many more years of experience that you?

a. Yes, I would.

It is unnecessary to yield to other professionals merely because of their degrees or years of experience. The essential factor is relevant knowledge and professional work. An appropriate reply could be:

A. I don't think I have to defer to the doctor. My training and clinical work are directly related to family problems, divorce, and children. I am very familiar with this case and I believe I have the expertise to assist in the matter before this court.

Rule 6: Maintain a Neutral Point of View

The mental health witness will often be asked to appear in court by a lawyer or a client and to advocate for one side of the issue (e.g., the custody of the children going to one of the parents). It is easy to be drawn into the role of arguing for the side who has requested you to testify in court, while debating with the opposing counsel. This approach should be avoided.

Q. You have testified that Mrs. Tanaka is the better parent for the children, Donna and Sharon, isn't that correct?

A. Yes.

Q. Who has asked you to appear in court today?

A. Mrs. Tanaka and her attorney.

Q. How many times have you met with Mrs. Tanaka?

A. About 10.

Q. And how many times have you seen the father, Mr. Tanaka?

A. About 3 or 4 times. He refused to come to the last several sessions.

Q. Wouldn't it be fair to say that you know Mrs. Tanaka better than Mr. Tanaka?

A. That's true.

Q. You are much more familiar with her good traits as a parent because you've talked with her more, right?

A. I agree.

Q. **If you had talked with Mr. Tanaka more, perhaps you could have become more familiar with his good traits as a parent, correct?**

A. Perhaps; he's not very communicative, you know.

Q. **At this point, isn't it fair to also say that you've gotten to like Mrs. Tanaka?**

A. I'd say that's true.

Q. **If you got to know Mr. Tanaka more, perhaps you would like him more, too, right?**

A. I don't know about that. I think I know a lot about him now and I'm not sure I'd like him more.

Q. **Well, then, wouldn't you agree that your liking Mrs. Tanaka more than her husband is a big reason why you think she's the better parent?**

a. My liking her has nothing to do with my opinion that she's the better parent.

The appearance of partisanship weakens the witness' professional credibility. Your responsibility is to provide objective opinions regarding the legal case and not to argue for one side. Consider this response:

A. My opinion regarding Mrs. Tanaka's superior parenting is based on the fact that she has spent more time helping the children with their schoolwork and sports activities, and because she communicates better with them.

Rule 7: Avoid Rendering a Legal Opinion

Mental health experts are expected to provide professional opinions within the scope of their specialized knowledge and skills. On the other hand, legal opinions such as whether a person is competent to stand trial or whether custody should be awarded to a parent are the ultimate responsibility of the court and outside the province of the mental health professional.

On occasion, clinical experts may be pressured to render legal judgments and should avoid offering conclusions on matters of law, which are the purview of the courts (Melton et al., 1987). Consider the following questions:

Q. **Sir, how well do you know Mr. Drew?**

A. I've known him for 6 months. He has been attending weekly sessions on anger management that I oversee.

Q. **What problems of anger does he have?**

A. He has difficulty communicating with his wife without losing his temper when she disagrees with him. It is worse when he has had a few alcoholic drinks.

Q. **Have there been incidents of violence?**

A. Yes. On at least 3 occasions, Mrs. Drew has required medical treatment because of the injuries she's sustained from being assaulted by her husband.

Q. Is he still showing violent behavior?

A. No. Since he's been coming to our sessions he's been controlling his anger much better. His wife has provided us with good follow-up reports.

Q. In your opinion, is Mr. Drew substantially improved with regard to controlling his temper?

A. Yes. Definitely improved.

Q. Is Mrs. Drew in danger of being assaulted by her husband?

A. I don't believe so.

Q. Then, are you saying that the restraining order on Mr. Drew can be lifted?

a. Yes.

A "yes" answer is a legal opinion and goes beyond the expert's training and experience, which are limited to behavioral and mental health issues. A better reply is:

A. The lifting of a restraining order is the responsibility of the court. That decision is beyond my skills as a mental health professional.

MISCELLANEOUS Q & A

Nondoctoral witnesses face a variety of challenges, such as the following. Note the weak answers as contrasted with the stronger replies.

Less Education

Q. Isn't it true that you have had fewer formal courses in psychology than a person with a PhD in psychology?

a. That's true but that doesn't mean that I don't have the expertise to testify today.

A. Although I've had fewer courses in psychology, I have had substantial continuing education activity and several years of clinical experience in the subject we are discussing today.

Nondoctoral Status

Q. You're not a doctor, are you?

a. No, I'm sorry. I'm just a counselor.

A. No. I am a certified pastoral counselor.

Professional Training

Q. **Are you aware of the studies that have shown that laypersons do as well as professional clinicians in predicting violence and detecting brain damage?**

a. No, I'm not aware of those studies.

A. I am aware of those studies. I am also aware of studies that show the diagnostic skills of trained clinicians. Would you like me to name some books on this subject? (Be prepared to support your response).

Experience

Q. **Years of experience by themselves don't make a practitioner better, do they?**

a. That's true. Some recent graduates are just as good as some of the old timers.

A. Not the years alone, but the continual feedback from my clients and my colleagues have helped me to improve as a practitioner.

Disagreeing With Authorities

Q. **Shouldn't the children be kept together as authorities recommend, rather than separate them between the parents as you suggest?**

a. I'm not sure. There are advantages to keeping them together as authorities say.

A. No. In this particular case, it is disadvantageous for one parent to manage the affairs of the 4 children. Dividing the children between their parents would have many benefits for all parties concerned.

Supporting Opinions

Q. **Can you explain your opinion about the mother's alcoholism?**

a. I'm certain she is an alcoholic and always will be. That's my professional opinion as a certified substance abuse counselor.

A. My opinion about her alcoholism is based on her many years of weekend binges, four traffic citations for driving under the influence of alcohol, and what her family told me about her frequent intoxicated behavior.

Using Jargon

Q. **Can you tell us what you do in counseling?**

a. Counseling is a very complex and dynamic counselor–client relationship in which the whole array of human emotions and cognitions interplay at varying levels of consciousness, with transference and countertransference phenomenon.

a. Well, it's too hard to explain to the court in just a few sentences. I'm sorry, it just can't be explained.

A. Clients come to us with personal and family problems. Through a series of talk sessions we try to help our clients understand the cause of the problems and, more importantly, to help them learn to cope with their problems in a more effective way.

Possibilities

Q. **Isn't it possible that the husband was extremely provoked by his wife so that he essentially struck back in self-defense?**

a. No. I don't think that's possible.

A. Yes, anything is possible. However, I don't have any facts to prove or disprove that possibility.

Hypotheticals

Q. **Would it change your prediction about this man if you found out that he had struck his previous wife as well?**

a. Yes. That would make me doubt his ability to control his anger.

A. I'm not sure. I would need more information to reconsider my opinions about him.

Confidentiality

Q. **Have you discussed this case with anyone?**

a. Of course not.

A. Yes. I've talked with my client's attorney. I've also discussed the issues of this case with colleagues for their feedback, but keeping the names of my client and his or her family confidential.

Yes or No

Q. **Psychological problems start in childhood, don't they? Please answer yes or no.**

a. Yes.

A. Frequently, yes.

Possibilities Versus Probabilities

Q. **Isn't it possible that Mr. Cox would be a better parent for the children?**

a. No, I don't think it's possible.

A. Many things are possible, but the probability is that he would not be the better parent for the children.

CLOSING ARGUMENTS

With the guidance of common law and the 1975 Federal Rules of Evidence, judges have welcomed an expert who has the knowledge, experience, and skills that will aid the triers of fact in their deliberation of a case. Doctoral degrees and titles are helpful but not essential, as the critical element is the expert's background that can help in clarifying technical information that is beyond the ken of the lay juror. Nonetheless, some jurisdictions require that clinicians meet specific educational or experiential requirements before they can be accepted as experts. Psychiatric social workers are generally acknowledged as experts in juvenile and domestic problems, and in certain jurisdictions they can offer opinions as to a defendant's competency to stand trial (Melton et al., 1987).

Not all authorities agree with simple rules of thumb, such as helpfulness or scientific observations, but they recommend that, for forensic purposes, any proffered scientific evidence be screened and subjected to strict peer review before being allowed in the courtroom (Ayala & Black, 1993). Moreover, other critics, like Faust and Ziskin (1988), suggest that mental health professional do not have sufficient certainty and do not have more accurate judgments than laypersons, and, therefore, fail to satisfy legal standards for expertise. The Faust–Ziskin position has been rejected by several authors as being extreme and one-sided (Brodsky, 1989; Matarazzo, 1991; Rogers, Bagby, & Perera, 1993), and Faust and Ziskin (1988) themselves admitted their explicit bias against the deficits of mental health clinicians.

This chapter offered several tips for the nondoctoral witness, including presenting an accurate profile of one's credentials, affirming one's expertise, and not deferring automatically to a doctor's opinion. Nondoctoral witnesses can expect aggressive probing by the opposing counsel into their education and training, in order to undermine their potential input into the trial proceedings. As always, a calm, self-assured professional manner is the desirable courtroom presentation to make.

There are no clear-cut guidelines to indicate when you can testify as an expert witness. The nature of the legal case and the background of the practitioner are the most relevant factors to consider. Moreover, opinions of doctoral and nondoctoral witnesses alike may carry different weight, depending on the level of acceptance by the jury members. Professionals who are truly qualified to offer expert opinions need not shy away from the task of aiding lay jurors. At the same time, those who enter the judicial arena need to appreciate the vast implications of their clinical judgments and must be conscious of the ethical requirements to testify only in matters within the scope of their training and skills.

CHAPTER 13

DEPOSITION

"You mean, this is your first deposition?"

The preparation phase that precedes the trial of a civil case consists of a discovery period, when attorneys present to each other written questions, or interrogatories, about the case. The legal counsels for each side also share lists of prospective witnesses who will appear in court. When expert witnesses are involved, the attorneys indicate which issues of the case the expert will address, and they have the right to subpoena all records related to the case.

In many instances, the opposing attorney is satisfied to receive a copy of the psychotherapist's treatment reports. Often, however, the opposing counsel obtains a court order by way of subpoena to query witnesses in an oral deposition, which is testimony taken under oath and transcribed by a certified court reporter. Typically, the opposing counsel will conduct a 1- to 2-hour deposition in the expert's office, with the attorney who represents the plaintiff or who is retaining the expert also being present. The main purpose of the deposition is to ascertain what the expert's opinions are and the bases for those opinions.

The attorney who represents the plaintiff or who is retaining the expert usually meets with the clinician before the deposition, to discuss potential issues in the case and to have a clear understanding of the major conclusions reached by the expert witness. If the attorney does not call to meet with you before the deposition, it is wise for you to schedule a predeposition meeting with the attorney to discuss the anticipated testimony.

The deposition is conducted with some of the courtlike formalities, beginning with a swearing in of the witness by the court reporter. As in the courtroom, testifying begins with the witness' professional qualifications being established, as described in chapter 2. If the witness' qualifications are found to be adequate, a detailed direct examination ensues. A cross-examination by the attorney retaining the expert is usually brief, as the strategy is to share as little as possible regarding the expert's findings. Redirect examination is also usually brief.

When the deposition is completed, the witness will be asked if reading and signing of the typed deposition is waived. You, as expert witness, are advised not to waive reading and signing of the deposition transcript, so that any errors in the typed transcripts can be corrected. Court reporters are not infallible, and the incorrect spelling or transcription of a single word can misrepresent the expert's opinion in a dramatic way.

The remainder of this chapter consists of a sample oral deposition taken from a psychotherapist who treated a person who was injured in a traffic accident. In order to incorporate as many different challenges as possible, the questions and responses are excerpts from the actual depositions of several different cases and blended into a single deposition.

The case involves a woman who suffered multiple physical injuries in an automobile accident and who was subsequently treated by several doctors, including a clinical psychologist. The patient, who filed a lawsuit claiming her injuries, gradually improved from her head, neck, and back trauma as well as from psychological reactions from the car accident. As her condition stabilized, the defense attorney subpoenaed the various physicians to appear for a deposition so that the nature and extent of the woman's injuries could be established before a final monetary settlement of the case could be reached. This deposition transcript is of the treating psychologist.

Different segments of the testimony comprise the typical areas of questioning the psychotherapist faces in a deposition including:

- deposition instructions
- witness qualification
- clinical examination
- psychological testing
- treatment
- causes of condition
- corroborative evidence
- malingering
- secondary gain, compensation neurosis
- cross-examination by plaintiff's attorney

EXAMINATION

By MR. WILLIAMS:

Q. Doctor, please state your full name for the record.
A. I'm Dr. Howard Anderson.

Q. And your business address, please?

A. I'm at Straub Clinic, 888 South King Street, Honolulu, Hawaii, 96813

Q. Okay. Doctor, I am Mr. Luke Williams and I represent the defendant in this case. Ms. F. Leigh McKinley who is also present is the attorney for the plaintiff and your patient, Mrs. Sandra Worthington.

A. I see.

Q. Now, Doctor, your deposition is being taken today because the records show that you're one of the physicians who have treated Mrs. Worthington. Is that correct?

A. Yes.

Deposition Instructions

Q. Doctor, I take it you've had your deposition taken before?

A. Yes.

Q. You understand that this is a legal proceeding in which your testimony is being taken as if you're testifying in a court of law?

A. Yes.

Q. Everything you say will be reduced to a transcript form. You'll have an opportunity to review that transcript, Doctor, but you understand if you make changes to that transcript, I can comment about it to the jury and the judge. So in order for that not to happen, you are required to testify to the best of your ability and your knowledge in this case. Is that understood, Doctor?

A. Yes.

Q. If I don't make myself understood in my questioning, please advise me. If you don't understand my question or my question is unclear to you, I'll try to rephrase it in some understandable fashion if I can.

A. Fine.

Q. One more thing. Plaintiff counsel may make an objection to my questions. This is because the objections must be made now, to preserve them for the record. You will be expected to answer the question anyway. Okay?

A. That's fine.

Witness Qualification

Q. Now, Doctor, can you briefly tell me what your educational background is, from the time of college onward?

A. Okay. I have a bachelor's degree in sociology from the University of Santa Clara, and a master's and a PhD in psychology— clinical psychology—from Fordham University.

Q. I see. And Doctor, how long have you bee n employed with Straub Clinic and Hospital?

A. Ten years.

Q. Do you have any certifications and licenses?

A. I have a license for the State of Hawaii as a psychologist.

Q. When did you obtain that license?

A. 1984.

Q. Do you belong to any medical societies or organizations?

A. I belong to the American Psychological Association and the Hawaii Psychological Association.

Q. Have you ever held any offices with any of those associations?

A. I was a representative-at-large of the Hawaii Psychological Association in the past.

Q. Now, Doctor, have you authored any articles in your field?

A. Yes.

Q. How many?

A. Five.

Q. Have you ever testified in court before?

A. Yes.

Q. On how many occasions do you recall testifying?

A. In court?

Q. Yes.

A. Twice.

Q. On each of those occasions, were you qualified as an expert in your specialty when you were testifying?

A. To the best of my knowledge, yes.

Q. Do you know whether you were or you weren't?

A. I was.

Q. You are a clinical psychologist, correct?

A. That's right.

Q. What is the difference between a clinical psychologist and a psychiatrist?

A. As far as the training goes, the psychiatrist is one who attends a medical school after college and then has about 3 years of psychiatric residency as a specialty in medicine. Therefore, he treats mental and psychiatric problems with medical techniques like medicines or hospitalizations or shock therapy. Clinical psychologists after college go through graduate school. And the average time of graduate school is about 6 or 7 years, during which time they take courses primarily in psychology and specifically in clinical psychology.

Q. You have a PhD?

A. That's right.

Q. And you are a psychologist and not a psychiatrist?

A. Yes. Right.

Q. **Are you a licensed neurologist or have you had any training in neurology?**

A. No.

Q. **Have you ever had any training in forensic psychiatry or forensic psychology?**

A. No formal training in those areas.

Q. **Earlier you gave me a copy of your vitae.**

A. Yes.

Q. **Let me just attach this as an exhibit to the deposition. You brought with you your file on Mrs. Worthington, didn't you?**

A. Yes.

Q. **Could I see that please?**

A. Sure. This is her Straub chart, which includes her visits with me as well as other Straub doctors, and other test reports and letters related to her care.

Q. **Have you reviewed this chart?**

A. Somewhat.

Q. **Could we have a copy of this attached as an exhibit to the deposition?**

A. Sure. Then this is her test folder, which contains the raw data of her psychological testing that's kept here in this department.

Q. **Thank you. And I also would like a copy of this attached to the deposition.**

A. Ethical considerations prevent me from handing over psychological test raw data, except to a professional capable of understanding and interpreting the test data. I am willing to make arrangements to share these results with a psychologist trained in psychological testing, with appropriately signed release forms.

Q. **I think I can make arrangements for that.**

A. Good.

Clinical Examination

Q. **Doctor, in the course of your practice here at Straub Clinic as a psychologist, you had the occasion to see Mrs. Worthington, right?**

A. That's right.

Q. **I see that you have your chart in front of you. Please feel free to refer to it as you need. When did Mrs. Worthington first come under your care? Her initial visit was on January 8, 1991, right?**

A. That's correct.

Q. **Would you tell me what transpired at that visit?**

A. Yes. That was a 1-hour interview with her in which I got a little bit of history as to her injury from an automobile accident that took place on April 28, 1990, the symptoms she had up to the present time in January

1991, and various questions about her health, her background, her work situation, and the treatment she had been receiving.

Q. Would you tell me what history you obtained from her?

A. All right. It's rather long. Would you like me go over that? It's not a problem for me to go over that.

Q. Would you, please?

A. Okay. She told me that she was in good health until the motor vehicle accident on April 28, 1990. This accident took place in town and she was a passenger in a car that was hit on the left front side, and she told me that she hit the windshield with the right side of her head. She didn't think she lost consciousness, but a few days later, she was in pain and she saw a chiropractor and that doctor treated her for about 2 months.

Her referral to me came from her neurologist, Dr. Leo Nakano, who had first seen her in May 1990. And Mrs. Worthington told me that she had a number of problems. One was lower back, upper back, and neck pain that was daily and constant. And she had daily and intermittent headaches. And as for treatment, she had received physical therapy and was mostly taking aspirin for her headaches, which helped a little. She had taken some Naprosyn in the past, but that wasn't too helpful.

She told me that she had some difficulty sleeping because of back pain and she was often very tired because she wasn't sleeping very well, that her back pain became worse with bending and lifting and raising of her arms or stretching, standing or kneeling too long.

She told me that she was having some marital difficulties because she was always tense, irritable, and grouchy because of the pain.

She was living in an apartment with her husband and their son who was then 12 years of age.

As far as her work situation, she told me she was not employed and was last employed 2 months earlier as a waitress.

In terms of earlier history, she was born in Honolulu and raised in Honolulu as well as in Colorado. She attended Kaiser High School but got her GED in 1981. That's about it from the initial interview.

Psychological Testing

Q. I understand that you administered the Minnesota Multiphasic Personality Inventory, or MMPI, when you first saw her in 1991; is that correct?

A. Yes. That's correct.

Q. For the record, what is the MMPI?

A. The MMPI is a psychological test that is basically a self-report inventory, consisting of 566 true–false items. These items or statements attempt to cover various emotional characteristics such as anxiety, depression, and anger. Also some health issues, as well as psychosocial relationships, general activity levels, and possible problems in thinking.

Q. **In general, Doctor, what were the results of the MMPI?**

A. Well, the MMPI verified the fact that she had significant psychological difficulties, primarily characterized by depression, anxiety, anger, and substantial health concerns.

Q. **Were there any scales on the MMPI to see if she was faking or malingering?**

A. Scales *L*, *F* and *K*, to the far left side of the graph, help us in this regard.

Q. **What were the scores on those scales?**

A. Her *L*, *F* and *K* scale scores were within the normal range.

Q. **That indicates that this was probably a valid MMPI result?**

A. Yes.

Q. **Does that cover all the testing that you did on Mrs. Worthington?**

A. Yes.

Q. **Did you reach any conclusions as a result of your initial examination and testing?**

A. Yes. Mrs. Worthington was suffering moderately severe emotional distress as a result of her car accident injuries, and she was feeling very frustrated, depressed, angry, and worried because her pain condition was not subsiding and her financial problems were mounting.

Q. **What was your *DSM–IV* diagnosis?**

A. The primary diagnosis was Major Depression, 296.22. The secondary diagnosis was Psychological factors affecting physical condition, 316.

Treatment

Q. **What was your treatment plan for Mrs. Worthington on that date in January 1991?**

A. To have her undergo psychotherapy for her emotional distress as well as biofeedback therapy, which is training her in muscle relaxation techniques, in order to reduce her headaches, neck, and back pain.

Q. **How did Mrs. Worthington respond to this treatment plan?**

A. She was very cooperative and appeared for therapy sessions regularly. She also followed instructions to listen to relaxation tapes at home daily. She participated actively in psychotherapy, venting her frustrations about her pain and the changed circumstances in her life. She interacted in a more positive way at home and worked with her new physical therapists to maximize recovery.

Q. **What were the results of the treatment she received here?**

A. After about 3 months, she began to report notable lessening of her headaches and neck pain, and eventually she said they faded away. The low back pain, however, persisted. As her pain went down, she found a new job as a restaurant hostess, at first part time, but for the past 2 years on a full-time basis. Her depression and anxieties have also lessened, including improvement in her marital relationship, and her sleep has been good.

Q. **Are you still seeing Mrs. Worthington?**

A. For the past 6 months she has come in once a month for follow-up. She is much better and benefits from the opportunity to talk about her continued back pain, inability to do many physical things she used to do, and dealing with the changes that have taken place at work and at home because of the injuries.

Q. **What is your prognosis for the patient?**

A. From a psychological standpoint, it looks good. We plan to end our therapy sessions by mid-year.

Q. **Will she have any permanent psychological problems?**

A. From what I know about the permanence of her low back condition, Mrs. Worthington will always feel a loss and frustrated that she can't do the things she's always enjoyed, like outdoor family activities. I do not expect her to require psychotherapy. I think she'll manage on her own.

Cause of Condition

Q. **Based on your examination of Mrs. Worthington as well as the many treatment sessions you have had with her over the past 3 years, can you state to a reasonable degree of psychological probability the cause for her psychological problems?**

A. The emotional difficulties she has had appeared to have occurred only since the car accident of 4/28/90. The difficulties she expressed are quite commonly seen with people who have serious headaches, back and neck pain, poor sleep, and the kind of family problems she was having.

Q. **Do you have any type of information concerning her psychological makeup prior to this accident?**

A. Not much. As far as I know, prior to the accident she never had the kind of emotional reactions she had after her car injuries.

Q. **So again this is based on information that she provided to you, is that correct?**

A. Yes, as well as some information from Dr. Nakano, and one visit that I had with her husband.

Q. **It is your opinion that the accident is the cause, is the sole cause of all of her emotional difficulties that you described?**

A. As far as I know.

Q. **Doctor, isn't it true that job stress and marital problems could also cause a certain amount of emotional difficulties in general?**

MS. MCKINLEY: Objection, asking the witness to speculate, no founda
tion, no reference to place, time, date, circumstance or
event.

Q. (by Mr. Williams) Please answer the question, Doctor.

A. Yes.

**Q. Were you able to assess whether any of Mrs. Worthington's emo-
tional difficulties could be associated with having a difficult job as a
waitress as opposed to anything having to do with this accident?**

A. I didn't think her emotional difficulties were related to her previous job.
She liked being a waitress, which she did for about 5 years.

**Q. Can you rule out the effect of her husband's being laid off from work
in 1990 as a factor contributing to the emotional difficulties Mrs.
Worthington was having?**

A. Well, as far as I know, the patient's husband was out of work for only 3
months in early 1990. I didn't think that the layoff affected her that much.
Her depression and anxieties peaked in late 1990 when she could see that
her pain problems weren't going away as was predicted by her doctors.
She had become irritable and grouchy because of the constant pain and
said her marriage began to worsen at that point.

Corroborative Evidence

**Q. Okay. Did you, in the course of treating the patient, speak with any
of the physicians to confirm Mrs. Worthington's impressions of her
medical condition?**

A. No.

**Q. Of course, not being a physician, you couldn't confirm Mrs.
Worthington's impressions of her physical condition, could you?**

A. That's right. I'm not qualified to conduct a medical examination.

**Q. Okay. How many treating physicians were there for Mrs. Worthington
from the date of her injury in 1990; can you tell me that?**

A. The names given to me by the patient were that of Drs. Nakano, Wedding,
Onorato, and Stoddard, so at least four.

Q. And you assumed that those were the only treating physicians?

A. No. These I would consider the major treating physicians.

**Q. Prior to rendering your opinion, did you speak with any of those
treating physicians?**

A. I did not.

**Q. Is there any particular reason why you did not speak with them to
determine whether the facts she had provided to them were different
from the facts she gave to you?**

A. No. I can't think of any good reason.

Q. Doctor, was there anything that prevented you from speaking with the prior physicians who had treated Mrs. Worthington over the previous 8 months?

A. I don't think so. I don't know that, but I don't think so.

Q. In the course of interviewing Mrs. Worthington, did you assume that the information and the history she gave you was accurate?

A. Yes.

Q. If Mrs. Worthington told other doctors things that differed from what she told you, would you change your opinion about her?

MS. MCKINLEY: Objection. States facts not in evidence. What things?

A. It depends on what she told them.

Q. As part of your examination do you assess a patient's credibility?

A. Yes.

Q. Did you do so in Mrs. Worthington's case?

A. Yes, I did.

Q. Now, at what point in time were you to make an assessment of her credibility, sometime prior to the interview, at the time of the interview, at the time of the treatment, or at some other time?

A. I would think around the time of the interview, but also in subsequent therapy visits.

Q. Now, Mrs. Worthington spoke of several complaints, correct?

A. Yes.

Q. Is it true that you took no steps to confirm the accuracy of the physical ailments of which she complained?

MS. MCKINLEY: Objection. Asked and answered.

MR. WILLIAMS: Go ahead, Doctor.

A. Yes.

Q. Doctor, let me ask you: In light of the fact that the credibility of the patient is one of the critical issues in a case like this, do you not feel it would have been more accurate to confirm the accuracy of the medical and physical complaints with a treating physician?

A. It would have been better.

Q. It would have been more accurate, too?

A. I think more data means more accuracy.

Malingering

Q. Thank you. Doctor, what I'm trying to find out is how you determine a patient's credibility. How do you do that?

A. There are different ways that credibility or malingering is evaluated. We want to see if a patient is consistent in reporting her symptoms, or if unusual patterns of symptoms are presented. Symptoms that don't make anatomical sense, or bizarre symptoms, indicate that the patient may not be credible.

Q. What source book or treatise or authority would support the position that you have just articulated?

A. There are not a lot of papers and research on the area of malingering and faking. Offhand I can't name a book or article that includes what I just said.

Q. Doctor, is there either a validated body of knowledge, demonstrated expertise, or special techniques to detect falsification of psychological disorders?

MS. MCKINLEY: Vague and ambiguous.

A. I believe that the literature I read indicates the presence of scientific data and valid approaches to evaluate faking psychological and medical disorders.

Q. Would you tell me today what is the authority that you refer to that demonstrates the ability to detect falsification of psychological disorders?

A. One book to refer to is by Rogers on malingering and deception.

Q. Anything else?

A. Various journal articles that have appeared through the years.

Q. Are you capable of reciting any other authors at this point?

A. No.

MS. MCKINLEY: For the record, if you want him to prepare the list, please ask for it affirmatively so we can keep tabs of the request. Otherwise, I will assume that you're not asking him to provide you with that information. Okay?

Q. (by Mr. Williams) How long would it take you to determine that fact?

A. I don't know. I do literature research all the time for various topics. It's never for just a few hours to be total and complete.

Q. Are you saying that it would take a couple of hours?

A. Oh, more than that.

MS. MCKINLEY: I think he said it would never be just a very few hours.

A. I would probably have to go to the university library.

Q. (by Mr. Williams) May I reasonably infer from your answer and your inability to recite to me authors or specific journals, that although there may be some periodicals or some specific papers, they are not of such notoriety that they come to your immediate attention?

A. Yes.

Secondary Gain, Compensation Neurosis

Q. Was there any indication to you, because of this car accident and the fact that she has filed a lawsuit, that there might be a secondary gain aspect to her pain syndrome?

A. I didn't think so.

Q. And why do you not think so?

A. Well, secondary gain is more apparent, of course, in patients who are not working at all and who are fully taking advantage of a pain problem by being completely disabled. Mrs. Worthington lost her job as a result of this accident, but she found a more appropriate job, given her injuries, as soon as she could handle part-time work. I see her as being a conscientious person.

Q. What about the fact that there is some monetary gain involved?

A. That's always a possibility with, I think, all lawsuits. I don't see her having any more concerns about winning money from her lawsuit than anybody else.

Q. Would there be any psychological test that would reveal a tendency?

A. The MMPI is helpful, and in her case there was no indication of faking or malingering.

Q. And so reiterate to me why you are not concerned with a secondary gain or malingering?

A. Okay. I think that becomes more of a concern for me, first, when the person is not working; and second, when the person seems to talk a great deal about lawsuits and monetary gain or talk about their lawsuit a lot. I didn't even know who her lawyer was. Third, secondary gain can occur when the patient is receiving unusual support and sympathy from her family, who may pamper the injured person. I don't see that happening. Those would be reasons.

Q. Are you aware that Dr. Stoddard opined that Mrs. Worthington has compensation neurosis?

A. No.

Q. Doesn't the fact that Mrs. Worthington is involved in ongoing litigation affect her emotionally?

A. Ongoing litigation would affect many people emotionally.

Q. Isn't that what is known as litigation neurosis?

A. No. Litigation neurosis implies high levels of emotional reactions, much more than would be ordinarily expected for persons involved in legal suits. I don't think Mrs. Worthington has litigation neurosis.

Q. Can you conclusively rule out compensation neurosis for Mrs. Worthington?

A. I think I did so.

Q. You conclusively ruled it out as a possibility?

A. Well, not as a possibility.

Q. All right.

MS. MCKINLEY: As a diagnosis?

THE WITNESS: Yes.

Q. Well, let me ask the question: You're not a medical doctor, are you?

A. That's right.

Q. **And you're not licensed to practice medicine, are you?**

A. That's right.

Q. **And you are not trained to render medical opinions regarding a physical condition, are you?**

A. No, I'm not.

MR. WILLIAMS: Okay. I see it is now 11:30, Doctor. I thank you for your time.

**CROSS-EXAMINATION
BY PLAINTIFF'S ATTORNEY**

By MS. MCKINLEY:

Q. **Doctor, are you satisfied with the information that you have on Mrs. Worthington and that the conclusions that you have offered today both in the form of your reports and the testimony that you have given is sound and has a reasonable basis in your training and clinical judgment?**

MR. WILLIAMS: I object to the form of the question. It is not only compound, but it totally begs the questions that have come up today and the testimony that this doctor has given.

A. Yes.

Q. **(by Ms. McKinley) You're satisfied with that?**

A. Yes.

Q. **Okay. Now, when you're testifying regarding an individual such as you've been asked to do here, and such as you have done in the past, there is a certain body of information that you would require prior to rendering any opinion in connection with that individual; is that correct?**

A. Yes.

Q. **Certain parameters that you have to cover?**

A. Yes.

Q. **A minimum amount of information must be obtained?**

A. Yes.

Q. **Okay. And you're aware of that and you try to acquire sufficient factual data on which to base your conclusions, do you not?**

A. Yes.

Q. **Now, as is the case with any type of an evaluation, the gathering of information could continue on endlessly into the future, could it not? I mean, it could be virtually endless, is that correct?**

MR. WILLIAMS: Object to the form of the question. It's a narration, it's a speech, and it is not a question.

Q. (by Ms. McKinley) Go ahead.

A. Yes.

Q. All right. In this case, you were asked about a patient's credibility, correct?

A. Yes.

Q. Okay. I believe you evaluate an individual's credibility, not only for litigation purposes but for other purposes; is that correct? Workers' compensation or some other purpose?

A. Yes.

Q. Do you evaluate each individual on a case-by-case basis?

A. Yes.

Q. (by Ms. McKinley) We may have covered this, Doctor, in your subsequent testimony, but there was a point where Mr. Williams asked a question about the malingering and the patient's credibility, and it seemed that you had something more to add but you didn't finish. Do you have anything more to add at this time in connection with the comments made about the malingering of symptoms?

A. I think I did later.

Q. You covered it later?

A. A couple of questions later.

Q. I just wanted to make sure that you felt now that you had an adequate opportunity to cover it.

A. Yes. If not, let me just state it real briefly. I do not think that Mrs. Worthington is malingering, or is obtaining secondary gain or has compensation neurosis.

MS. MCKINLEY: Thank you very much.

FURTHER EXAMINATION

By MR. WILLIAMS:

Q. Doctor, have you ever been manipulated by a patient?

A. Yes.

Q. Did you find any signs of manipulation on the part of Mrs. Worthington?

A. No.

Q. Do you consider Dr. Stoddard to be an experienced psychiatrist?

A. Yes.

Q. Do you consider him one of the better qualified psychiatrists in the state?

MS. MCKINLEY: Vague and ambiguous. Do you mean better qualified by having better credentials, better skills, or by having a busier practice?

MR. WILLIAMS: Better credentials.

A. I would say especially in the area of forensic work.

Q. Yes?

A. Yes.

MR. WILLIAMS: Thank you.

MS. MCKINLEY: Thank you very much, Doctor.

CLOSING ARGUMENTS

The oral deposition is an essential part of the litigation process, especially in civil tort cases. The work of a defense attorney is often incomplete without obtaining a sworn statement from critical experts as well as non-expert witnesses. In most instances, after vital information is obtained from a deposition the legal case is settled out of court or by an arbitration hearing, and a trial is averted. Consequently, you are likely to submit many more sworn statements in depositions in your office than in an actual courtroom.

Although the deposition is conducted in the safe and secure environs of your own working place, you must be alert to avoid casual clinical observations and speculations, and you must provide well-founded and thoroughly reasoned forensic testimony as would be profferred in the presence of a judge and jury. In fact, if the case proceeds to trial, the deposition transcripts are utilized to assure that you do not express opinions that deviate from the testimony given in the oral deposition. Any changes in the facts or conclusions offered by you may be justification to impeach your testimony altogether.

The sample deposition in this chapter included the common forms of questioning that occur in depositions of mental health professionals. The opposing attorney will ask questions regarding witness qualification, how the evaluation and treatment of the patient was conducted, the causes of the emotional injuries, any corroborative evidence obtained, and how malingering, secondary gain and compensation neurosis issues were addressed.

The oral deposition usually lasts an hour or two. In cases involving high monetary stakes (e.g., hundreds of thousands of dollars or more) and where psychological testimony plays a vital role, the deposition could last 3 or more hours, with vigorous and complex challenges by experienced and skilled opposing attorneys. The mental health professional who has well-documented treatment records and who has conferred with the referring attorney about the relevant issues in the case has little to worry about, except to provide calm, nondefensive and nonargumentative responses to the questions put forth in the deposition.

APPENDIX

ANNOTATED REFERENCE LIST

BOOKS

The Psychologist as Expert Witness (Blau, 1984) is one of the standard texts on forensic psychology. It contains a brief review of the court system, and provides practical advice about many aspects of forensic work, from preparing a case folder, to conducting an evaluation and testifying in court. Areas covered include competency to stand trial, the insanity defense, custody disputes, and personal injury litigation. It contains numerous sample forensic evaluations and examples of court dialogue. The useful appendices report important cases and contain a glossary.

Testifying in Court (Brodsky, 1991) has become an instant "classic." It contains numerous nuggets of wisdom and advice covering a broad range of topics of interest to the mental health expert.

Forensic Psychological Assessment (Shapiro, 1991) focuses primarily on criminal forensic psychology. Topics covered include competency to stand trial and criminal responsibility. There are also chapters on being an expert witness and on professional liability.

Psychological Evaluations for the Courts (Melton et al., 1987) is a comprehensive handbook of forensic psychological assessment. It contains a useful overview of the law and its relationship to the mental health professions. It has detailed chapters on competencies in the criminal process, mental state at the time of offense, and sentencing. Civil commitment, civil competencies, com-
206

pensation for mental injuries, child abuse, and child custody are also thoroughly covered. A variety of sample reports are provided.

Coping with Psychiatric and Psychological Testimony (5th ed., 3 vol.; Ziskin, 1995) is the classic book for attorneys to help neutralize opposing mental health experts by focusing on the limitations of psychiatric and psychological evidence. The suggestions on how to challenge the expertise of psychiatrists and psychologists can be helpful reading.

The Mental Health Professional and the Legal System (Group for Psychiatry and the Law, 1991) provides a brief overview of the legal system in relation to mental health. The role of the expert witness from initial contact with attorney, through the forensic examination, report writing, preparation for deposition or trial, and testifying. A list of "trick" questions used by cross-examining attorneys is provided. The reading list of the Accreditation Council of Fellowships in Forensic Psychiatry is in an appendix.

Forensic Psychiatry (Sadoff, 1988) covers a variety of issues involved in psychiatric consultation to attorneys. These include the forensic psychiatric interview, evaluation of criminal defendants, determining dangerousness, assessment of mental competency, custody issues, and traumatic injury.

Clinical Handbook of Psychiatry and the Law (Applebaum & Gutheil, 1991) is a comprehensive, general text on legal issues in psychiatry. Topics include confidentiality, commitment, suicidality, dangerousness, malpractice, and civil competence. Several chapters address forensic evaluations and testimony.

A Clinician's Guide to Forensic Psychological Assessment (Maloney, 1985) addresses legal insanity, competency to stand trial, commitment, competency to confess, and forensic psychological evaluation of sex offenders, violence potential, and malingering. Workers' compensation, personal injury, and custody evaluations are also discussed. There is a brief chapter at the end of the book on expert testimony.

The MMPI, MMPI-2 & MMPI-A in Court (Pope et al., 1993) focuses primarily on the use of these tests in forensic psychology. Nevertheless, it also contains general information about forensic psychology including suggestions about working with attorneys, planning and conduction assessments, and report writing.

Court Testimony in Mental Health (Vandenburg, 1993) provides a brief introduction to forensic practice and very brief descriptions of areas of forensic assessment.

Clinical Psychiatry and the Law (Simon, 1992) addresses ethical and legal issues of providing psychiatric care.

The Psychologist's Legal Handbook (Stromberg et al., 1988) provides a comprehensive coverage of legal and ethical issues encountered in psychological practice. These include licensure, business, confidentiality, dangerousness, and civil commitment. One chapter addresses issues in forensic psychology.

Evaluating Competencies (Grisso, 1986) reviews techniques and instruments used for evaluation of competencies to stand trial, to waive right to legal counsel and to consent to treatment. Assessment of criminal responsibility, parenting capacity, and capacity to manage property and care for self is also covered.

Volumes such as the *Handbook of Psychology and Law* (Kagehiro & Laufer, 1992) and *Law and Psychology: The Broadening of the Discipline* (Ogloff, 1992) address issues such as eyewitness evidence and testimony, competencies in the criminal process, privacy torts, children as witnesses, copyright protection of scientific research data, therapeutic jurisprudence, and psycholegal education and may be of interest to forensic psychologists specializing in these areas.

JOURNALS AND ORGANIZATIONS

Journals of interest include *Law and Human Behavior, Behavioral Science and the Law, Law and Psychology Review, American Journal of Forensic Psychology, Forensic Reports, Journal of Psychiatry and Law, Bulletin of the American Academy of Psychiatry and the Law*, and *International Journal of Law and Psychiatry*.

Organizations of interest include the American Psychology-Law Society (Division 41 of the American Psychological Association), American College of Forensic Psychology, American Academy of Psychiatry and the Law, American Academy of Forensic Sciences, and National Association of Forensic Social Work.

REFERENCES

American Psychiatric Association. (1974). *Report of the task force on clinical aspects of the violent individual* (Task Force Report No. 8). Washington, DC: Author.

American Psychiatric Association. (1994). *Diagnostic and statistical manual of mental disorders* (4th ed.). Washington, DC: Author.

American Psychological Association. (1978). Report of the task force on the role of psychology in the criminal justice system. *American Psychologist, 33,* 1099.

American Psychological Association. (1994). *Guidelines for child custody evaluations in divorce proceedings.* Washington, DC: Author.

Anastasi, A. (1988). *Psychological testing* (6th ed.). New York: Macmillan.

Anderson, R. M. (1994). *Practitioner's guide to clinical neuropsychology.* New York: Plenum.

Applebaum, P. S., & Gutheil, T. G. (1991). *Clinical handbook of psychiatry and the law* (2nd ed.). Baltimore: Williams & Wilkins.

Ayala, F. J., & Black, B. (1993). Science and the courts. *American Scientist, 81,* 230–239.

Blau, T. H. (1984). *The psychologist as expert witness.* New York: Wiley.

Brodsky, S. L. (1989). Advocacy in the guise of scientific advocacy: An examination of Faust and Ziskin. *Computers in Human Behavior, 5,* 261–264.

Brodsky, S. L. (1991). *Testifying in court: Guidelines and maxims for the expert witness.* Washington, DC: American Psychological Association.

Clingempeel, W. G., & Respucci, N. D. (1982). Joint custody after divorce: Major issues and goals for research. *Psychological Bulletin, 91,* 102–127.

Committee on Ethical Guidelines for Forensic Psychologists. (1991). Specialty guidelines for forensic psychologists. *Law and Behavior, 15,* 655–665.

Cornell, D. G., & Hawk, G. L. (1989). Clinical presentation of malingerers diagnosed by experienced forensic psychologists. *Law and Human Behavior, 13,* 375–384.

Couric, E. (1988). *The trial lawyers.* New York: St. Martin's Press.

Dahlstrom, W. G. (1993). Tests: Small samples, large consequences. *American Psychologist, 48,* 393–399.

Dershowitz, A. M. (1982). *The best defense.* New York: Random House.

Ewing, C. P. (Speaker). (1985). *Ten commandments for the expert witness* (cassette recording). Sarasota, FL: Professional Resource Exchange.

Faust, D., & Ziskin, J. (1988). The expert witness in psychology and psychiatry. *Science, 241,* 31–35.

Faust, D., Ziskin, J., & Hiers, J. B. (1991). *Brain damage claims: Coping with neuropsychological evidence.* Los Angeles, CA: Law and Psychology Press.

Garb, H. N. (1992). The trained psychologist as expert witness. *Clinical Psychology Review, 12,* 451–467.

Garfield, S. L., & Bergin, A. E. (1986). *Handbook of psychotherapy and behavior change* (3rd ed.). New York: Wiley.

Goldstein, J., Freud, A., & Solnit, A. J. (1973). *Beyond the best interests of the child.* New York: The Free Press.

Graham, J. R. (1993). *MMPI-2: Assessing personality and psychopathology* (2nd ed.). New York: Oxford University Press.

Grisso, T. (1986). *Evaluating competencies: Forensic assessments and instruments.* New York: Plenum.

Grisso, T. (1988a). *Competency to stand trial evaluations: A manual for practice.* Sarasota, FL: Professional Resource Exchange.

Grisso, T. (1988b). *Preparing for a forensic mental health practice* (cassette recording). Sarasota, FL: Professional Resource Exchange.

Group for the Advancement of Psychiatry. (1991). *The mental health professional and the legal system.* New York: Brunner/Mazel Publishers.

Hambacher, W. O. (1994). Expert witnessing: Guidelines and practical suggestions. *American Journal of Forensic Psychology, 12,* 17–35.

Hare, R. D. (1991). *Manual for the revised Psychopathy Checklist.* Toronto: Multi-Health Systems.

Jenkins, J. A. (1989). *The litigators.* New York: Doubleday.

Jenkins v. United States, 307 F.2d 637 (D.C. Cir. 1962).

Kagehiro, D. K., & Laufer, W. S. (Eds.). (1992). *Handbook of psychology and law.* New York: Springer-Verlag.

Kaplan, H. I., & Sadock, B. J. (1991). *Synopsis of psychiatry* (6th ed.). Baltimore: Williams & Wilkins.

Klawans, H. L. (1991). *Trials of an expert witness: Tales of clinical neurology and the law.* London: The Bodley Head.

Klerman, G. L. (1986). Drugs and psychotherapy. In S. L. Garfield & A. E. Bergin (Eds.), *Handbook of psychotherapy and behavior change* (pp. 777–820), New York: Wiley.

Kreitman, N. (1961). The reliability of psychiatric diagnosis. *Journal of Mental Sciences, 107,* 876–886.

Lanyon, R. I. & Goodstein, L. D. (1982). *Personality assessment* (2nd ed.). Lanham, MD: University Press of America.

Larrabee, G. J. (1990). Cautions in the use of neuropsychological evaluation in legal settings. *Neuropsychology, 4,* 239–247.

Maloney, M. P. (1985). *A clinician's guide to forensic psychological assessment.* New York: The Free Press.

Mangiaracina, M. (1991). *Courtroom survival guide.* San Clemente, CA: Qwik-Code Publications.

Matarazzo, J. D. (1990). Psychological assessment versus psychological testing: Validation from Binet to the school, clinic, and courtroom. *American Psychologist, 45,* 999–1017.

Matarazzo, J. D. (1991). Psychological assessment is reliable and valid: Reply to Ziskin and Faust. *American Psychologist, 46,* 882–884.

McConnell, J. V. (1969). A psychologist looks at the medical profession. In A. G. Sugerman (Ed.), *Examining the medical expert: Lecture and trial demonstrations* (pp. 61–84). Ann Arbor, MI: Institute of Continuing Legal Education.

McNeil, D. E., & Binder, R. L. (1991). Clinical assessment of the risk of violence among psychiatric inpatients. *American Journal of Psychiatry, 148,* 1317–1321.

Melton, G. B., Petrila, J., Poythress, N. G., & Slobogin, C. (1987). *Psychological evaluations for the courts.* New York: Guilford.

Melzack, R., Katz, J., & Jeans, M. E. (1985). The role of compensation in chronic pain: Analysis using a new method of scoring the McGill Pain Questionnaire. *Pain, 23,* 101–112.

Mendelson, G. (1986). Chronic pain and compensation: A review. *Journal of Pain Symptom Management, 1,* 135–144.

Miller, H. (1961). Accident neurosis. *British Medical Journal, 1,* 919–925, 992–998.

Miller, L. (1990). Litigating the head trauma case: Issues and answers for attorneys and their clients. *Cognitive Rehabilitation, 8,* 8–12.

Monahan, J. (1984). The prediction of violent behavior: Toward a second generation of theory and policy. *American Journal of Psychiatry, 141,* 10–15.

Moore, J. W. (1985). *Moore's federal practice: Federal rules of evidence.* New York: Matthew Binder.

Moss, D. (1994). Assessing predictions of violence: Being accurate about accuracy. *Journal of Consulting and Clinical Psychology, 62,* 783–792.

Musetto, A. P. (1985). Evaluation and medication in child custody disputes. In C. P. Ewing (Ed.) *Psychology, psychiatry, and the law: A clinical and forensic handbook* (pp. 281–304). Sarasota, FL: Professional Resource Exchange.

Ogloff, J. R. P. (1992). *Law and psychology: The broadening of the discipline.* Durham, NC: Carolina Academic Press.

Pope, K. S., Butcher, J. N., & Seelen, J. (1993). *The MMPI, MMPI-2, and MMPI-A in court: A practical guide for expert witnesses and attorneys.* Washington, DC: American Psychological Association.

Report of the Division 40 Task Force on Education, Accreditation, and Credentialing. (1989). Guidelines regarding the use of nondoctoral personnel in clinical neuropsychological assessment. *The Clinical Neuropsychologist, 3,* 23–24.

Report of the Division 40 Task Force on Education, Accreditation, and Credentialing. (1991). Recommendations for education and training of nondoctoral personnel in clinical neuropsychology. *The Clinical Neuropsychologist, 5,* 20–23.

Rogers, R. (1984). Towards and empirical model of malingering and deception. *Behavioral Sciences & the Law, 2,* 93–111.

Rogers, R. (1987). Ethical dilemmas in forensic evaluations. *Behavioral Sciences & the Law, 5,* 149–160.

Rogers, R. (Ed.). (1988). *Clinical assessment of malingering and deception.* New York: Guilford.

Rogers, R., Bagby, R. M., & Perera, C. (1993). Can Ziskin withstand his own criticisms? Problems with his model of cross-examination. *Behavioral Science and the Law, 11,* 223–233.

Rogers, R., & Mitchell, C. N. (1991). *Mental health experts and the criminal courts.* Ontario, Canada: Thomson Professional Publishing Canada.

Rosenthal, R. & Rosnow, R. L. (1991). *Essentials of behavioral research: Methods and data analysis* (2nd ed.). New York: McGraw-Hill.

Sadoff, R. L. (1988). *Forensic psychiatry: A practical guide for lawyers and psychiatrists* (2nd ed.). Springfield, IL: Charles C. Thomas.

Sattler, J. M. (1992). *Assessment of children* (3rd ed.). San Diego, CA: Jerome M. Sattler.

Shapiro, D. L. (1991). *Forensic psychological assessment: An integrative approach.* Boston: Allyn & Bacon.

Simon, R. I. (1992). *Clinical psychiatry and the law* (2nd ed.). Washington, DC: Amercian Psychiatric Association.

Spitzer, R. L., & Fleiss, J. L. (1974). A reanalysis of the reliability of psychiatric diagnosis. *British Journal of Psychiatry, 125,* 341–347.

Stromberg, C. D., Haggerty, D. J., Leibenluft, R. F., McMullin, M. H., Mishkin, B., Rubin, B. L., & Trilling, H. R. (1988). *The psychologist's legal handbook.* Washington, DC: Council for the National Register of Health Service Providers in Psychology.

Sue, S., Fujino, D. C., Hu, L., Takeuchi, D. T., & Zane, N. W. S. (1991). Community mental health services for ethnic minority groups: A test of the cultural responsiveness hypothesis. *Journal of Consulting and Clinical Psychology, 59,* 533–540.

Trimble, M. R. (1981). *Post-traumatic neurosis: From railway spine to whiplash.* New York: Wiley.

Vandenburg, G. H. (1993). *Court testimony in mental health: A guide for mental health professionals and attorneys.* Springfield, IL: Charles C. Thomas.

Warshaw, B. G. (Ed.). (1984). *The trial masters: A handbook of strategies and techniques that win cases.* New York: Prentice-Hall.

Weitzman, L. J., & Dixon, R. B. (1979). Child custody awards. *University of California, Davis Law Review, 12,* 473–521.

Weller, M. P. (1985). Head injury — organic and psychogenic issues in compensation claims. *Medical Science and Law, 25,* 11–25.

Ziskin, J., & Faust, D. (1988). *Coping with psychiatric and psychological testimony* (Vols. 1–3, 4th ed.). Los Angeles, CA: Law and Psychology Press.

Ziskin, J. (1995). *Coping with psychiatric and psychological testimony* (Vols. 1–3, 5th ed.). Los Angeles, CA: Law and Psychology Press.

AUTHOR INDEX

❖ ❖ ❖

SUBJECT INDEX